Al Jazeera and the Global Media Landscape

This book analyzes how and why Al Jazeera English (AJE) became the channel of choice to understand the massive protests across the Arab world in 2011. Aiming to explain the 'Al Jazeera moment,' it tracks the channel's bumpy road towards international recognition in a longitudinal, in-depth analysis of the channel's editorial profile and strategies. Studying AJE from its launch in mid-November 2006 to the 'Arab Spring,' it explains and problematizes the channel's ambitious editorial agenda and strategies and examines the internal conflicts, practical challenges, and minor breakthroughs in its formative years.

The Al Jazeera phenomenon has received massive attention, but it remains under-researched. The growth of transnational satellite television has transformed the global media landscape into a complex web of multi-vocal, multimedia, and multidirectional flows. Based on a combination of policy-, production- and content-analysis of comprehensive empirical data, the book offers an innovative perspective on the theorization of global news contraflows. By problematizing the distinctive characteristics of AJE, it examines the strategic motivation behind the channel and the ways in which its production processes and news profile are meant to be different from its Anglo-American competitors. These questions underscore a central nexus of the book: the changing relationship between transnational satellite news and power.

Tine Ustad Figenschou is a Postdoctoral fellow at the Department of Media and Communication, University of Oslo, Norway.

Routledge Advances in Internationalizing Media Studies

Edited by Daya Thussu, University of Westminster

Al Jazeera and the Global Media Landscape

The South Is Talking Back

Tine Ustad Figenschou

Routledge
Taylor & Francis Group

NEW YORK AND LONDON

First published 2014
by Routledge
711 Third Avenue, New York, NY 10017

Simultaneously published in the UK
by Routledge
2 Park Square, Milton Park, Abingdon, Oxon OX14 4RN

*Routledge is an imprint of the Taylor & Francis Group,
an informa business*

Library of Congress Cataloging-in-Publication Data

Figenschou, Tine Ustad.
    Al Jazeera and the global media landscape : the south is talking back / by
Tine Ustad Figenschou.
        pages cm. — (Routledge advances in internationalizing media studies ; 11)
    Includes bibliographical references and index.
    1. Al Jazeera English (Television network)   2. Television broadcasting
of news—Political aspects—Qatar.   I. Title.
    PN1992.92.A393F55 2013
    079.17'4927—dc23
    2013018905

ISBN: 978-0-415-81443-0 (hbk)
ISBN: 978-0-203-06732-1 (ebk)

Typeset in Sabon
by Apex CoVantage, LLC

Printed and bound in the United States of America by Publishers Graphics,
LLC on sustainably sourced paper.

Contents

Figures

Acknowledgements

First and foremost, I would like to thank the informants at Al Jazeera English for sharing their professional insights, honest opinions and precious time. A special thanks goes to the Al Jazeera Network's Ezzeddine Abdelmoula, Lana Khachan and Sebastian Ford for arranging the interviews and facilitating access to the network's headquarters in Doha and London, and to Christina Aivaliotis for helping out with the final fact check.

I am very grateful for the support from series editor Dr. Daya K. Thussu and the editors at Routledge/Taylor & Francis Books, Felisa Salvago-Keyes and Nancy Chen.

My partner in crime, Nina Bigalke, has read the manuscript thoroughly and given invaluable feedback. Thank you.

The point of departure for this book is my PhD research (2006–2010) at the Department of Media and Communication, University of Oslo. My two excellent supervisors, Professor Espen Ytreberg (University of Oslo) and Dr. Naomi Sakr (University of Westminster); all the hardworking assistants involved in various parts of the project: Sarah Chiumbu, Elin Strand Hornnes, Turid Edvardsen, Marthe Ødegaard and Alix Dunn; and my dear colleagues in Oslo have all been crucial in completing this analysis. I have also benefited from pep talks and discussions with Kjersti Thorbjørnsrud, Audun Beyer, Unn Haukvik, Ole Johan Mjøs and Alexa Robertson at different stages of the writing process. Thank you all.

Researching this book has taken me on a long journey, to Qatar, the United Arab Emirates, Israel and the Palestinian Territories, the UK, the US, Germany, Finland and Sweden. It would not have been possible to conduct extensive fieldwork, to present my work internationally or to complete the manuscript without the financial support from the Faculty of Humanities (University of Oslo), The Sasakawa Young Leaders Fellowship Fund, The Leiv Eiriksson Mobility Programme (The Norwegian Research Council), The Norwegian Non-Fiction Writers and Translators Organisation (NFF) and The Freedom of Expression Foundation (Fritt Ord). Thank you.

Most of all, I thank my family—Simen, Sylvia and Olivia—for coming with me to the dry Doha desert, for the lovely time in London and New York and for providing a home wherever we are.

Oslo, June 2013
Tine Ustad Figenschou

1 Introduction
The Al Jazeera Moment

"Al Jazeera is not a tool of revolution. We do not create revolutions. However, when something of that magnitude happens, we are at the center of the coverage," said Wadah Khanfar, Al Jazeera Network's Director General from 2003–11, in his TED talk from March 2011. Interviewed after the talk, he described the enormity and the importance of the Arab uprisings in almost poetic terms:

> Actually, this may be the biggest story that we have ever covered. We have covered many wars. We have covered a lot of tragedies, a lot of problems, a lot of conflict zones, a lot of hot spots in the region, because we were centered at the middle of it. But this is a story—it is a great story; it is beautiful. It is not something that you only cover because you have to cover a great incident. You are witnessing change in history. You are witnessing the birth of a new era. And this is what the story's all about. (Khanfar, 2 March 2011)

For the network's English news channel, Al Jazeera English (AJE), the uprisings represented a 'perfect media storm' as the channel capitalized on a set of comparative advantages making them *the* international news channel to go to. This book analyzes *how* and *why* AJE became the channel of choice to understand the massive protests across the Arab world. Aiming to provide a comprehensive understanding of the 'Al Jazeera moment,' it tracks the channel's bumpy road towards international recognition in a longitudinal, in-depth analysis of the channel's editorial profile and strategies. Studying AJE from its launch in mid-November 2006 to the 'Arab Spring' and beyond, it explains and problematizes the channel's ambitious editorial agenda and strategies as well as examines the internal conflicts, practical challenges, and interim successes in its formative years.

To understand the role of the new and old media during the Arab Spring, it is important to recognize the complex and contradictory characteristics of the wider Arab public sphere. The present chapter first maps recent localization trends in the global media landscape. Second, it discusses the strengths, weaknesses, and democratic potential of the Arab public sphere, with particular emphasis on satellite news channels, expectations of a 'satellite democracy,' and popular participation and mobilization. It aims to demonstrate that neither the naïve beliefs in media effects in the Arab world nor popular mobilization and protest are a new phenomenon in the Arab public sphere, although the pace, scale and magnitude of the Arab uprisings were unprecedented. The third part of the present chapter situates Al Jazeera English in the global news landscape and outlines the channel's comparative advantages over its international competitors in the dramatic last couple of years.

THE LOCALIZATION OF GLOBAL NEWS

Al Jazeera English's coverage of the Arab uprisings has been seen as a powerful demonstration of the channel's emerging role as a major international player (Miles 2011, Ricchiardi 2011, Seib 2012). And yet, there can be no static definition of what such a role might entail at any given time, as the international media ecology (and with it the implications of what it may mean to successfully compete within it) is constantly evolving. However, there are certain recurring trends and themes. As I will outline in the following, in the past decades, international media outlets oscillated between efforts to globalize and efforts to localize.

In today's complex satellite news landscape, the technological developments, the plurality of news outlets, new patterns of global ownership, new global media institutions and new financial hubs and emerging media centers blur the traditional dichotomy between dominant Western news flows and its challengers. The growth of transnational satellite television has transformed the global media landscape into a complex web of multivocal, multimedia and multidirectional flows (Chalaby 2005b, Rai & Cottle 2007, Sinclair et al. 1996, Straubhaar 2007, Thussu 2007b). Today, 24-hour news channels compete in a very crowded, highly competitive market, and in addition to overlapping each other, they also compete with an ever-increasing number of state and local news channels (Cushion 2010: 23). These complexities have revealed the shortcomings of existing theoretical approaches and paradigms in the global news field (Cottle & Rai 2008, Rai & Cottle 2010) and the present study is one attempt to illuminate the complexity of the current satellite news landscape. Recent years have shown an unprecedented growth of localized international news satellite channels stressing distinctive news perspectives and challenging the commercial Anglo-American news media. As the most ambitious of these satellite news contra-flows, the rise of the Al Jazeera Network epitomizes the dramatic changes in the global television news landscape.

In the early 1990s, the original ideal type of transnational satellite news channel was promoted as deterritorialized and cosmopolitan, disrupting the relationship between place and time.[1] The deterritorialized channels in the first generation of transnational news channels had less time-specific, 24-hour-oriented programming schedules for a multinational audience and internationalized patterns of production. Deterritorialization implies a weakening or loss of the 'natural' relationship of culture and media to geographical and social territories (Rantanen 2005: 96). In the first phase of satellite news, politicians, business executives and academics in the tradition of the global public sphere (see Volkmer 1999, 2000, 2002) shared a strong belief in global news. In the early days of satellite television, it was widely believed in corporate circles that the boundaries between cultures were quickly disappearing and that a global, cosmopolitan culture was emerging (Chalaby 2005b: 53). Cosmopolitanism symbolizes an exciting and glamorous lifestyle, travel between and intermingling with different cultures, and a broad-minded, urbane and worldly attitude. Consequently, it was criticized for being elitist and Western (Rantanen 2005: 119–22).

The logic behind this first phase of satellite news broadcasting was best symbolized by the instant, initial success of CNN International's (CNN) 24/7 breaking news coverage in the early 1990s. Foreign news reporting had previously been defined largely within the scope of the nation-state, but the international strategies of CNN rapidly established the network as a global news leader in the coverage of world crises. The earliest 24/7 satellite news channels were heralded as symbols of the global news organizations. The satellite news pioneers, CNN International, later followed by BBC World,[2] demonstrated the potential of satellite technology to broadcast a common set of programming across a range of television markets around the globe (Rai & Cottle 2007). In response to the continuous production demands of the 24/7 news genre, CNN developed three new journalistic styles and types of news presentation: breaking news, live coverage and fact journalism (Volkmer 1999: 139). In particular, CNN's live reporting of global breaking news and international crises gave it an unparalleled position in international communication in the 1990s. At the outset of the first Gulf War, CNN was ahead of its competitors with its live coverage of the conflict, advanced presentation techniques, and extended access to US military sources (El-Nawawy & Powers 2008: 12). The emergence of CNN as a major influential satellite news network produced a new communication approach to international relations known as the "CNN effect" (Gilboa 2005b: 326), discussed in more detail below.

Emphasizing their global orientation, CNN and the BBC exhibit a cyclicity in their schedules with a preference for half-hour programs and no identifiable prime-time period. Furthermore, the schedules of both channels are often subject to change as they make way for live coverage of breaking news events (Rai & Cottle 2007: 68). In her analysis of CNN's organization and strategy, Küng-Shankleman (2000) argued that its concentration on news made the channel a unique global product, but also resulted in uneven ratings, advertiser unattractiveness, accusations of sensationalism and the challenge of balancing fixed schedules with breaking news (ibid.: 194–9). In particular, the CNN *World Report* has been highlighted as a typical example of the emerging global public sphere and the de-Americanization of the channel (Flournoy & Stewart 1997, Kraidy 2005: 100, Volkmer 1999).[3] According to scholars of political economy, such as Thussu (2007c: 69), the initial success of CNN resulted in the "CNNization" of international news and the launch of a number of new satellite news channels inspired by the CNN model, such as Sky News, the BBC and ITV. Further, he argues that the fierce competition among increasing numbers of satellite news networks encouraged them to provide news in an entertaining manner, as global infotainment, "the globalization of US-style ratings-driven television journalism, which prioritizes privatized soft news . . . over news about political, public and civic affairs" (ibid.: 8). On the other hand, in their study of the global 24/7 news channels CNN, the BBC, Sky News and Fox News, Cottle and Rai (2008: 176), found an "inherent complexity in the communicative structures of global TV news and the ways in which these deliver, deliberate and display conflicts and cultural differences in and around the contemporary world."

In their empirical mapping of the reach, access and ownership of satellite news channels, Rai and Cottle (2007, 2010) identify the structural limitations in the global news ecology. They conclude that only a few of the contemporary satellite news channels are indeed global in reach: CNN, BBC, CNBC, Bloomberg TV and Fox News (Rai & Cottle 2010: 55–64). All of the global channels are major Western players, thereby lending credence to the thesis of continued Western dominance in the news market (ibid.). There are over 100 satellite news channels, cutting across virtually every region of the globe, with many of them broadcasting in different languages and the vast majority operating principally at regional, national or subnational levels. This suggests an increasing localization of the 24/7 news genre. Second, Rai and Cottle accentuate satellite news ownership. They find considerable evidence that major Western corporations dominate ownership at the global level. At the regional and national levels, however, they find that ownership patterns reveal an increased complexity and heterogeneity. They argue that this offers a less Western-dominated reading of news flows and formations than has been proffered by traditional geopolitical economy approaches (Rai & Cottle 2007: 60). The contemporary satellite news landscape is dynamic and rapidly expanding, with information flows increasingly overlapping and intersecting both within and across regions. Third, Rai and Cottle underscore the structures of distribution and access that reinforce the dominance of the major Western satellite news channels. Satellite news channels are generally accessible only via subscription (with some exceptions) and face considerable structural hurdles when it comes to distribution (Parker 1995 in Rai & Cottle 2010: 67). The global players, such as the BBC and CNN, are available all over the world without difficulty, whereas the choice of regional and national satellite channels on offer differs by area.[4] These structures reinforce traditional political economy arguments, highlighting the continuing supremacy of the major Western players (ibid.). Following this argument, the ability of non-Western news channels to create contra-flows is called into question by these structural inequalities of access (ibid.). At the same time, Rai and Cottle (2010: 69–70) note these distribution structures are creating "an interesting paradox in which the news markets of the non-Western world, in many cases, are more pluralized, offering a mix of regional and national channels alongside the major Western players."

Over time, the globalization strategy in the first phase of satellite broadcasting (offering the same menu to more and more people) turned out to be a failure as the big Western news channels struggled to attract a broader global audience (Hafez 2007, Hjarvard 2001, Sparks 2005). Audience numbers were lower than the global public sphere advocates might have expected, and viewers were predominantly male, well-educated and well-off and represented a global elite (Sparks 2005: 42). One of the main limits to globalization in the media is the fact that relatively few people have a primarily global identity (Straubhaar 2007: 6) and, in general, local, national, and regional media and identities have not been eroded by the competition from global media. On the contrary, the new global and transnational media have actually helped strengthen and created new national and regional media in many parts of the world (Hafez 2007, Rantanen 2005). Moreover, Sparks (2005: 38) showed that although satellite news channels are often perceived as primary agents of global media, they are never free from national restrictions: all signals must be linked up from somewhere, and nowhere is unregulated. Satellite channels operate under national and regional political and economic constraints. The state's influence over satellite broadcasting is particularly strong in the Arab world, where the Arab states have been and remain a determining factor, initiating and shaping satellite broadcasting.

In contrast to the global public sphere proponents, who argue that the conventional distinctions between the foreign and the domestic are irrelevant in deterritorialized satellite news, more recent academic contributions argue that the domestic frame has remained present in global news. The second phase of satellite broadcasting has been characterized by two interconnected and corresponding developments in transnational television. First, the major global transnational channels initiated different processes of localization in the shape of a centralized approach to local adaptation (Chalaby 2005b, Straubhaar 2007, Thussu 2007b).[5] Today, global audiences are increasingly stratified by media output, which is specifically geared towards national or regional interests (Chalaby 2003, 2005a/b, Clausen 2003, 2004, Hafez 2007, Kraidy 2005, Straubhaar 2007). The two major global news channels CNN and the BBC have chosen different localization strategies (Chalaby 2003: 466–7, Thussu 2007c: 66). CNN gradually localized its feeds, introduced local and/or regional language news slots, and developed an international network of regional and local channels (Chalaby 2003). In contrast, the BBC has broadcast the same news to everyone while varying the current affairs, documentary and lifestyle programming (ibid.), and their news has been broadcast mainly in English, with the exception of limited dubbing in Japan and Spanish subtitles in Latin America (Thussu 2007c). As emphasized by Hafez (2007: 13), one result of the localization of the global channels is that there are many regional versions of the global channels, but no completely global program. According to El-Nawawy and Powers (2008), these localization and domestication processes cause the global media to reflect and speak to "particular national discourses with little regard to each other" (El-Nawawy & Powers 2008: 14). Scholars of political economy, such as Thussu (2007b), argue that these localization processes are central to the acceleration of Western or Westernized media flows around the globe, and that media output and services are being tailored to specific cultural consumers as a commercial imperative.[6] The localization of the global satellite channels, exemplified by CNN International and CNN (the domestic US channel), arguably weakens the 'global public sphere' argument (Sparks 2005: 41): why does the leading satellite channel strategically differentiate the material it broadcasts to the most powerful television market (the US) from the material it broadcasts to the rest of the world if international communication is characterized by a strong and vibrant global public sphere?

Secondly, there has been an unprecedented growth of more localized transnational satellite channels since the mid-1990s. Aware of the structural limitations in the global news system, these newcomers have been targeting specific national, regional or geocultural audiences. Researchers have identified a growth in localized transnational channels, particularly in the last ten years (Rai & Cottle 2007, 2010, Straubhaar 2007, Wessler & Adolphsen 2008). In contrast to the first generation of global satellite channels, which mainly expanded from a national base or market where they remained strong and profitable, the second generation targeted regional and/or international audiences from the very beginning (Straubhaar 2007: 55–6). Regionalism has been a strong trend in the international media since the 1990s, and the dynamic regionalist view of international media structures has been investigated in a growing number of publications (Hafez 2007, Moran 2009, Sinclair et al. 1996, Straubhaar 2007, Tunstall 2008). The aforementioned Arab satellite 'revolution' is a pivotal illustration of the development of regional markets of localized transnational satellite channels.

In the Arab context, CNN's coverage of the Gulf War in 1991 highlighted the contrasts between Arab state television's coverage of the war, giving static, censored versions of the dramatic events, and the live coverage of CNN (Sakr 2001). Western media were generally seen as having more credibility than Iraqi and Arab media. Still, many Arabs were disappointed by the Western bias in the war coverage, and the need for stronger Arab media was apparent (Ghareeb 2000: 1). The presence of CNN helped to forge a market for a new kind of Arabic broadcasting, for leading Arab entrepreneurs had watched CNN and recognized how powerful satellite television could be as a political and commercial vehicle (Rugh 2004: 211). The CNN model inspired the development of Arab satellites, and these were deployed to suit the interests of those who controlled individual stations. In most cases, this meant limiting the model in some way (Sakr 2001: 97). From the mid-1990s to the present, there has been an explosive growth in Arab satellite channels competing for Arab viewers, ranging from news channels to family channels, religious channels and music television (Sakr 2007b). Furthermore, in the last decade there has been an unprecedented boom in Arabic-language television channels operated by non-Arab states: Al-Hurra (*The Free One*), funded by the US congress; Rusya al-Yawm (*Russia Today*), funded by the Russian government; al-'Alam (*The World*), owned by the Iranian state; BBC Arabic, funded by the UK Foreign Office; and CCTV Arabic, funded by the Chinese government—in addition to the Arabic versions of Deutsche Welle World TV (German government) and France 24 (French government) (Kraidy & Khalil 2009: 125).

In addition to the rapid growth in the Arabic-language market, there has been an unparalleled growth in recent years of localized international news satellite channels stressing alternative news perspectives vis-à-vis Western mainstream news outlets. Both governments and private corporations have acknowledged the plurality of voices and recognized the need to broadcast their own perspective on global events. A prominent example is the Spanish-language Latin American news channel, Telesûr (2005), launched under the catch phrase "Nuestro Norte es el Sur" ("Our North is the South") (Boyd-Barrett & Boyd-Barrett 2010, Burch 2007). Although these channels are established to target international audiences, they differ markedly from the cosmopolitan ideal viewers that theorists have associated with CNN and other global networks in the first generation satellite channels (Rai & Cottle 2007), and they could be understood as defensive and even reactionary to the growing influence of the global Western channels (ibid. 2010: 72). Today, a growing number of channels are competing for English-speaking audiences worldwide, offering English-language alternatives to the Anglo-American satellite news channels, e.g., France24 (2006) ("worldwide news with French eyes"),[7] Russia Today (2005) ("the Russian point of view"), Deutsche Welle TV (from 1953) ("German and other positions on important issues"), Chinese CCTV 9 ("your window on China and the world") and the Iranian Press TV (2007) ("unbiased reporting of controversial global news"). These channels offer a variety of combinations of information about internal events and domesticated perspectives on international affairs.

Al Jazeera English (AJE) represents the most ambitious of these channels and is the object of analysis in this book. AJE was launched on 15 November 2006. At present, the channel employs over 1,000 employees from over 50 nationalities, covering the world 24/7 from the channel's four broadcasting centers in Doha, Kuala Lumpur, London and Washington D.C. and from the Al Jazeera Network's more than 70 bureaus in the field (AJE press office information request, May 2013). As of May 2013, it is being distributed to over 260 million homes in over 120 countries (ibid.).

AJE is the first English-language satellite news channel headquartered in the Middle East,[8] and, in order to situate the channel within the Arab regional context, the major developments in and key characteristics of the Arab public sphere will be outlined in the next section.

PARTICIPATION, PROTEST AND AUTHORITARIAN RULE: THE ARAB PUBLIC SPHERE

From the mid-1990s, optimistic expectations of a kind of 'satellite democracy' were nurtured by the new editorial line of the Arab satellite networks, the geographical reach of the new networks, and their ability to speak to the wider Arab community and to reunite regional communities scattered by war, exile and labor migration (Sakr 2001, 2007a). With this line, the Arab satellite news channels, such as Al Jazeera Channel, Al Arabiya Channel and Abu Dhabi TV, posed new challenges to government censors that encouraged analysts to hope for political reform. The aim to change the region was also strongly emphasized in survey studies of Arab journalists stating that driving regional political and social change was their key mission (Pintak & Ginges 2008) and, for as many as three out of four Arab journalists, encouraging political reform represented the most significant job of a journalist (Pintak 2011: 156). In the short term, however, the political effects of satellite television seemed to be limited. The regional governments remained in office, they did not change their foreign and domestic politics and the satellite media did not empower any new powerful or lasting coalitions (Lynch 2011a: 302). Overall, after the first initial shock, the governments seemed to respond to and counter the media pressure from the new media and the stability of Arab authoritarianism reemerged as the central thesis of the political science theory (Lynch 2011a). Consequently, media scholars became more moderate and realistic in their analysis of the political implications of the new Arab media, and the academic debate on the political potential of the Arab satellites moved from trying to identify direct political implications of these new media outlets to a more general debate on the satellite channels' contribution to the emergence of a new Arab public sphere (for in-depth analyses of this aspect, see also the studies of Hafez 2006, 2008, Lynch 2005a/b, 2006, 2007, 2008, Sakr 2007a).

To understand this complex, contradictory new Arab public sphere, it is vital to understand that the Arab satellite media were established primarily as tools for regional governments to use to pursue their own domestic and foreign policy objectives (Sakr 2008). Even today, two years after the Arab uprisings brought down and challenged authoritarian rulers, the political elite's influence over the regional media should not be underestimated. Although most of the new satellite channels were started as 'private' undertakings, their owners have strong connections to Arab political leaders (Pintak & Ginges 2009: 169, Rugh 2004: 218), a system that Pintak (2011: 72) has characterized as "corporate feudalism." In Arab satellite media, the dividing line between state and private channels is not always clear cut because there is a web of connections between private owners and holders of political power (Sakr 2002). Overall, Arab elites across the region have managed to influence and shape the media, including the regional satellite channels. Thus, "editorial content is ultimately attributable not to people outside the elite, but to political agendas that reflect patterns of elite ownership and control" (Sakr 2007a: 6). Sakr further argues that divisions and realignments among the ruling elite drive the developments in Arab satellite broadcasting more than popular mobilization and participation (Sakr 2001, 2005, 2007a). According to Pintak and Ginges (2009: 169), this "feudal corporatist model" is replacing state media control in the region, and it has been particularly strong in the Gulf kingdoms. The elite dominance of Arab satellite news is reflected in a survey study of Arab journalists, in which government control, media ownership and corporate pressure were ranked among the top challenges to Arab journalism (ibid.)

Most of the Arab satellite channels are dependent on financial subsidies, and there is a general consensus that none of the Arab satellite broadcasters earn enough from advertising revenues to break even (Rugh 2004: 218, Sakr 2008: 190). There are several reasons for this. First, the region as a whole is not wealthy, the advertising market in general is weak, and the competitors are increasingly numerous. Second, due to a lack of audience data produced within the media industry itself, mirrored by a lack of scholarly research on audience demographic profiles, there are no professional independent rating systems for the Arab market that allow reliable tracking of media consumption patterns over time. Consequently, the advertisers do not know much about whom they are targeting. Many companies prefer to advertise in Western outlets, and politics steers advertisements to regime-loyal outlets (Alterman 1998, Lynch 2008, Rugh 2004: 219, Sakr 2008). Thus, most channels are dependent on financial support from powerful private entrepreneurs, politicians and wealthy governments in order to survive. Such financial dependencies make satellite channels vulnerable to outside pressures, from the richer states in general and Saudi Arabia in particular (Alterman 1998: 51). The politics of the poorer Arab states, on the other hand, are continuously criticized in order to give the impression that the media are free, critical and independent (ibid.: 52). Poorer states have served as "laboratories for the political effects of press freedom" and will be the targets of more aggressive regional coverage (ibid.: 53). This has been particularly evident in the Arab satellite news channels' extensive critical coverage of "weak and disintegrated" states such as the occupied Palestinian Territories and Iraq (Figenschou 2007). Hafez (2006) characterizes this structural paradox of Arab satellite television as a "double curse." The market orientation of the state-backed, private Arab satellite channels reinforces the populist trend in Arab television, but the Arab satellites are only allowed to be market-oriented as long as they do not challenge the interests of their government sponsors. In other words, although this populism interferes with objectivity about culturally resonant issues, epitomized by the Palestine problem, the dependency on state subsidies could prevent the satellites from acting as critical and outspoken advocates of political change.

Sponsored by political and business elites, the new Arab media landscape has been characterized by an unprecedented plurality of media outlets: the increasing number of players on the sender side as well as on the receiving end drives the development of the new Arab public sphere (Zayani 2004). In April 2009, the Arab television industry comprised 470 transnational satellite channels (Kraidy & Khalil 2009: 3), ranging from rebroadcasts of terrestrial state television to commercial networks, news channels, family channels, religious channels and music television (see Kraidy & Khalil 2009 for a discussion of the Arab television industry). Among the newcomers in this crowded news market, worth noting is Sky News Arabia (Abu Dhabi Media Investment Corporation and UK-based BSkyB)(2012). The extant academic literature on the Arab media strongly highlights the ways in which the new Arab satellite media have opened up the Arab public sphere.

First, the Arab world shares a common language: there are 250–300 million Arabic-speaking viewers in the Middle East and worldwide (Kraidy & Khalil 2009: 31). To attract audiences from the entire region, an increasing number of new satellite channels broadcast their news and political debates in Modern Standard Arabic (MSA). MSA is the language shared, despite some nuances, by all Arabs, at least passively. The use of MSA by an Arab staff recruited from different Arab countries has highlighted the pan-Arab character of these channels (Mellor 2005: 120).

Second, researchers have called attention to a feeling of common identity among Arabs congregating around the new media (Mellor 2005, Lynch 2005a, 2006). According to Lynch (2005a), the news coverage, paired with the political talk shows, established a common, core Arab narrative. The regional Arab emphasis was also apparent in Pintak and Ginges' (2008: 197–200) survey of Arab journalists, in which they found that Arab journalists most closely identified with the pan-Arab region and the broader Muslim world rather than the nation state. Moreover, the surveyed journalists found political reform, human rights, poverty, and education as the most profound challenges for the region (Pintak 2011: 155). This feeling of a common Arab identity and destiny has nurtured the return of a sense of pan-Arabism to the region. The new Arabism can be described as a rising sense of regional solidarity—as "Arabism from the ground up" led by the people rather than by the leaders of the state (Alterman 2002). It has also been characterized as "McArabism," a form of imagined Arab and Islamic communities, conveyed through Arab transnational television (Rinnawi 2006: 54). Critics argued that the discussion of this new Arabism was characterized by the treatment of the new regional identity as an end in itself rather than a means to other ends. For a long time, the political, social and economic implications of the new regional identity remained unexplored and empirically unsubstantiated (Hafez 2006). The manifestation of the new popular pan-Arabism as a "unified narrative of change" during the Arab uprisings (Lynch 2011b), thus represented a new and more internally-focused stage of the identity that had been formed over a decade. The pace, scale and profound political changes caused by the uprisings surprised analysts, politicians and the media, but the ideas, the pan-Arab "media-fueled narrative of change," had been circulating in the Arab public sphere for almost a decade (Lynch 2011b).

Third, the new Arab media are broadening the range of topics that people in the Arab world can talk about publicly. It is worth noting that, before 9/11, Al Jazeera Arabic was almost unanimously applauded outside the Arab world for its ability to criticize Arab governments and break taboos. Traditionally there were four 'red lines' or taboos in the Arab state media that could not easily be crossed due to regional censorship and self-censorship practices. First, the media should be cautious not to promote oppositional forces, particularly not the Islamist opposition. Second, the ruling family should not be criticized. Third, the media should be careful when they cover issues of a religious nature to avoid the eruption of any undue dissension. Islam is the majority religion in the Arab world, but there is disagreement within and between countries on various religious matters. Fourth, strong social and sexual taboos still exist in the region regarding pornography, other aspects of sexual relations and intra-family relations that should not be talked about in public (Alterman 1998: 46–7). Although there remain severe restrictions on media freedom in the region, these taboos are regularly challenged by the increasing plurality of voices in the new regional media (Pintak 2011: 50–3). Over time, Lynch (2005a) emphasized, the legitimacy of disagreement demonstrated in the Arab satellite media would strengthen the long-term foundations for a more pluralistic political culture in the autocratic Arab world.

Fourth, there has been a fundamental change in the dynamics of the traditional sender–receiver relationship. In terms of format, programs became increasingly interactive and participatory, qualities that were generally lacking in regional politics (Kraidy 2007, 2010, Kraidy & Khalil 2009). According to Kraidy (2007), the pluralistic, non-hierarchical "Arab hypermedia space" has been demonstrated in various types of communicators using e-mail, mobiles, text messaging, digital cameras, electronic newspapers and satellite television (ibid.: 140). Due to broadcasters' reluctance to measure ratings, advertisers' reluctance to advertise without ratings, and the widespread piracy of pay TV, the satellite channels have sought to capitalize on the huge growth in the mobile industry (Sakr 2008: 195). The Arab public was invited to call in their questions and views to studio debates, to participate in phone or online polling and to comment directly on screen by text messaging in an increasing number of media outlets (Ayish 2005, El-Nawawy & Iskandar 2002, Kraidy 2007, 2010, Kraidy & Khalil

2009, Lynch 2005b). Among the most debated 'Arab' issues were Palestine, Iraq and the question of political reform, and all elections in the Arab and Muslim world received considerable attention (Lynch 2005a). Moreover, the relatively rapid diffusion of Internet in the Arab world (Khamis & Vaughn 2011) and the falling costs of mobile phones with video, photo and Internet capability (Tufecki & Wilson 2012) facilitated the audience's ability to document and share content (Kraidy 2008). With time, Kraidy (2010) concluded, hypermedia space could act as a potential incubator of social change. Over the last decade, there have been several examples of protest movements in which Arab protesters have employed, tested and refined their media literacy tools in popular protests. Primarily, these popular street protests have been over foreign policy issues that Arab governments have been able to control without risking their own legitimacy (Lynch 2006). First and foremost, Israel's reoccupation of the Palestinian West Bank in 2002 and the US-led war in Iraq caused massive popular mobilizations across the region and widespread protests, although this critique of Israel and the US was followed by demands for political reform (Lynch 2011a: 303). Secondly, the Lebanese 'Cedar revolution' (2005), protesting and ending Syria's longtime military presence (Khatib 2007, Pintak 2011); the various social movements in Egypt from 2004–11, including the 'Kefaya ("Enough") movement'; the 'April 6 Youth' and 'We are all Khaled Said' (see Lim 2012 for an analysis of online activism in Egypt from 2004 to 2011); and the 'Green revolution' in Iran, protesting the election results in the summer of 2009 (Lynch 2011a) were prominent examples of protest movements' pioneering the use of social media and mastering the use of potent symbolism that communicated to regional and international media and publics (Lynch 2011a/b, Pintak 2011).

In the decade leading up to the Arab uprisings of 2011–12, a critical change narrative evolved in the new Arab public sphere, relentlessly confronting the status quo, desiring political change, yearning for democratic freedoms and possibilities, and increasingly identifying with other Arabs (Lynch 2011b). Within the new Arab public sphere, these ideas were strong, but nevertheless, mostly contained by national authoritarian governments due to the striking paradoxes of the regional public sphere: In the new Arab public sphere, the Arab public inside and outside the region could seek information from a variety of new outlets and express their opinions on numerous new media platforms. At the same time, powerful media owners (the political elites and businessmen with close ties to regional governments) have remained in control of the various media outlets, and each of the pseudo-independent regional media outlets is still ideological and politically tinted (Pintak 2011: 75). Added together, however, the expansive Arab media landscape has provided the Arab public with comprehensive and pluralistic regional and international news. These complex media-elite relations underscore a core question of this book: the changing relationship between transnational satellite news and power.

FROM A CNN EFFECT TO AN AL JAZEERA EFFECT?

'The satellite media effect' hypothesis illustrates the widespread assumption that satellite news channels alter the elite domination of mainstream news. In the first phase of satellite news broadcasting, CNN's breaking news coverage of international events seemingly altered the political elite–media power relations. The 'CNN effect' concept was initially used by politicians and officials haunted by the myth of 'the Vietnam syndrome' (see chapter 7, this volume, for discussion) and uncertain how to respond to the confusion of the post-Cold War era and the communications revolution (Gilboa 2005a: 37). Since then, the phrase has become a generic term for the ability of the news media to provoke major responses from domestic audiences and political elites to global and national events: an argument that has later been contested and moderated (see, among others, Bahador 2007, Gilboa 2005a/b, Robinson 2002, 2005, Thune 2009).

Although the CNN effect has become the term for describing the influence of international news media on international politics, the precise meaning of the popular concept is far from clear (Thune 2009: 39). Research on international media–politics relations has employed a number of confusing definitions and reaches different conclusions (Gilboa 2005a: 29). In his meta-analysis of the field, Gilboa (2005a/b) concluded that academic studies of the CNN effect have yet to present sufficient evidence to validate the existence of such an effect, that the studies have exaggerated the CNN effect, and that numerous attempts to clarify the CNN effect have only achieved minimal success (Gilboa 2005a: 38). Adding to the conceptual argument about inconsistency and uncertainty, Thune (2009: 41–2) argued for steering clear of the CNN effect as a concept and analytical tool. For one thing, he regarded the CNN effect as too contextual and historically too specific, inevitably closely associated with CNN itself and its coverage of a few US-led military operations in the early 1990s. Furthermore, the CNN effect indicates a particular one-way, mechanical, direct relationship between news media and politics (ibid.). Critics, such as Thune (2009) and Cottle (2009), support a more general mediatization thesis—a broader, more complex understanding of the ways in which the media logic influences conflict, crisis and (foreign) policy. In his revision of the CNN effect after 9/11, Robinson (2005: 348) concluded that the Bush administration forged a new consensus between journalists and policy-making elites. He found that the "war on terror" diminished the priority given to humanitarian concerns in the US foreign policy agenda and that the humanitarian war discourse has been a legitimating device used by political elites to justify military action. Another development mitigating the CNN effect involves the accelerated attempts by governments to manage and control the information environment (ibid.: 347).

In the complex contemporary international news landscape outlined above, the intensification, diversity and complexity of the contemporary global news media have contributed to an increased awareness of 'other' news perspectives (Liebes & Kampf 2009, Orgad 2009) or a "new visibility" (Thompson 2005). After the terrorist attacks of 9/11, scholars and media reports have talked about an "Al Jazeera Effect" (El-Nawawy & Gher 2003, Pintak 2010, Powers & El-Nawawy 2008, Seib 2008). According to El-Nawawy and Gher (2003), the idea behind this term "is the visible regional and global presence established by Al Jazeera and the vital role it plays as a pan-Arab network in broadening the scale of Arab cross-border interaction." In his book *The Al Jazeera Effect* (2008: 175), Seib argues that Al Jazeera is "just the most visible player in a huge universe of new communications and information providers that are changing the relationship between those who govern and those who are governed." To varying degrees throughout the world, Seib (2008) writes, the connectivity of new media is superseding the traditional political connections that have brought identity and structure to global politics. Rather than testing the Al Jazeera Effect empirically on particular political contexts or crises, the literature has employed the term to stress the broader expansion of the Arab public sphere discussed above, epitomized by the controversies surrounding and the success of AJA.

During the Arab Spring, there were once again strong claims of an Al Jazeera Effect (see, among others, Miles 2011 and Ricchiardi 2011). In general terms, there are four distinct ways by which the new Arab satellite and Internet-based social media has challenged and keep challenging Arab states, "1) promoting contentious collective action, 2) limiting or enhancing the mechanisms of state repression, 3) affecting international support for the regime, and 4) affecting the overall control of the public sphere" (Lynch 2011a: 304). Due to the highly visible activity on social Internet-based media such as Twitter, Facebook, and YouTube, a wave of academic publications has sought to measure, characterize or question how these new media mattered in the different Arab uprisings and protest movements. Most researchers agree that social media mattered, but they have different views on the direct impacts for new media on the Arab uprisings—more precisely, how and to what extent social media contributed to the organization and promotion of the protests (Aday et al. 2012, Alterman 2011).[9]

More importantly for this book, most researchers find that the old media, satellite television in general, and Al Jazeera Arabic in particular, as well as the new social media, reinforced each other and that it is increasingly difficult to separate old and new media from each other in the Arab public sphere (Aday et al. 2012, Alterman 2011, Kallander 2013, Lynch 2011a, Robertson 2012, Tufecki & Wilson 2012). Warning against ignoring traditional media such as television and less accessible new media such as mobile phones, researchers call for a more integrated examination of the media's role during the dramatic uprisings (Aday et al. 2012, Alterman 2011). There are several vital insights worth emphasizing here: First, survey studies have found that two thirds of the Tunisian respondents (Kallander 2013) and over 90 percent of the Egyptian respondents (Wilson & Dunn 2011) relied on television for information during the uprisings, in combination with personal communication, other traditional media and social media. And this documents that television (and to lesser extent other traditional media) still plays a ubiquitous and powerful role in the Arab public sphere (Alterman 2011). Second, social media supplied the rolling television coverage with new material—exposing the images and voices that the authorities wanted to stop (Alterman 2011: 112). And furthermore, while the Al Jazeera channels and other satellite television channels leaned heavily on Twitter and other online sources, new media often referred back to those same television networks. Aday et al., in their (2012) study of shared links from the uprisings, document how social media activists were reflective of the mainstream media, often referred to as and linked to mainstream media sites (ibid.: 9). Among the most popular bit.ly links outside the Arab region were links to live streaming video from the scene of the protests provided by mainstream media outlets, among them Al Jazeera's live feed from the protests (ibid.: 14). Third, the new and old media together drew international attention to the regional uprisings (Aday et al. 2012: 9, Alterman 2011: 113). Studying the location-specific patterns of online links, Aday et al. (2012: 12–14) find that most of the bit.ly traffic occurred outside the Arab region. They conclude that the social media mainly functioned more as a megaphone broadcasting information to a wider international audience than a rallying cry mobilizing the Arab public (ibid.: 13).

In the Arab Spring context, the term Al Jazeera Effect has mainly been used with two slightly different meanings. The first has emphasized the Al Jazeera Arabic's (AJA) key role in the Arab uprisings (see Miles 2011). Researchers argue that the AJA and other regional satellite channels drove the protestors, framed them, legitimized them, and broadcast them to a larger audience (Alterman 2011: 114). In his analysis, Alterman (2011) stresses that the protests soon became an emotional, dramatic, telegenic media event (ibid.: 111). For example, AJA almost immediately framed the Egyptian uprising as a revolution, and throughout the protests it gave generous headcounts to the Egyptian protests (ibid.). The channel's validation of the protest movements has fueled the debate over whether its coverage could best be characterized as campaign journalism (see, among others, Mair 2011, Mir 2011 and Rinnawi 2012 for further discussion). During and after the Arab uprisings, the concept of the Al Jazeera Effect has also been frequently employed to underline the key role played by Al Jazeera English (AJE), bringing the drama of the Arab streets to audiences, politicians and journalists worldwide (see Ricchiardi 2011 for an example). This understanding of the term does not claim a direct regional or international political effect of AJE's coverage, but rather is a generic term underlining the AJE's comparative advantages covering the 2011–2012 Arab uprisings.

THE PERFECT MEDIA STORM: AL JAZEERA ENGLISH'S COMPARATIVE ADVANTAGES

Introducing an edited volume on Al Jazeera English, Philip Seib characterizes the Arab uprisings as an opportunity the channel news executives dream about:

> It was the biggest story of the century, it was happening on home territory, and the channel had the expertise and the reportorial staff on the ground at levels its competitors could not match. For English-speakers around the world, AJE was the indispensable, go-to source of information about what was happening in the streets of Tunis, Cairo, Sanaa, and elsewhere in the suddenly rebellious region. (Seib 2012: 1)

In its ambitious editorial agenda, AJE states that it aims to challenge the dominant Western news flows, challenge power elites, and report international news from a southern, grass-roots perspective (see chapter 3, this volume, for a comprehensive analysis of the channel's news agenda). Striving to meet these ambitious goals, AJE has employed a set of alternative production strategies. When the Arab uprising story broke in 2010–11, it could capitalize on these production strategies, giving it considerable comparative advantages over its Western competitors.

First, AJE has an extensive network of bureaus and correspondents around the world, especially in the Global South, where its competitors are much more scarcely represented. AJE has put much of its newsgathering capacity in the South with an extensive network of permanent correspondents and a decentralized, resource-intensive production structure. This southern presence, with many correspondents available in its 'home region' gave AJE a head start on its competitors. To sum up, AJE has more correspondents on the ground than most of its Western competitors, and it has also had an active policy of countering the location practices of the Western news media, which are mostly located in financial hubs in the US, Europe and Asia. Being on the ground in the right place at the right time has been a fundamental success strategy for AJE's predecessor and sister channel Al Jazeera Arabic (AJA). Analyzing the Al Jazeera Network's editorial success strategy,[10] Zayani and Sahraoui (2007: 35–42) highlighted its instinct for breaking news, its dynamic production practices, its individual freedom, and the channel's wide-ranging presence on the ground, with a special concentration of bureaus and correspondents in the Arab and Muslim world. In AJE's coverage of the start of the uprisings (January 2011), they had a noticeable presence where the story unfolded and had reporters on the ground in 9 out of 10 stories, compared to the BBC, who were on site in two-thirds of all its reports (Robertson 2012: 12); and AJE had noticeably more reporters on the ground than CNN, which largely covered the uprisings from its studios (ibid. 2013).

Second, another and related strategy is the channel's policy of hiring local correspondents to cover their home country or region, again particularly in the Global South. There is a widely shared belief within the channel that local, permanent correspondents are better equipped to grasp and convey the realities on the ground than international, rolling (foreign) correspondents. According to this strategy, correspondents 'who have lived the story' are better qualified to communicate the channel's editorial core values. Since local correspondents are permanently based in the field, they have a better understanding of the context and complexities of a running news story. The local correspondent speaks the local language(s); knows the culture, religion and way of life; has personal experience and a deep understanding of the challenges of the community; navigates the system and knows how to deal with local authorities; has more extensive and alternative source networks; respects local sensitivities; and strives to give a fair representation of the local point of view. Many of AJE's most prominent correspondents and news anchors covering the Arab uprisings had a professional or personal Middle Eastern background. Compared to the BBC, AJE used more female correspondents and local correspondents to report the uprisings, and fewer middle-aged, white, male correspondents (Robertson 2012: 12).

Third, in covering the Arab Spring, AJE could also benefit greatly from being part of the Al Jazeera Network. Cooperating and coordinating the resources within the "Al Jazeera Family" has been a third editorial strategy for AJE that is particularly valuable in the coverage of the Arab and the Muslim world. the Arabic channel has been the most popular, hard-hitting and controversial Arab satellite news channel for over 15 years. Primarily, its Arab staff on the ground, extensive network of sources and contacts, and regional experience and expertise proved valuable during the dramatic uprisings. Moreover, the Arabic channel had broad experience navigating and working in the often dangerous, difficult and contradictory regional political context. During the uprisings, the authorities have tried to shut down the new media communication, ranging from unprecedented complete shutdowns of the mobile networks and the Internet, in addition to expelling, attacking and arresting news media staff (Lynch 2011a). AJA had over 15 years of practice in how to circumvent regional censors and how to continue covering Arab realities after being banned or shut down from various countries and areas, and they had become an important outlet for the aforementioned "narrative of change" (Lynch 2011b). Throughout AJE's almost seven years on air, these progressive and ambitious production strategies have often been demanding to put into practice, and these editorial challenges and dilemmas are explored in depth in chapter 3, this volume. During the Arab uprisings, however, the benefits arguably exceeded the costs, and both AJE and AJA became leading news organizations internationally and regionally.

In the chaotic, unprecedented wave of protests shaking the Arab world in 2011–12, the editorial agenda and strategies enabled AJE to emphasize, explain and voice the protesters' perspective through its alternative source hierarchies, dramatic visualization and criticism, and exposure of the authorities' official version of the uprisings.

Reflecting AJE's ambition to find alternative sources to voice their opinion on air, the channel invited grass-roots networks, activists and critics of the political establishment on air. The AJE teams inside the region had extensive local knowledge and experience and, together with their colleagues from the Arabic sister channel, they had extensive access to a variety of sources on the ground. More importantly, when their international competitors covered the story from hotel rooftops or from inside their news studio, AJE was in the streets among and with the protesters. In her comparative analysis of the Arab Spring coverage on AJE and the BBC through January 2011, Robertson (2012: 9) finds that, for both channels, the majority of the sources invited to voice their opinion were non-elites, primarily activists and people who had taken to the streets to join the protesters or to witness and document the events themselves. In a closer narrative analysis, however, she concludes that AJE had a grass-roots perspective in contrast to the BBC's white, male elite focus. The high number of critical voices is confirmed in another comparative study, finding that AJE gave more time to neutral sources (almost 50 percent), and anti-government sources (36 percent) than pro-government sources (Loughborough University 2012: 83). During the Arab uprisings, AJE established an alternative source hierarchy of independent (elite) sources, "people on the streets, rather than politicians in official buildings" (Robertson 2012: 15). Robertson further underlines that AJE did not only interview protestors in the Arab world, but also paid attention to democratic demonstrations in other regions, especially in Eastern Europe (ibid.).

To access and identify these alternative voices and grass-roots perspectives, AJE developed routines to (re)broadcast online eyewitness reports, integrate social media content such as YouTube clips and Twitter updates into their coverage, accord authority to activists, and, by this, to offer a platform for the social media protest that both validated and magnified the uprisings' reach and influence. In a quantitative, comparative analysis of how often social media were used as a source of content or the extent to which social media was the topic of the story, Robertson (2013) finds that AJE used social media more actively than their international competitors CNN and the BBC. AJE explicitly focused on the social media's importance and role in the uprisings, and used, acknowledged and incorporated information from blogs and tweets in their reporting (ibid.). Having said that, Robertson (2013) underlines that, although AJE outclassed the Western media, social media items amounted to less than 4 percent of all items in her January 2011 sample.

Writing about how the AJE newsroom in Doha integrated eyewitness accounts and updates from the ground into their rolling news coverage, senior AJE correspondent Alan Fisher (2011: 151) states that social media was used to "source and corroborate, and in return, gave people a feeling of involvement and engagement in the news gathering process." He characterizes this news gathering process as circular, with news being constantly shared and exchanged between people, using new media and traditional outlets (ibid.: 152). As discussed above, the Al Jazeera Network integrated and validated social media into their newscasts at the same time as social media activists actively linked to Al Jazeera links and output. Early into the uprisings, AJE set up a desk in the newsroom to work exclusively towards the social media: the team monitored Twitter, Facebook, YouTube and Flickr and looked for updates, conversations and trends in the material, which was then either summarized in the hourly 'web desk' updates or, for the most dramatic and significant, included as updates in the main report of the hour edited together by the Doha news desk (ibid.).

For AJE, having local editorial staff on the ground inside the Arab region and on the web desk also became crucial when deciding which videos, eyewitness accounts and images they perceived as reliable. The local staff could establish authenticity through their knowledge of places/local geography and local accents, and the web desk also used their audience for corroboration through crowdsurfing (Fisher 2011: 155). During the uprisings, AJE was temporarily shut down or banned from reporting from the protests by Arab military and political authorities, and, due to the difficult working conditions, social media became a vital source of material. The Al Jazeera Network was banned from Tunisia from the start of the uprisings and had to cover the conflict through a network of bloggers. According to Fisher (2011: 152), these bloggers had been sources and established as credible and reliable in the days and weeks before the uprising. Channel correspondents made direct contact with bloggers and online activists so that they could keep communication lines open in case they were blocked or shut down (Minty in Mir 2011: 165). As the conflict escalated, the channel started to smuggle in correspondents traveling on tourist visas to report undercover. Similarly, the channel also had to rely more on user generated content (UGC) when Egyptian authorities closed down their Cairo bureau, suspended the accreditation of the journalists, blocked its signals and detained some of the staff. The channel correspondents kept reporting among the protesters, primarily over the phone and via social media, with their identities hidden (Fisher 2011: 153). During the uprisings, the correspondents on the ground were themselves 'embedded' in the crowds and experienced the authorities' threats and violence themselves (Cottle 2011: 207), and critics have noted that AJE reporters became participants as well as observers and reporters during the intense first phase of the uprisings (Robertson 2013). Particularly when they reported undercover, hidden among the protestors, the AJE correspondents became part of the story they reported. Symptomatic of the many bonds between the AJN staff and the protestors, activists mobilized on Twitter to release high-profile AJE correspondent Ayman Mohyeldin from his detention by the Egyptian military (Fisher 2011: 154). Another example of the tight bonds was the Al Jazeera Network's controversial and risky decision to provide Egyptians on the ground with Flip cameras (see Fisher 2011 and Mair 2011 for debate).

Another key characteristic in AJE's coverage of the uprisings was the channel's raw, direct and constant visual documentation of the events on the ground. Researchers have underlined how the increased visibility of events on the ground, documented by mobile phones, amateur cameras and the AJN cameras, gave unprecedented documentation of the demonstrations and the military and political authorities' sanctions and reactions to the popular uprisings. The most prominent example is the Al Jazeera Mubashir (Live) Channel's live stream from Tahrir Square. The cameras raised the costs of repression, as police brutality was recorded on mobile phones and Al Jazeera cameras and was repeatedly exposed and widely distributed to local, regional and international media and publics (Alterman 2011, Cottle 2011, Lynch 2011a: 305). Particularly striking were the images documenting the massive, brute violence by government-backed thugs attacking demonstrators in Tahrir Square on 1 February 2011 (Cottle 2011). The UGC videos documenting violence and repression have had a clear effect on how regional and international audiences understand the conflicts and realities of the uprising. There seems to be a qualitative change in the way protestors, authorities, external publics, and the international community now responds to such documentations of violence (Aday et al. 2012: 20). During the uprisings, the gulf between the official and semiofficial media and the independent media, satellite media and social media was striking (see, among others, Hamdy & Gomaa 2012 for a comparative content analysis). On AJE, this gulf was effectively demonstrated as the channel repeatedly included dramatic visual documentation from the ground in interviews with government officials, or when contrasted to the government's official or semiofficial media. By including the documentation from the ground, AJE's' live footage from the ground and/or images of atrocities and brutality served to undermine and expose the sanitized, official version of the uprisings. Moreover, the visual documentation of the protestors both scaled up local protests into a broader democracy movement and localized broader episodes as the protesters adapted similar symbols, language and protest methods, competing for the same cameras (Lynch 2011a: 305), building on and extending the lessons from the Arab hypermedia space. Overall, the massive popular, peaceful mobilizations contrasted with the authorities' brutality made powerful, emotional, and engaging images and gave front-row seats to AJE viewers as witnesses of this telegenic media event (Alterman 2011).

Analyzing why the Western media had covered the Arab uprisings uncharacteristically sympathetically and in a humanizing way, Cottle (2011) argues that the role of the new media in disseminating voices of dissent and potent images, the symbolism and dramaturgy of the peaceful protests, and the role of the correspondents who experienced and witnessed repressive state violence appealed to media and audiences worldwide. In the Arab world, the international media attention most probably gave confidence to the protest movements competing for the television cameras and possibly mobilized larger crowds as this was a story many wanted to take part in, and, more importantly, it constrained the governments' ability to use force (Alterman 2011). Traditionally, protest movements and radical movements in the Arab and Muslim world have received minimal but critical coverage in mainstream Western media. In the Arab uprisings, the Al Jazeera Network, particularly through its English news channel and English web site, played a key role in explaining the demonstrations as legitimate, peaceful movements for democracy (Alterman 2011, Robertson 2012). More than anything, AJE's integration of UGC, continuous flow of images from the ground and intense updates from its extensive network of correspondents made the coverage more connected to the experiences of those on the ground. During the uprisings, AJE used live streaming, live blogs and live tweets as a way of enhancing their regular reporting with perspectives from the ground (Mair 2011: 176), and, in particular, the live streaming (monitoring the events 24/7) and the live blogs (where the very latest developments on the ground were updated frequently on a 24/7 basis) became very popular during the uprising (Mair 2011: 176, Randree in Mir 2011: 163). According to Fisher (2011: 156), social media tools were key in circumventing censorship and restrictions on the ground, getting the channel's coverage out to audiences worldwide, increasing the breadth and scope of the reporting, and engaging those participating in the dramatic events.

BOOK OUTLINE: EXPLAINING EDITORIAL STRATEGIES AND PRACTICES

The academic debate on the role of social media in the Arab uprisings illustrates the political potential of the Arab public sphere, but it also problematizes the technological optimism and the methodological and empirical challenges in the analysis of the new Arab media phenomenon. In his razor-sharp criticism of those Western media and analysts that have pointed to the Internet as a key instigator of the Arab uprisings, Alterman (2011: 106) argues that these analysts fell prey to numerous logical fallacies. Basically, he argues, because social media made the uprisings accessible to the analysts, they perceived it as fundamental to the movement; that Western-centric analysts wanted sexy, social media to matter in the Middle East and to export Western technologies and freedoms; and that analysts were swept off their feet by the likable, young, Westernized Internet activists they could instantly connect with ("not only do they speak English much of the time, but they are youthful, full of energy, and they wore jeans" [ibid.]). This critique of the tendency to overestimate the political effects of new media in the Arab context is very timely in the wake of the Arab uprisings, but it is, unfortunately, not a new phenomenon.

Overall, much of the literature on the Arab media developments have been written within an essayistic culture that has demanded popularized accounts and edited volumes: formats providing a fascinating overview of the issue, often at the expense of theoretical and empirical depth (see Hafez 2006 for a critique). And especially the academic and political discussions of the ways in which Arab audiences are influenced by the new media have largely been empirically unsubstantiated and are often based on anecdotal evidence or content analysis (Hafez 2006, Lynch 2008). The discussions have arguably, therefore, assumed a unilinear, causal, direct media agenda-setting effect on a passive audience—an oversimplified and basic understanding of the media-effect thesis which has been nuanced, refined, problematized and tested empirically since the 1930s (Esser 2008). It is a paradox that these assumptions of a passive Arab audience have influenced most of the discussions about media effects in the Arab world. This pertains to both the optimistic claims of an 'Arab satellite revolution,' the Western-mediated public diplomacy strategies towards the region, and the criticism of the Arab satellite news channels for radicalizing the 'Arab street.' This paradox is pointed out by Hafez (2008: 1), noting that "in most Arab countries, which are still characterized by authoritarian rule and stagnation of political development, more is expected of the media than in the postmodern Western world." One particularly striking example is the assumption that the widely popular pan-Arab talent reality shows like *Super Star* and *Star Academy* would teach Arab viewers to vote and thus have Arabs embrace democracy (see Kraidy 2010 and Lynch 2005b for analysis of this debate). It is necessary to reiterate the need for humble, empirically grounded and methodologically sound analysis in the writings about the Arab uprisings (see Aday et al. 2012: 14–21 for discussion about methodological concerns in analyzing the new media effects during the Arab uprisings).

This book aims to explore AJE as a satellite news contra-flow, building on key works from a broad range of disciplines. Aiming for an empirically grounded discussion of AJE's editorial agenda, strategies and output, the present book combines extensive empirical data analyses that pose methodological challenges to the researcher. All in all, close to 100 hours of AJE, CNN and BBC news, 45 qualitative interviews with AJE/AJA editorial staff and management, 20 editorial meetings, and a number of policy documents, editorial guidelines, and evaluations, as well as promotional products were analyzed for this book (see Figenschou 2010b: 63–78 and 2010c for a detailed discussion of methodological challenges, triangulation of methods and the complementarity of this integrated design). The empirical data includes both intense periods of international wars and conflicts, but also the channel's regular day-to-day coverage over longer periods of time. Based on a combination of policy-, production- and content analysis of comprehensive empirical data, the book offers an innovative perspective on the theorization of global news contra-flows. It challenges the extant news-flow literature by going beyond the directionality of news flows and focuses on the political and/or commercial strategies behind the production process involved in and forming the content of satellite news contra-flows. By problematizing and investigating the distinctive characteristics of Al Jazeera English, it examines the strategic motivation behind the channel and the ways in which its production processes and news profile are meant to be different from dominant flows.

Aiming to explain the channel's comparative advantage and key role during the Arab uprisings, the second chapter analyses why the Al Jazeera Network has the ability to maintain its resource-intensive news production. The network is financed and owned by the Qatari royal family and chapter 2 (this volume) discusses Al Jazeera English's relationship with its Qatari owners, the structural limitations affecting the channel, and the ways in which the Qatari ownership interests affect the channel's editorial line. In recent years, the debate over Qatari–Al Jazeera relations has been brought up to date with numerous WikiLeaks cables concerning Qatar's use of the channel for political purposes, and most recently as Qatar took a new and more aggressive role in the Arab world during the Arab uprisings and internal conflicts in Libya and Syria. It argues that Al Jazeera English is a strategic communication tool for Qatar, reflecting and promoting the tiny petro-state's ambitious and unpredictable foreign policy agenda and massive place-branding campaigns. For Qatar, the Al Jazeera Network serves as one of many 'showcases of reform,' demonstrating the Gulf kingdom's freedom and modernity. For Qatar Al Jazeera is both the messenger and the 'message.' Combining the extant political science literature and media system theory, the chapter argues that the Al Jazeera Network is fully dependent on the Qatari royal family, who can close down the network overnight should they want to. At the same time, the network is only useful for Qatar as long as it is perceived as credible and independent.

As demonstrated above, AJE's production strategies and alternative editorial line gave it significant comparative advantages in its coverage of the Arab uprisings of 2011–12. Building on interviews with editorial management and staff in Doha and London, internal documents and observation of editorial meetings, chapter 3 explores AJE's ambitious editorial agenda and strategies outlined in this introduction in more detail. The chapter problematizes the channel's editorial line and practices with a particular emphasis on three of these strategies: its southern presence, the policy of employing local correspondents and the channel's tense cooperation with its Arabic sister channel. The chapter analyzes the challenges and practical dilemmas these strategies of 'reporting back' raise in the channel's newsrooms.

Aiming to meet the call for more systematic content analysis of the Al Jazeera phenomenon (Hafez 2006, 2008, Lynch 2008), it has been a primary objective in this project to provide a comprehensive overview of the editorial profile of AJE and to study the ways in which the channel's editorial distinctiveness is expressed in its news coverage. Chapters 4–7 aim to examine how this editorial agenda is reflected in AJE's newscasts, paying particular attention to its geographic emphasis (chapter 4), sourcing practices (chapters 5 and 6) and visual profile (chapter 7).

Chapter 4 synthesizes and reviews the relevant research on dominant media flows and contra-flows and problematizes the 'South' and the 'North' as analytical concepts. Against this background, it analyzes AJE's intended 'Southern perspective' through a quantitative mapping of the channel's news geography and news topics. It finds that the channel has more news from the Global South than the Global North in its regular day-to-day coverage, and that the South is covered in more in-depth news formats, with more correspondents on the ground. The news geography analysis also finds that AJE has more in-depth reports and a greater presence on the ground in its home region—the Middle East.

For AJE sources, the South is more than geography, and a Southern news perspective is also about giving a voice to the voiceless, the underprivileged and the subaltern. The channel aims to have a "grass-root perspective" on the world, to "focus attention on the margins, not just the corridors of power." The fifth chapter discusses to what extent the channel's self-declared bottom-up perspective is reflected in its sourcing strategies and practices. Based on the literature on mediated power and political elites, it examines how Al Jazeera English struggles to implement its emphasis on the voiceless in an elite-dominated international news landscape. The channel aims to include dissenting, conflicting voices. There is a shared understanding across AJE that the channel needs to be bolder and have a broad agreement about voicing 'the other opinion,' but there are conflicting interpretations of what this means in journalistic practice.

News media organizations demonstrate their weaknesses and strengths in times of crisis and conflict. Prior to the Arab uprisings, AJE's potential as an alternative contra-flow in global news was demonstrated most clearly through the channel's coverage of the January 2009 war on Gaza. Chapter 6 analyzes the channel's war coverage, in comparison with the Gaza coverage on the BBC and CNN. It discusses the channel's coverage in relation to the extant literature on mainstream Western and pan-Arab coverage of the Israel-Palestinian conflict, with emphasis on sourcing patterns, information strategies and access to the battlefield. As a result of Al Jazeera English's production strategies, it was the only international broadcaster present inside Gaza after Israeli forces closed the borders. AJE had more Palestinian sources than Israeli, it challenged the official Israeli framing of the war, and documented the atrocities and civilian suffering on the ground.

The current academic debate on mediated death and distant suffering has been largely Western-centric, documenting an increasing sanitization of media images and emphasizing the distance between media professionals, audiences, and the victims on the screen. In contrast, AJE literally zooms in. The visualization of suffering and death has become increasingly politicized, particularly in times of conflict and war. The seventh chapter thus explores the AJE's dramatic visualization of suffering and death based on data from its Gaza (2009) coverage and problematizes the ethical aspects of this controversial and risky editorial policy.

2011 was an extremely dramatic year for both for the Al Jazeera Network and Qatar, and the way the trials of the Arab uprisings have put pressure on the Qatar–Al Jazeera relations is explored in Chapter 8. The events of the Arab Spring have positioned Qatar as a controversial, unconventional regional power, and both the country's involvement and military intervention and its position among the repressive Gulf Cooperation Council (GCC) states should be investigated thoroughly by international media. At the same time, changes in the Al Jazeera Network's top management have increased the international scrutiny of the network's economic and political bonds with its owner. Since former Director General Wadah Khanfar was replaced with a member of the ruling family in September 2011, it has become more important than ever to prove the Al Jazeera Network's editorial independence. To do so, it has to cover the new aggressive Qatari foreign policy and the counterrevolution in the Arab Gulf comprehensively.

2   A Strategic Contra-Flow?
Al Jazeera–Qatari Relations

Late 2010/early 2011, two sets of controversial, leaked confidential documents showed the Al Jazeera Network at its best and its weakest.

In January 2011, Al Jazeera launched "the largest-ever leak of confidential documents related to the Israeli-Palestinian conflict" (AJE 2011a) in a series of special programs entitled *The Palestine Papers*. According to the Al Jazeera English website, the nearly 1,700 files, dated from 1999 to 2010, detailed the inner workings of the Israeli–Palestinian peace process (ibid.). The Palestine Papers angered both the Palestinians and the Israelis as they exposed the double standards, desperation and weaknesses of the involved parties. In many ways the network's critical coverage of the issue represents its brave, independent, alternative journalism at its very best. Acknowledging the sensitivity and controversy surrounding the thousands of pages of leaked embassy documents, Al Jazeera English carefully argued the journalistic value of presenting the papers. The channel stated the materials will prove to be of value to journalists, scholars, historians, policymakers and the general public. Moreover, it underlined that presenting the papers is a reflection of the network's fundamental belief "that public debate and public policies grow, flourish and endure when given air and light" (ibid.).

These fundamental journalistic principles of transparency and openness were strikingly absent in the network's coverage of the second set of leaked documents—the US embassy cables written by American diplomats based in Qatar leaked by WikiLeaks in December 2010. Whereas the international media dwelled on the American diplomats' analysis of the Qatari–Al Jazeera relations, the network itself did its best to ignore the Doha embassy cables, as it exposed its close ties to its Qatari owners. In a document dated 1 July 2009, Doha-based American diplomats characterized Al Jazeera as a network that "is heavily subsidized by the Qatari government and has proved itself a useful tool for the station's political masters" (Booth 2010). Moreover, the American diplomats claimed that Al Jazeera's ability to influence public opinion throughout the region "is a substantial source of leverage for Qatar, one which it is unlikely to relinquish." In another classified document from the US Embassy in Qatar, dated 19 November 2009, Qatar's use of

Al Jazeera (particularly its Arabic news channel) as a diplomatic and foreign policy tool is discussed in more detail. According to American diplomats, the network is an "instrument of Qatari influence, and continues to be an expression, however uncoordinated, of the nation's foreign policy" (Booth 2010). It is further underlined that Qatar will continue to use Al Jazeera as a "bargaining tool to repair relationships with other countries, particularly those soured by Al Jazeera's broadcasts, including the United States" (ibid.). It is a well-acknowledged fact that the Al Jazeera Network cannot be fully understood independently from the politics of Doha (Da Lage 2005), and the Doha cables once again revived the debate over the networks editorial independence.

Qatar, a small peninsular state bordering Saudi Arabia in the Persian Gulf, is an absolute monarchy governed by the Al Thani family, and Al Jazeera received its initial funding from the Qatari Emir, Sheikh Hamad bin Khalifa Al Thani, in November 1996. The Emir paid an initial $140 million to help launch and subsidize the channel over a five-year period through November 2001 (Al Thani & Iskandar 2002: 33). The Emir wanted an Arab station with Arab talent and expertise. The cousin of the Emir, Hamad bin Thamir, became the Chairman of the Board. Muhammad Jasim al-Ali was chosen Director General (Ghareeb 2000: 406).

According to the founding document displayed at the network's entrance, the Al Jazeera Network is an "independent public institution," and this chapter problematizes Al Jazeera–Qatari relations and the structural limitations of Al Jazeera English's (AJE) independence. According to the Al Jazeera Centre for Studies: "Al Jazeera is state-funded in terms of financial resources, but independent operationally. It's public in terms of ownership (no private owners). In real terms, this means that the budget comes from the government, but the editorial line and policy is set independently from any governmental interference" (e-mail to author, 17 April 2010). From the launch of Al Jazeera Arabic (AJA) to 2011, the network's only formal connection with the Qatari government was its funding—the interest-free loan from the government (which officially fell due after a period of five years) as well as continuing government subsidies. The financial responsibility for Al Jazeera was initially delegated to the accounting section of Qatar's governing council (Ghareeb 2000: 406). The financial model has benefitted both the network executives, who protect their journalistic credibility by pointing out that it is an independent network, and the Qatari authorities who can argue that they do not control the network and thus are not responsible for its often controversial editorial decisions.

Although both Al Jazeera and Qatari officials stress that the network is politically and editorially independent, it is vital to point out that—in the authoritarian Qatari political context—this independence is relative and conditional. To understand the subtle ways in which the Qatari ownership interests may affect AJE's editorial line, the present chapter first outlines the major developments in, and key characteristics of, the Arab satellite landscape. It further situates the Qatari media system in the Arab media typology, describes the political system in Qatar, and indicates the inherent contradictions in the Qatari media system. Furthermore, it elucidates Qatar's multi-faceted strategic interests in the Al Jazeera Network and discusses whether AJE serves as a public diplomacy tool for the Qatari authorities. It argues that AJE is a strategic communication tool for Qatar, reflecting and promoting the tiny petro-state's ambitious foreign policy agenda, public diplomacy and place-branding campaigns.

ORIGINS OF THE ARAB SATELLITE ECOLOGY: A STATE-BACKED MEDIA REVOLUTION

The first Arab Satellite Communications Organization (Arabsat) agreement was signed in 1976. Saudi ownership dominated Arabsat, and its headquarters were situated in the Saudi Kingdom. During its first five years, Arabsat was markedly underused for telecommunications, regional exchanges, and domestic networks (Sakr 2001: 10). As emphasized in chapter 1, CNN's innovative live coverage of the 1991 Gulf War inspired Arab governments and entrepreneurs to invest in satellite broadcasting. In addition to the political motivation, technological developments facilitated the Arab expansion. Following the war, the transformation of the Arab media landscape gathered speed, involving the physical expansion of satellite capacity serving the area, a rapid increase in the number of channels, and a matching growth in the size of the satellite audience (ibid.: 12). The technological developments were driven by the emergence of a substantial class of Arab professionals who had studied and worked in the West before returning to their countries of origin (Alterman 1998: 16). These groups constituted the audience and the staff for the first satellite channels in the region.

Overall, Arab satellite television has largely been launched, developed and financed by regional governments or entrepreneurs with close ties to governments. The aim has been regional political influence (Alterman 1998, Amin 1996, Hafez 2006, Kraidy & Khalil 2009, Pintak & Ginges 2009, Rugh 2004, Sakr 2001, 2002), and there is a remarkable concentration of satellite channels in Saudi hands (Hammond 2007, Kraidy 2007, Sakr 2001: 42). One fruitful analytical approach, represented by Sakr (2001), is to interpret the initial development of satellite television as a political struggle between Egypt and Saudi Arabia over regional influence. The Egyptian film and television industry has played a historically dominant role in the Arab broadcasting industry (Amin 1996: 102). After the oil crisis in 1973–74, with the vast transfer of wealth to oil-producing Saudi Arabia and the other Gulf states, the balance of power in the Arab world moved eastwards, and the Kingdom challenged Egypt as the pivotal state in Arab politics (Zahlan 1998: 148).

During the 'European phase' of Arab satellite broadcasting, the Saudi-owned channel MBC (1991) was broadcasting from London while ART (1994) and Orbit (1994) were transmitting from Rome. Europe was selected for its editorial and creative freedom; it was geographically proximate to the Arab world, and offered attractive logistics and human resources (Kraidy & Khalil 2009: 19). The first three Saudi satellite channels shared important features. From their European headquarters, based outside the Arab world, the broadcasters avoided domestic Arab media laws. Started by private entrepreneurs with close connections to the Saudi ruling family, the companies enjoyed some logistical support from government quarters (Sakr 2002). Even though the different branches within the extended Saudi royal family may have diverging aims, they all represent a shared overall interest in safeguarding the supremacy of the royal family as a whole (Hammond 2007, Sakr 2001: 49). Similarly, the development of all of Egypt's satellite channels was geared to a particular official view of Egypt's role in the region and the world. Therefore, Egyptian television soon became an effective arm of government policy and national projection in the region (Amin 1996: 102). Egypt, once the leader of Arab media in the 1950s and 60s with its 'media of mobilization' and Arab nationalist political ideology, established satellite channels to provide a counterweight to Saudi Arabia and to promote Egypt's future economic development by opening up to the West (Hammond 2007: 2, Sakr 2001: 39).

Another analytical approach to the developments in Arab satellite television, as represented by Kraidy (2007, 2010), has the convergence of Saudi capital and Lebanese talent as a starting point. During the Lebanese civil war (1975–90), political parties and warring factions launched numerous unlicensed radio and television stations, developing a pool of creative and managerial talent (Kraidy 2007: 142). After the war, the Lebanese Audio-Visual Media Law was hailed as the first broadcasting law in the region, but its implementation favored fewer, larger channels, owned by leading politicians and left hundreds of Lebanese media professionals unemployed (ibid.). The majority of this qualified and available Lebanese media expertise were recruited by Saudi entrepreneurs, particularly to the increasing number of entertainment and family channels, offering steady employment and competitive salaries (ibid.). With the growing number of satellite channels, many top editors still bemoan the shortage of experienced Arab media professionals and the relative trickle of newly educated journalists emerging from Arab journalism schools (Pintak & Ginges 2009: 164).

Paradoxically, Qatar was amongst the latest Arab states to establish a national channel (Kraidy & Khalil 2009: 31). In 1991, the Qatari government opened the airwaves and made it possible for viewers to receive CNN on their local TVs. This service was closed when the Gulf War ended, but it was an eye-opener for Qatari viewers and authorities (Rugh 2004: 238). The Al Jazeera Channel (today known as Al Jazeera Arabic) was developed in opposition to the Saudi media dominance and could therefore be understood as Qatar's voice in the regional power play. Like the Saudi channels, the Al Jazeera Channel grew out of the combination of local (Qatari) capital and pan-Arab (largely Palestinian, Lebanese and Iraqi) expertise. Al Jazeera managers recruited a group of Arab media professionals who were left unemployed after the termination of cooperation between the Saudi-financed Orbit Channel and the Arabic TV division of the BBC News Service. The BBC and Orbit clashed over the issue of editorial independence. This disagreement led the Saudi investors to withdraw financial support only 20 months after the initial deal between the two channels was signed (El-Nawawy & Iskandar 2002: 31). Al Jazeera Channel executives, who were already in the process of planning and structuring the channel, hired the 20 Arabic-language media professionals who had lost their jobs at BBC Arabic TV (ibid.) as well as administrative staff. Initially, the idea had been to modernize Qatari TV and to broadcast via satellite. The Qataris, however, decided to launch a completely new news channel in order to be more competitive (Bahry 2001: 89).

Emerging out of this particular context, the vast bulk of the Al Jazeera Arabic staff consisted of Arabs who had lived in the West. Many had been trained in Western newsrooms and Arab newsrooms abroad, and the diversity within the staff helped create the channel's pan-Arab identity. In 2005, 75 percent of the editorial staff in the Al Jazeera Channel were Arab expatriates (Miles 2005: 33). Since its launch in 1996, Al Jazeera Arabic has become one of the world's best-known brand names (Brandchannel. com 2004) and has expanded into a multi-channel global network. In addition to the news channel in Arabic and Al Jazeera English (2006), Al Jazeera Network has also launched a variety of specialized channels, such as Al Jazeera Sports Channel (2003), Al Jazeera Sports Plus 1 and 2 (2005), Al Jazeera Mubasher (Live) (2005), Al Mubasher Al Misr (a version of Mubasher focusing on Egypt [2012]), Al Jazeera Children (with the Qatar Foundation, 2005), and Al Jazeera Documentary (2007). In recent years, the network is targeting regional markets outside the Arab world such as Al Jazeera Balkans (2011) and the planned launch of Al Jazeera Turk and Al Jazeera America (Al Jazeera America, AJE 2013). Moreover, the network is expanding across multiple platforms, including the Internet and mobile phones (Kraidy & Khalil 2009: 96) and is in the process of strengthening its knowledge-building and training programs through its center of studies and its training and development center (AJN 2009a: 6).

QATAR IN THE ARAB MEDIA TYPOLOGY

Arab media have certain characteristics that set them apart from other media systems (Rugh 2004). Rugh's influential Arab media typology places the Arab media systems in four categories: mobilization, loyalist, diverse and 'transitional.' The media typology, which was updated in 2004 to include the satellite media, is an Arab adaptation of the classic four theories of the press: authoritarian, libertarian, social responsibility, and totalitarian (Siebert et al. 1956). Both the four theories of the press and Rugh's typology, as well as Hallin & Mancini's (2004) seminal characterizations of media systems,[1] have been criticized for overlooking non-Western media modalities (Iskandar 2007: 4, Mellor 2005: 49–74). In the Arab context, Rugh's Arab media typology has been examined, adapted, revised, and critiqued by media scholars both within and outside of the Arab world.[2]

According to Rugh, most national Arab media systems are variations on the authoritarian model (Rugh 2004: 23), and he proposes four categories: mobilized press, loyalist press, diverse press, and transitional press (ibid.: 25–26). Rugh (2004: 59–85) has characterized the national Qatari media system prior to 1995 as a "loyalist broadcasting system." The loyalist system was found in countries such as Morocco, Tunisia, Jordan, Kuwait, Saudi Arabia, Bahrain, Qatar, the UAE, Oman and North Yemen. The loyalist system is characterized by governments with little interest in active social engineering of the masses that are less intrigued by the idea of using the media as tools to promote social change. Due to political sensitivities, media content tends to be characterized by less politically motivated programming and more entertainment and culture (ibid.: 190). In contrast, governments in the strict-control systems mobilize mass audiences in support of leftist, anti-imperialist, Third World agendas (ibid.: 184). Rugh identifies five mechanisms that secure the loyalist system: First, systems rely on anticipatory self-censorship practices based on sensitivity to the political environment. Second, the regime publicizes its priorities and official line through policy statements and appointments. Third, the government operates national news agencies and thereby signals to the private media what to emphasize. Fourth, government officials brief editors and media owners from time to time (informally and privately) on official policy on specific issues. Fifth and last, the government has certain powers under the law that it uses when it believes direct action must be taken against a disloyal media outlet (ibid.: 82). In a more recent update on the typology, Rugh (2007: 9) found that since the political conditions in the Arab world have not changed substantially, the Arab media system typology has survived the rapidly changing regional satellite landscape.

In his essay on the typology of Arab media, Iskandar (2007) pointed towards differences between Arab and Western media as well as the need for alternatives to Western theoretical approaches as the academic lens through which media systems are being looked at. Specifically, whereas foreign typologies of Arab media are concerned with the systematic analysis of each nation-state as a singular media environment, regional (Arab) media view them as transnational broadcasters with programs that cross borders and reach a pan-Arab audience (Iskandar 2007: 16). Furthermore, he argued that in light of the increasingly strong call to de-Westernize media studies, the Arab media system must be interpreted as reflecting regional resistance to the Western models and not solely be understood within the linear development scheme that articulates a passage toward Western democratization (ibid.: 24). Iskandar also pointed out that prevailing notions that the media systems in the West and in the Arab world are on a collision course only serve to reify and ossify the categorical distinctions between the media systems 'here' and 'there' (ibid.: 25).

QATAR'S POLITICAL SYSTEM: POLITICAL REFORMS, AUTOCRATIC RULE

The Arab world has been governed by authoritarian regimes, and the stability of the autocratic oil monarchies in the Gulf has been particularly striking. In Qatar, the Emir, Sheikh Hamad, replaced his father in a palace coup in June 1995 and has been perceived as a representative of a new, progressive generation of Arab Gulf leaders (Blanchard 2008, Da Lage 2005, Fromherz 2012, Wright 2009). The Emir is the head of the executive branch of the Qatari government and appoints members of the Al Thani family and other notables to a governing Council of Ministers (a cabinet headed by the Prime Minister and the Foreign Minister) (Blanchard 2008: 2). Qatar's permanent constitution of 2005 formalized the Qatari tradition that the rule of the state is hereditary within the Al Thani family, added clarity to Qatar's political system, and underlined the importance of the rule of law (Wright 2011: 122). The constitution's other main innovation was an advisory council (see Wright 2011 for details), in which 30 of the 45 members will be elected by direct universal suffrage, and the Emir directly appoints the remaining 15 from among ministers and other political elites. When implemented—the election has been postponed several times—the Advisory Council will have oversight authority over the Council of Ministers. Another key element in the top-down reforms has been the status of women, particularly through female enrollment in higher education and work (Berrebi et al. 2009), the high-profile role of the royal females, and the expansion of women's political rights (Bahry & Marr 2005, Lambert 2011).

Sheikh Hamad and his advisors initiated a limited reform program designed to gradually make Qatar's government more participatory and accountable. In 2004, the Emir issued a new labor law, which protects the labor rights of Qatari nationals but does not protect Qatar's large foreign workforce (Blanchard 2008: 4). Furthermore, the Emir and prominent Qatari women started to reform the education sector through the Qatar Foundation and the new 'Education City' in particular (a state-of-the-art campus complex outside Doha that offers degrees from prestigious US universities such as Cornell, Georgetown and Carnegie Mellon) (Blanchard 2008: 6, Eakin 2011). Although the legislative constitution and political reform program were significant steps, the Emir seemed to slow down the pace of constitutional, democratic reform in his final years in office, consolidating his power (Fromherz 2012: 86). In late June 2013, the Emir Sheikh Hamad bin Khalifa Al Thani stepped down and handed over power to his son, heir apparent Sheikh Tamim, in a peaceful abdication.

Today, Qatar remains an absolute, hereditary monarchy. The Emir exercises full executive power, and the ruling elite is also the de facto owner of the country's vast economic resources, which derive mainly from Qatar's unique position in the international gas markets with the world's third largest gas reserves (after Russia and Iran) (Mansour 2007, Wright 2009) and from being the world's leading exporter of liquefied natural gas to European and North-American markets (Eakin 2011) and increasingly to Asian countries (Ulrichsen 2012: 6). Although a series of national elections have been held in Qatar, the government maintains strict limits on freedom of assembly and association. In Qatar, there are no elections for national leadership, political parties are outlawed, and civil society organizations are heavily regulated. A series of new laws allow individuals to organize public gatherings, but organizers must obtain a permit from the government in order to do so. All private professional and cultural associations must register with the state; they are monitored, and Qatari authorities may impose restrictions on the topics of discussion (Blanchard 2008: 3). The state has initiated a number of well-funded, government-controlled 'NGOs,' primarily institutions engaging in charity and outreach efforts, thus forestalling the emergence of politically autonomous organizations (Kamrava 2009: 407). As will be explored in more detail below, the Qatari elite has developed an open environment for debate, social freedom, creativity and religious freedom as long as these debates do not address internal Qatari affairs or the positions and practices of the elite (Fromherz 2012: 28).

Overall, Qatar's rulers are under little if any internal political pressure (Ehteshami & Wright 2007, Kamrava 2009). The Qatari state has significant capacity and power in relation to Qatari society (Kamrava 2009: 405): The small size of the country's population, combined with its vast oil and gas resources, has made it easy to establish a comprehensive welfare system (Dargin 2007) and has made Qataris among the world's wealthiest citizens (Berrebi et al. 2009). Compared to its Gulf neighbors, Qatar is relatively ethnically and religiously homogenous (Rabi 2009). The royal Al Thani family has not faced any serious competition to the throne from other powerful families, the religious establishment has not created an independent power base, and the family has managed to centralize power and develop extensive patronage networks undermining the "potential emergence of an autonomous, politically independent Qatari civil society" (Kamrava 2009: 406). In particular, the Qatari elite has benefitted strongly from the country's rapid development and thus actively support the large-scale modernization processes (Fromherz 2012, Kamrava 2009). Underlining that the Qatari political landscape is more complex than it seems, however, Fromherz (2012: 129–44) finds that the power of the Emir is circumscribed by internal arrangements of a highly local, tribal and informal nature.

Analysts have characterized Qataris as "politically apathetic" (Ehteshami & Wright 2007), with low "political consciousness" (Lambert 2011), and popular demands for democratization or increased women's rights have been practically nonexistent (Kamrava 2009: 417, Lambert 2011: 96). The recent Arab Youth Surveys (2011, 2012) have demonstrated that democracy ranked lowest among young Qataris of all countries polled (see Lambert 2011 for discussion). Historically, the only group that has challenged Qatar's political stability has been the ruling family itself, and before the recent peaceful transition of power, all of the last three leadership transitions (1949, 1960 and 1995) have been results of forced abdications (Kamrava 2009: 412). The question of Qatari government-initiated political reforms have puzzled political analysts, although most conclude that the controlled, top-down political reforms amount to pragmatic measures initiated by the Qatari elite to increase their own legitimacy (Ehteshami & Wright 2007, Kamrava 2009, Lambert 2011). Kamrava (2009) argues that it was internal royal factionalism that forced the Emir to make promises of political liberalization in order to bypass the criticism of the royal family's more conservative elements (supported by neighboring GCC ruling elites). Fromherz (2012: 94) argues that Qatar's political reform agenda has served to distinguish and contrast Qatar from its powerful neighbor, Saudi Arabia. Similarly, Lambert (2011) explains the reform initiatives as instrumental in bolstering Qatar's external legitimacy—and ultimately the tiny country's security—by adopting international norms on democracy and gender equality. Qatar can best be characterized as a 'democratic autocracy'—an autocratic state where the rulers legitimize their rule by maintaining some form or semblance of a democratization process, such as elections, a conditional press freedom, a semi-independent judiciary, etc. (Rønning 2009: 31). As underlined by Lambert (2011), most regimes in the Middle East/North Africa region allow some form of electoral policies although many of them have used political participation to avoid (proper) democratization.

QATAR'S AMBITIOUS FOREIGN POLICY LINE

After the end of the Iran-Iraq War (1988) and the Gulf War (1991), Qatar developed a more autonomous foreign policy conducted largely on the basis of Qatar's own interests, which have been characterized as "pragmatic" (Wright 2009), "ambitious" (Dargin 2007), "independent" (Blanchard 2008), "intricate" (Rabi 2009) and "chaotic" (de Lage 2005). After Qatar gained independence in 1971, Qatari authorities have striven to balance three foreign policy considerations: on the one hand, Qatar's foreign policy interests largely coincide with those of the other Gulf Cooperation Council (GCC) members in (1) their role as strategic energy exporters, (2) their strategic relationship with the US in terms of security and political and economic considerations, (3) their collective, independent roles within the Middle East subregion, (4) their domestic social, political and economic dynamics, and (5) their personalized, elitist, political decision-making processes (Wright 2009: 3–4). Overall, there has been a general recognition among GCC ruling elites that their survival is "interlinked"—that they can rely on each others' support in the face of serious domestic crisis (Kamrava 2009:404). In the first years after independence, Qatar acted under the Saudi/GCC umbrella, and its security became linked to that of its powerful neighbor (Zahlan 1998: 153).

On the other hand, Qatar's foreign policy has been shaped by its need for protection from its powerful Gulf neighbors, Iran and Saudi Arabia (Dargin 2007). Qatar's pragmatic strategy of using an external foreign power as a guarantor of its security has been a key characteristic of its foreign policy from the periods of the Ottoman Empire (late 1860s–1916) and the British Empire (1916–71), to the contemporary American military presence (1996 to the present) (Wright 2009: 9). In May 2003, US President Bush hosted the Emir of Qatar, thanking him for his steadfast support during Operation Iraqi Freedom and praising his role as a reformer (Blanchard 2008: 14). The US embassy was established in Doha in 1973, but US relations did not become more cordial until after the 1991 Persian Gulf War. Qatar first signed a defense cooperation agreement with the US in 1992, but it was not until Sheikh Hamad took power in 1995 that the "foundations were set for a changed foreign policy strategy of seeking a long-term hard-security arrangement to offset the geopolitical threats that were being faced" (Wright 2009: 15). The high construction costs of the al Udeid airbase facility (widely reported as costing Qatar over USD 1 billion at a time when the country had experienced years of government deficits), illustrated the strategic importance of coming under the American security umbrella (ibid.: 16). After September 11 2001, the al Udeid facility gained significant status in US military planning of the "war on terror" (Blanchard 2008: 9). At this time, US–Saudi relations were deteriorating because Osama bin Laden and the majority of the hijackers were of Saudi origin, and Saudi authorities, given the growing internal Islamist opposition, were reluctant to participate in the impending attack on Iraq (Wright 2009: 16). Consequently, the US administration redeployed its military forces from the Prince Sultan airbase in Saudi Arabia to al Udeid and decided that the facility should become the Headquarters of the US central Command (ibid.: 17). Over the last 15 years, Qatari–US defense relations have expanded to include cooperative defense exercises, the prepositioning of equipment, and base access agreements (for details on this defense cooperation and counterterrorism, see Blanchard 2008: 10–14). During the US-led war against Iraq in 2003, Qatar and Kuwait were the only neighboring states that offered military basing rights to the US, thereby departing from the GCC consensus (ibid.). It is noteworthy that, although tensions between the Arabic Al Jazeera Channel (AJA) and the US Administration grew during the war in Iraq (see Figenschou 2005 for discussion), diplomatic relations remained stable (Powers 2012). Challenging Arab norms, Qatar's unique, albeit controversial, bilateral ties with Israel have been another much-discussed feature: "Qatar has used both normalization with and estrangement from Israel as policy tools, calibrated to maintain its visibility in a constantly changing geopolitical environment" (Rabi 2009: 459). The fact that Qatar shut down the Israeli interest office in Doha during the Gaza War in January 2009 shows that even Qatar's flexible diplomacy has its limits (Fromherz 2012: 103). Moreover, there is reason to believe that Qatar has also had strategic contacts with controversial non-state actors such as Al-Qaeda and various opposition groups in exile have sought refuge in Doha (ibid.).

Since the mid-2000s, Qatar has strategically sought greater international recognition and harbors aspirations of playing a proactive global and regional role in conflict resolution. This key facet of its foreign policy is explicitly laid out in the Qatari constitution of 2004, stating:

> The foreign policy of the State is based on the principle of strengthening international peace and security by means of encouraging peaceful resolution of international disputes; and shall support the right of peoples to self-determination; and shall not interfere in the domestic affairs of states; and shall cooperate with peace-loving nations. (Article 7, Government of the State of Qatar 2004)

To date, Qatar has become one of the world's most active mediators in the Middle East and Africa, most notably in Lebanon, Yemen and Sudan (Kamrava 2011), but also in Libya, Iran/UAE, Iraq, Palestine, Sudan, Djibouti/Eritrea, Morocco/West Sahara and Afghanistan (Eakin 2011, Fromherz 2012, Kamrava 2011, Wright 2009).[3] Explaining the Qatari mediation efforts, analysts again point to the particular Qatari combination of small-state survival strategies and a desire for international prestige (Kamrava 2011, Wright 2009). Qatar's 'niche diplomacy' has been characterized by a combination of intense personal diplomacy and engagement by prominent Qatari leaders coupled by promises (implicit or explicit) of vast Qatari investments if/when the dispute settles ("business or checkbook diplomacy") (Kamrava 2011, Rabi 2009). The strategy is made possible due to the country's perceived impartiality in regional politics and vast gas reserves—a strategy that can be summarized as: wealth, will and vision (Barakat 2012: 12). But Qatar's small size, its lack of experienced diplomats and relatively-short history of diplomatic initiatives have made it difficult to move beyond mediation to successful conflict resolution (Barakat 2012: 22–5, Kamrava 2011: 552–6).

THE PARADOXES OF THE QATARI MEDIA SYSTEM

Mass media in Qatar were initially started for the purpose of building a modern nation, planned and initiated by the former Ministry of Information (Arafa 1994: 230). The Qatari Press and Publication Law of 1979 stated that the media should not publish news that could harm the Emir, undermine the established order, or endanger the political regime. The press law also stated that the authorities had the right to censor media that did not comply with these regulations (ibid.: 231). After Sheikh Hamad replaced his father, the new Emir eased press censorship and abolished the Ministry of Information. Qatar became the first Arab government without such a ministry. According to the official website of Qatar's Ministry of Foreign Affairs (MOFA), "Censorship was lifted from local press in accordance with the eminent directive of His Highness the Emir since October 1995. Law No 5 of 1998, which abolished the Ministry of Information and Culture, distributed some of its departments and transformed others into independent bodies complemented the move" (MOFA 2010). At the same time, however, the Emir created a new General Association for Radio and Television to supervise the government-owned terrestrial broadcasting facilities (Rugh 2004: 205). The national broadcaster, Qatar TV, started transmitting in the early 1970s and by satellite since 1998. Broadcasting has been a priority for Qatari authorities, and in addition to the national television channel, Qatar General Broadcasting and Television Corporation runs the national radio Qatar Radio (QBR)(1968), Sout al Khaleej Radio (music and entertainment starting in 2002), and two sports channels (starting in 2008). Additionally, Qatar News Agency (QANA) covers both Qatari interests and affairs worldwide and seeks to promote the country to foreign media (MOFA 2010). Furthermore, the influential and controversial Islamic web site, IslamOnline, is based in and funded by Qatar (Fromherz 2012: 109).

The Qatari constitution of 2004 provides for freedom of speech and the press, but the government has limited those rights in practice. According to MOFA's presentation, "Local press has flourished in recent years, benefiting from the prevailing democratic atmosphere and available incentives to grow and spread to cover all social and economic areas of interest" (MOFA 2010). However, the US Bureau of Democracy, Human Rights, and Labor found that: "Journalists and publishers continue to self-censor due to political and economic pressure when reporting on government policies, material deemed hostile to Islam, the ruling family and relations with neighboring states" (US Bureau of Democracy, Human Rights, and Labor 2009: 3). There were reported cases where security personnel threatened both individuals and organizations against publishing certain articles, and the interference of media owners in media content was prevalent. Ironically, one of the issues in which the state has instructed national media was women's political rights and candidature for office (Lambert 2011: 93). Although Qatar's seven daily national newspapers are not state-owned, the owners are members of the ruling family or closely connected to government officials (US Bureau of Democracy, Human Rights, and Labor 2009: 3). State-owned broadcasting reflects government views, although callers to the morning radio show frequently criticize government inefficiency and related topics (ibid.: 4). The government also restricts Internet access and monitors and blocks political, religious and pornographic content through a proxy server (ibid.). The government censors imported foreign publications, and objectionable sexual, religious and political content is removed or scrawled in black. Moreover, Qatar customs and the censorship office in the Qatar Radio and Television Corporation checks imported foreign broadcasting for sensitive content (ibid.: 4). Qatar was ranked 110 out of 179 countries in the Reporters Without Borders annual index of press freedom 2013 (Reporters Without Borders 2013). All in all, the Qatari national media maintain a polished, loyalist news agenda—publishing stories of ministers and members of the royal family shaking hands with visiting state leaders—and selective, positive résumés of the government affairs of the day.

At the same time, with its innovative media projects, of which Al Jazeera is the prime example, Qatar aims to play a role as a regional patron of media freedom. Most recently, Qatari authorities distinguished themselves from their Arab neighbors by declining to sign the 2008 Arab Satellite Charter, citing potential conflicts with their own media laws (Kraidy & Khalil 2009: 142). Whether symbolic or a concrete step toward a more repressive regional media-policy regime, the charter represents the first formal pan-Arab regulatory text and indicates the policy agendas of the majority of the Arab governments, which aim to reassert control over the transnational media scene (ibid.: 144). Other examples of Qatar's media initiatives are The Doha Debates (a collaboration between the Qatar Foundation and BBC World, hosted by Tim Sebastian and broadcasted on the BBC since 2004) and The Doha Centre for Media Freedom (opened in April 2008). The Emir's motives in launching and expanding these initiatives are not entirely clear, but most researchers conclude that they are related to Qatari foreign policy interests and thus act indirectly as a soft power tool (see discussion below) (Telhami 2004: 84, Wright 2009).

The 2009 controversies related to the Doha Centre for Media Freedom illustrate the contradictions between policy declarations and political practice in Qatar's media policy. The centre was set up with support from Reporters Without Borders in cooperation with the Qatar Foundation, which is headed by Sheikha Mouza (Emir Sheik Hamad's second wife and mother of the current Emir Sheikh Tamim). The Doha Centre's stated purpose was to provide physical refuge to endangered journalists and strengthen press freedom (MOFA 2010). Although the center, headed by international freedom of the press campaigner Robert Ménard, played a regional role and helped over 250 endangered journalists, they encountered difficulties when they criticized Qatari conditions. The center was openly critical of media developments in Qatar, and in its February 2009 report titled Media Freedom in the Middle East and North Africa, it asserted that the Qatari media are greatly affected by self-censorship (MENA Report 2009: 17). In June 2009, Ménard and his staff left the Doha Centre, and Reporters Without Borders withdrew its support.[4] The Qatari authorities' inconsistencies with regard to the Doha Centre, first inviting the center to open and then sabotaging its work, are hard to explain. One possible explanation may be that the authorities were taken by surprise by the Doha Centre's lack of self-censorship so that they felt the need to restrict the center's activities. What's more, different factions within the royal family may have held diverging opinions on media freedom. In the above-mentioned report, the Doha Centre for Media Freedom called attention to the striking contrast between Al Jazeera's boldness in its coverage of international affairs and the cautiousness they and other Qatari journalists exercise when it comes to internal Qatari matters (MENA Report 2009: 17). After an almost two-year hiatus, the center was relaunched in April 2011, and, according to the Doha Centre website, the new director Dutch Jan Keulen was granted full freedom and promised to push for greater media freedom in Qatar.

ANYWHERE, BUT HERE: AL JAZEERA–QATARI RELATIONS

Al Jazeera Network officials are not willing to comment on the amount of financial backing they receive from Qatari authorities and are very secretive about their budgets, but it is vital to note that the Arab news networks (including Al Jazeera) have to rely on the deep pockets of political patrons (Kraidy & Khalil 2009: 97). Although Al Jazeera is partly commercial, the advertising revenue alone rarely covers the large expenses associated with satellite links, bureaus, journalists and high-value news production (ibid.). According to Al Jazeera sources interviewed for this book, only a small portion of the budget comes from commercial revenue (around 15–20 percent), and the network remains funded by the government.

Advertising in the Arab world is politicized. As discussed above, there is a lack of rating information and audience profiles, the regional advertising market is scanty, and competition is increasing among a growing number of networks (Sakr 2002).[5] In the wealthy Arab countries, the governments continue to dominate the economy, and privatization has generally meant transferring state assets to the ruling family. The placing of lucrative advertisements has thus been used more for "political leverage than as a means of communicating with consumers" (ibid.). Consequently, Al Jazeera Arabic has lost many of its commercial advertisers due to pressure exerted by the Gulf Cooperation Council (GCC) member states spearheaded by Saudi Arabia. Initially, the channel sold advertisements to Saudi companies, but when relations between Qatar and Saudi Arabia froze, the contracts were cancelled. A meeting of the GCC in 2002 issued a call to boycott advertisers who bought time on Al Jazeera, and Saudi and Kuwaiti authorities discourage their citizens from advertising on the channel (Bahry 2001: 95, El-Nawawy & Iskandar 2002: 211, Hammond 2007: 9). Even as AJA became the most watched Arab satellite channel, advertisers avoided it in fear of alienating the Saudi authorities and risking their access to the lucrative Saudi market.

After the Arabic channel's controversial coverage of the wars in Afghanistan and Iraq, major companies regionally and globally have become concerned that Al Jazeera's shaky relationship with Arab governments could harm their business interests. Consequently, the Al Jazeera Network has a low advertisement dependency, and this has given them greater editorial freedom compared to commercial media. On the other hand, the low level of advertisement results in a high sponsor dependency that may potentially influence the editorial line.

Furthermore, for private advertisers following commercial logic, the Al Jazeera Network and other Arab satellite channels represent a risky investment. In general, the increased commercialization of the Arab television industry, the introduction of product placement and the growth of regional advertising budgets have not been matched by reliable audience measurements, and pan-Arab audience research remains underdeveloped when compared to the satellite industry (Kraidy & Khalil 2009: 116–122). Most Arab-based satellite media do not have detailed audience profiles, and the Al Jazeera Network is no exception. To take AJE as an example, although it is a commercial English-language channel open to advertisers worldwide, the channel management does not have a distinctive conception of who their viewers are. In written internal editorial guidelines, the audience is described broadly as 'worldwide, English speakers.' In the official information for potential advertisers, AJE emphasizes that the channel is available (to potential viewers) in over 260 million households in over 120 countries (AJE press office information request, May 2013).

The overall impression is that the channel is dependent on the Qatari elite, not only through the government subsidies, but also through its 'private' advertising. The channel airs remarkably few advertisements, and the majority of the advertising time is used to air promos for the channel and upcoming programming. In addition, most of the sponsors are national Qatari interests and businesses, such as Qatar Airways and Qatar Gas, whereas other significant Qatari companies such as Qatar Petroleum and Qatar Financial Centre had frequent advertisements on the channel in its first years on air.

Moreover, for the majority of Al Jazeera Network employees who are expatriates, their relations with their employer have a direct impact on their rights to work and live in Qatar. In the Arab Gulf kingdoms, the kafala, or sponsorship system, regulates the rights of all expatriate workers (Dresch 2005: 23). These sponsorship laws tie all non-Qatari workers' residence visas to a specific employer, or sponsor, who controls their status, visa, salary, working (and often living) conditions and potential expulsion—and often has authority over the expatriate workers' personal documents (Fromherz 2012, Nagy 2006). Naturalization of foreign residents is very rare, especially for non-Arabs or non-Muslims, and the majority of foreign workers occupy the status of eternal visitors (Nagy 2006: 122). Over time, the sponsorship system maintains a subtle social hierarchy that elevates the Qataris above the expatriate workers and secures significant economic benefits for the national sponsors (Davidson 2012). In the sponsorship system, openly disagreeing with a sponsor may entail a high degree of personal risk. The dilemmas and challenges concerning the expatriate population's relations with Qatari authorities and native population will be explored more in detail in chapter 8, this volume.

As outlined in the beginning of this chapter, the growth of Arab satellite news channels has been driven by inter-Arab political rivalries. Most critical investigations of the ways in which the Qatari ownership interests have been reflected in the editorial line of the Al Jazeera Network have analyzed Al Jazeera Arabic's critical coverage of Saudi Arabia. The Saudi case illustrates the ways in which Qatari authorities have used AJA in the regional rivalry by exposing the negative developments and problems of their mighty neighbor. The relations between Qatar and Saudi Arabia were not normalized until a deal was struck in late September 2007 (Blanchard 2008, Fandy 2007, Hammond 2007, Wright 2009). Another primary focus in the literature has been on AJA's controversial coverage of the US-led war on terror, elucidating Qatar's pragmatic relationship with the US. America's Arab allies in the Gulf have always struggled to balance the need for protection and support with the growing unease about dependence on the West (Sick 1998: 79). This dilemma is reflected in Qatari–US relations, where Qatari authorities pragmatically balance external and internal pressures. First, the presence of American military bases on Qatari soil, which provides security against the wrath of powerful neighbors, has secured the Qatari goals of political autonomy and regime security (Telhami 2004, Wright 2009). Second, AJA's critical coverage of the US-led war on terror has won support from broader Arab and Muslim audiences and served a domestic purpose by shaping opinion and fostering legitimacy against charges of being overly aligned with a perceived imperialist power (Telhami 2004). Third, by publicly refusing to interfere with Al Jazeera Network's editorial line, Qatari authorities enhance their image as a brave supporter of freedom of the press.

The network channels have repeatedly been challenged for their neglect of domestic issues and negative developments in Qatar. According to Fandy (2000), Al Jazeera suffers from what he characterizes as the 'anywhere but here' syndrome in the Arab media: frequently criticizing the politics of other Arab countries, while remaining silent about domestic issues (Fandy 2000). In particular, Al Jazeera Arabic's news broadcasts have a long history of infuriating, provoking, and frightening regional governments. When their legitimacy is brought into question, Arab governments have often taken action (Telhami 2004: 82). Much of the criticism against AJA has been directed towards debates and talk shows; for instance, the channel is frequently criticized for being sensationalist, populist, and speculative, rather than informative, investigative and serious (Ayish 2005, El-Nawawy & Iskandar 2002, El Tounsy 2002). It is also charged with preferring conflict to dialogue and compromise, inviting guests who represent extreme opinions while neglecting the moderates (ibid.). Al Jazeera has also been criticized for using Western news agencies and Western standards, thereby alienating viewers from Arab culture and society (Bahry 2001: 96).

With a few noteworthy appearances of high-ranking Qatari officials on AJA's talk show *Without Borders*, Qatar's foreign policy is barely covered on the network in any breadth or depth (Zayani 2011: 190). According to Al Jazeera Network officials, Qatar has not been a priority for the network because it is not a national news network but rather a regional and international network broadcasting for regional and international audiences. When criticized for muting Qatari affairs, Al Jazeera officials reiterate that they are governed by newsworthiness. Qatar is a small country with little news of regional or international importance. They assert that if something were to happen in Qatar that had regional or international implications, the network would cover it on the basis of its news value. In the quantitative content analysis of Al Jazeera English's flagship news over a period of five months in 2007–2008, Qatari domestic affairs were not an issue in any of the more than 1300 news items analyzed (see chapter 4, this volume). This may signal that the channel is truly global in its approach, as emphasized in the channel's production strategies (see chapter 3, this volume for discussion). Alternatively, it could strengthen claims that the Al Jazeera Network is a foreign policy tool of the Qatari authorities (Da Lage 2005) and that the limited coverage of domestic Qatari affairs is the result of self-censorship. However, the news items in which Qatari diplomats and interests were involved were related to the Qatari authorities' proactive role in conflict resolution in Yemen and Lebanon. Qatar's role in the negotiations during the political deadlock in Lebanon in May 2008 was given particular priority on AJE. Thus far, the high-profile, Doha-brokered agreement between the contesting Lebanese groups in May 2008 has been the most noteworthy Doha initiative. To reach an agreement on Lebanon, Qatari authorities flew all parties to Doha and thereby demonstrated their readiness to engage in high-profile summit-style diplomacy (Wright 2009: 26). Thus, AJE's coverage of the negotiations on Lebanon highlighted Qatar's most recent diplomatic success and reflected its foreign policy interests.

In the examples above, the Al Jazeera project seems to correspond with Qatari foreign policy by strengthening Qatar's position (towards Saudi Arabia), by balancing Qatari needs in the country's controversial partnerships (with the US), or by emphasizing Qatari initiatives (and highlighting the proactive Qatari role in regional conflict resolution). Primarily, Al Jazeera's political attitude can be regarded to some extent as the result of a policy of putting Qatar on the map by emphasizing the ways in which it diverges from its neighbors and challenges regional and global powers. By these means, Qatari political elites use Al Jazeera to stir up controversy in a controlled way (Rugh 2007: 12).

IS AJE A QATARI PUBLIC DIPLOMACY TOOL?

For an adequate discussion of AJE in relation to Qatari foreign policy, it is fruitful to employ the growing literature on mediated foreign policy initiatives. The US administration's intensive public diplomacy campaign towards the Arab public epitomized the renewed awareness of soft power (Nye Jr. 1990, 2004a/b, 2008), public diplomacy (see Gilboa 2008, Leonard 2002, Leonard & Smewing 2003) and place branding (Ham 2008) in the last decade. Soft power is "the ability to affect others to obtain the outcomes one wants through attraction rather than coercion or payment" (Nye Jr. 2008). Public diplomacy has a long history as a means of promoting a country's soft power. Public diplomacy signifies various efforts to inform and influence public opinion in other countries—to win hearts and minds by means of information activities, educational and cultural exchange, and international broadcasting (see Gilboa 2008, Leonard 2002, Leonard & Smewing 2003). Theories on place branding consider a place brand to be an intellectual property—the strategic image, brand building, and reputation management of a place and/or state. Place branding and public diplomacy both combine foreign policy goals with internal soft power strategies and objectives (Ham 2008: 135).

In spite of the renewed academic and political interest in public diplomacy, the literature on the field lacks a substantial theoretical structure (Entman 2008, Gilboa 2008). According to Entman, the current scholarship on public diplomacy has been too broad and has been based on the false assumption that if only foreign elites and publics had access to better factual information, they would become more supportive of American policy (Entman 2008: 88–90). In an effort to operationalize and theorize public diplomacy strategies toward foreign media, which he labeled mediated public diplomacy, he elaborated an extension of the cascading networks model (see chapter 5, this volume, for further elaboration). The success of these strategies, he hypothesized, depends most importantly on political and cultural congruency between the sender and the target nation, as well as on the strategy, power and motivations of foreign elites to promote positive news about the sender. In the current global visibility, however, there seems to be an inherent tension between the effect of cultural proximity and the persuasive needs of public diplomacy. It is increasingly difficult to keep the local home audience and the foreign audiences separated (Sheafer & Shenhaw 2009: 277–80). Examining mediated public diplomacy empirically, Sheafer & Gabay (2009) demonstrated that political and cultural congruency between the sender country and the target country is a decisive factor, but they also documented that foreign media and governments do not play a passive role in the process, but rather strive to promote their own interests (ibid.: 463–4).

Public diplomacy strategies also include international broadcasting, most recently in the form of state-sponsored satellite news channels launched for the purposes of public diplomacy. In the limited research literature that analyzes Al Jazeera in a public diplomacy perspective, the channel has mainly been studied as a platform for public diplomacy initiatives for Western governments or as a platform for dialogue. These studies conclude that Western and/or American officials need to intensify their diplomacy efforts to communicate with the Arab people through effective existing media channels like AJA (El-Nawawy & Gher 2003, Figenschou 2005, 2006, Lynch 2003, Rugh 2009). Another body of literature finds that AJE has a potential to bridge East and West and that the channel can be characterized as a conciliatory medium (El-Nawawy & Powers 2008, 2010, Khamis 2007, Powers & Gilboa 2007). A third research tradition analyzes AJA as a political actor, arguing for a new public diplomacy that is no longer confined to the domain of nation-states. In the case of transnational media organizations like AJA, Powers & Gilboa (2007: 74–5) found that Al Jazeera is not merely a transnational media organization, but also a network that acts and is treated as a political actor in international politics. They argued that it has adopted a political agenda with regard to both internal Arab politics and Arab–Western relations and that the channel use public diplomacy to achieve this agenda (ibid.). The problem with Powers & Gilboa's (2007) study is their neglect of the important role and strategic political interests of the Qatari authorities highlighted in this chapter.

In the following, I argue that Al Jazeera has to be understood in terms of a dialectic of autonomy (organizational and journalistic) and dependency (economic and political) that results from a complex interplay between national, regional and international factors and aspirations. As mentioned at the beginning of this chapter, Al Jazeera is an independent public institution. Both government and Al Jazeera officials maintain that the network is independent and that its only connection to Qatari authorities is through its funding. There is a broad consensus that the network has revolutionized Arab television news as the first Arab channel based on Arab soil that is explicitly critical of Arab regimes and governments. Furthermore, the level of individual editorial freedom within the Al Jazeera Channel has been emphasized in studies of the channel (Zayani & Sahraoui 2007). Having said that, in the authoritarian Qatari political context—where the ruling family and elite both have monopolized executive political power, regulate the contradictory Qatari media system and operate as the de facto 'owners' of the network—it is obvious that this independence is somehow relative and conditional. The limits of this independence will be tested more frequently and thoroughly if Qatar's regional and international role grows. The most up-to-date example will be the tiny nation's preparation for and hosting of the 2022 World Cup. Can and will AJE cover Qatar's achievement as the host nation independently and critically? And to give another related example, if Qatar gains a position as a key regional peace negotiator, can AJE scrutinize its strategies and initiatives?

At the same time, as a public diplomacy tool, the Al Jazeera Network only serves Qatar as long as it maintain its editorial independence, or at least is perceived to be editorially independent by the outside world. According to the official narrative, Al Jazeera is a symbol of the progressive reform line of the Qatari Emir, but a closer investigation reveals that the interests in launching and expanding the Al Jazeera Network are more multifaceted. It is therefore fruitful to distinguish between the intra-Gulf, regional and global levels in order to understand Qatar's Al Jazeera project.

First, in recent years there has been a national revival throughout the Gulf kingdoms: a rebranding of the region and the relatively young individual nation states, which has involved the invention and reinvention of traditional culture. A prominent argument in Fromherz' (2012) history of modern Qatar is the fact that Qatar has maintained a very traditional society throughout its rapid growth and modernization, or, rather, constructed a tightly controlled, sanitized, neotraditional national identity. One example is the adoption of the 'traditional' national dress code, which distinguishes the national population from the expatriates (Davidson 2012: 60–1). Considerable spending on museums, the staging of heritage events and the sponsorship of traditional literary and cultural productions are examples of this revival of tribal history, which reminds the national population of the historical roots of the ruling family's legitimacy (Davidson 2009: 133, Fromherz 2012: 29). At the same time, to diversify the petroleum-based economies and rebrand Gulf identity, the ruling families in the Arab Gulf kingdoms have launched impressive modernization strategies (Baabood 2008, Davidson 2008, 2009, Hvidt 2011, Mattern 2008, Wright 2009). Following what Hvidt (2009, 2011) has described as the "Dubai model" (a more production-oriented economic model), all the Gulf kingdoms seem to be in the process of preparing their economies to become more competitive, diverse and more reliant on the private sector. In particular, Qatar, the UAE, Saudi Arabia and Oman have made their economies increasingly open and attractive to international investors, although rolling back 30–50 years of rentierism is neither an easy nor a quick task (Hvidt 2011: 102).

For Qatar, the modernization strategy includes a massive program of infrastructural development to boost the tourism sector, such as its world-class national air carriers (Qatar Airways) and airports, striking architecture (the glass skyline of The West Bay and the artificial island the Pearl), luxurious leisure facilities, impressive sporting facilities and academies (Aspire Academy and Sport City), and high-profile international competitions (the Asian Games, 2006, and, more than anything, the upcoming 2022 FIFA World Cup). The unprecedented investment in sporting infrastructure and the staging and sponsorship of the world's leading sports has made researchers talk of a 'sportification' of the region (Amara 2006). The Qatar Investment Authority has invested in cultural institutions, real estate and prestigious companies worldwide, with trophy acquisitions such as Harrods (London, UK) and Volkswagen/Porsche

(Germany) (Davidson 2012). Among its main investments in culture, Qatar hosts the Doha Tribeca film festival (an offshoot of the New York event) and the Museum of Islamic art.

The large-scale investments showcase modern Gulf culture, express the Arab Gulf kingdoms' national identity, project their self-image and, thereby, serve as a means by which the region can engage with the rest of the world (Davidson 2009). They also serve as an example of what has been characterized as a "place branding frenzy" in the contemporary mediatized global economy (Ham 2008: 133). By aiming to manage their nation brand equity, governments seek to strengthen both their power and identity and to increase the inhabitants' sense of belonging (ibid.: 131). Qatar's massive investment in regional and international satellite news media is part of this intra-Gulf rivalry for regional and international media attention, both because it demonstrates Qatari modernity and because it is an efficient platform to promote national development and success in other sectors.

Second, on the regional level, Al Jazeera (particularly through the Arabic-language channel) has been a tool for the Qatari authorities in the intra-Arab political rivalry across the Arab region, between Qatar and the regional superpowers, between Qatar and its powerful neighbor Saudi Arabia, and among the smaller Gulf kingdoms. In this regional struggle for influence outlined in the beginning of this chapter, Al Jazeera has the only influential English-language news channel, which demonstrates the global ambitions of the Qatari authorities. All in all, there is a feeling among Gulf Arabs that the rest of the world, including other parts of the Middle East, have tended to be dismissive of and condescending to the indigenous Gulf culture. Furthermore, in the wider MENA region, the large media investments in the Gulf challenge traditional regional Arab media powers, such as Egypt, Lebanon and Saudi Arabia.

Third, after Al Jazeera launched its English-language website (March 2003) and news channel (November 2006), the network increased its potential global audience and influence and thereby helped put Qatar on the international map. Through its distinct, alternative agenda in international affairs analyzed throughout this book, AJE demonstrates its editorial boldness and Qatari 'media freedom' in practice, and the editorial distinctiveness of the channel has attracted vast international media interest with mostly positive spillover effects on its owner. All in all, it is through AJE's role as a satellite news contra-flow (see chapters 3–7, this volume, for discussion) that it serves Qatar's strategic interests. In order to reflect the national strategies underlying AJE's role of providing contra-flow and shed light on the structural contradiction between AJE's alternative agenda and its autocratic owner, the channel's purpose has been described as *strategic* contra-flow. Qatari interests in AJE are communicated through a subtle, public diplomacy strategy in which AJE systematically neglects critical coverage of Qatari affairs at the same time as Qatar is promoted through channel design (the Doha skyline is a key element in the Doha news studio design), positive infomercials and sponsor activity. AJE could therefore be understood as a key component of Qatar's broader place-branding strategy within the Gulf region, in the Arab world, and on a global level. Qatar is projecting its political influence transnationally without formally owning or operating the satellite network. Moreover, with its editorial emphasis on Qatar's proactive role in regional and international politics, in combination with the many advertisements for the Qatari oil and gas, business, transport, financial and education sectors, the Al Jazeera Network gives Qatar a stronger voice than the country could ever hope to achieve through traditional diplomacy.

The Qatari–Al Jazeera public diplomacy model diverges from Western models of public diplomacy in that it is *outward looking.* In contrast to the international broadcasting strategies of the great powers, such as American, British, French, or German international broadcasting, which promote, highlight, and explain national models and values, Qatari society and values have been largely ignored on AJE. Qatar is a tiny, wealthy, young nation that primarily aims for international recognition and economic and political attention. Consequently, Qatar has a different agenda than traditional power centers, which are striving to change largely negative perceptions of their foreign policy, best symbolized by the US public diplomacy campaigns in the Arab world after 9/11. As demonstrated in the news flow debate examined in chapter 4 (this volume), a microstate like Qatar does not traditionally attract news coverage in major foreign or international media. By circumventing the news agenda in mainstream international media, the Al Jazeera project both increases Qatar's newsworthiness and offers Qatari authorities a platform from which to discretely promote and frame the Qatari success story (its expansive economy, booming gas exports, health care system and investments in higher education and architecture) to an international audience. According to this idealized marketed image of Qatar, Fromherz (2012: 2) writes, "Qatar seems full of venues for dialogue that enhance Qatar's image and the image of the ruling Al Thani family." For the ruling family, the Al Jazeera Network serves both as a demonstration of, and channel to inform regarding what has been labeled Qatar's many "showcases of reform" (Bahry & Marr 2005: 108). The fact that few of these reforms represent substantial societal changes is purposely omitted from the marketed Qatari image.

The analysis of Qatari–AJE relations in this chapter provides new insight into the research on mediated public diplomacy and elucidates the ways in which satellite broadcasting can be utilized for the purposes of foreign policy, public diplomacy and place branding. Second, it demonstrates the ways in which AJE's alternative editorial line and its identity-news contra-flow paradoxically serve the purposes of the autocratic Qatari government. Third, it demonstrates the ways in which national governments aim to influence the global satellite news ecology through state-sponsored satellite news channels. These findings illustrate the need to conduct critical examination of strategic media ownership in the analysis of the current boom in second-generation satellite news channels. As long as Al Jazeera is financially and politically dependent on the Emir, any serious domestic political change in Qatar may have an impact on the network. After the 'Arab Spring' uprisings shook the region in 2011–12, the longtime stability of the Gulf kingdoms has been questioned by political analysts. The challenges to the ruling Al Thani family and the Qatari system, and how these challenges may influence the future of the Al Jazeera Network, will be discussed in the concluding chapter.

3 Editorial Strategies
The Challenges of 'Reporting Back'

"The feature channel," he said. "I call it the feature channel." The senior editorial manager at Al Jazeera Arabic could not hide a smirk, knowing he had put his finger on a sore spot. His comment echoed the repeated criticism of both Al Jazeera English's many in-depth feature reports, its boring, politically correct "Bob Geldof TV" and, worse, the fact that the channel's content was characterized as irrelevant by external analysts (Pintak 2008). His comment also reflected the internal fear of becoming irrelevant that was prevalent among many Al Jazeera English staff interviewed for this book, who found it difficult to achieve a balance between being a competitive 24-hour international news channel and being an alternative to those channels.

The production level has been largely ignored in current scholarship on global news flows and contra-flows (Hanusch & Obijiofor 2008, Hjarvard 2002, Paterson 2011). This chapter addresses the acute need for studies that examine journalists' reflection on their role in the new Arab media (Mellor 2008) and gives unprecedented empirical insights into the discussions and concerns in the Al Jazeera English newsroom during its first years on air. Al Jazeera English's editorial agenda and production strategies are analyzed primarily in relation to alternative media production and traditional foreign correspondence. It explores how channel employees struggle to make sense of what it means to be and practice a southern alternative in a mainstream 24-hour news landscape. Based on qualitative interviews with 45 members of the channel staff and management, document analysis and observation during editorial meetings, it discusses the production strategies that are crucial to the channel's identity as an alternative, southern news channel in its formative years. It demonstrates how reporters from various backgrounds struggled to adapt to the channel's idealized role of a 'local' reporter and to redefine their role within the larger, international 'interpretive community' of foreign correspondents (Berkowitz & TerKeust 1999, Zelizer 1993).

ALTERNATIVE MEDIA MODELS AND PRODUCTION STRATEGIES

Throughout AJE's existence, there have been arguments about whether AJE—given the rare combination of rich resources and a counter-hegemonic remit—qualifies as 'alternative' or 'mainstream' media. In the following, I will discuss in more detail some of the underlying reasons for the diverging opinions in this debate.

Alternative media have traditionally been examined as campaigners for social protest and as critics of dominant ideologies. In early dichotomous models, alternative media were characterized as democratic, open and non-hierarchical, using collective modes of organization with a radical political agenda and close bonds to social movements. The idealized alternative media were contrasted with the mainstream media, which were characterized as monolithic, profit-seeking and hierarchically organized, with a routinized and professionalized journalism that was implicitly elitist and exclusive. This dichotomization has been criticized for presenting alternative media as an ideal type of 'purer' media, contrasted with the elitism of professional media (Atton 2002b), as the strong focus on media elitism ignored both the democratization of mainstream media and the subversive use of mainstream media products and processes (ibid.: 152). It should be noted, however, that the categories of mainstream and alternative media are not rigid but fluid (Bailey et al. 2008: 151). In his later works, Downing (2001: ix-x), himself an early proponent of the dichotomous approach, acknowledged that this "slippage toward binarism" overlooks the actual spectrum of alternative media.

Since the turn of the millennium, scholars have paid great attention to alternative forms of media (see Rauch 2007 for an overview). Current academic contributions have stressed the multiple, competing meanings of 'alternative' in alternative media and examined the concepts of alternative and mainstream as a continuum rather than as absolutely opposed categories (Atton 2002a/b, Atton & Wickenden 2005, Bailey et al. 2008, Downing 2001, Harcup 2003, Rauch 2007). Bailey et al. (2008: xii) argued that the identity of alternative media "should be articulated as relational and contingent on the particularities of the contexts of production, distribution, and consumption." Moreover, they stressed the elusiveness of alternative media, which are not only articulated in relation to the mainstream media, but also as community media, civil society media and rhizomatic media. In essence, media that are regarded as 'alternative' in certain contexts could be defined as 'mainstream' in others (ibid.: 18). Emphasizing that "everything, at some point, is alternative to something else," Downing (2001: ix-x) argued that content, context and consequences must be primary guidelines when conceptualizing radical alternative media.[1]

Consequently, a media organization's position on the mainstream-alternative-continuum may change according to the context (Bailey et al. 2008: 70).

Transnational media can cross borders between mainstream and alternative media in both the original (sending) country and wherever it is received. And, more importantly, it can be redefined by the particularities of production, distribution and consumption contexts. In essence, AJE may be perceived as mainstream news in some parts of the world and as alternative when accessed by news media, Diaspora groups or the general public in the West. A related example is the BBC in America during the last decade, what Bicket and Wall (2009: 376) characterize as a "super-alternative" news medium, albeit an alternative source with enormous resources and high credibility, within the context of an expanding public sphere in the US. They argue that the BBC in the US context represents a media production that challenges actual concentrations of media power in the US. Moreover, the BBC's "alternativeness," the authors claim, is "a temporary condition, made possible by a confluence of larger changes in international relations, global journalism, and communicative practices and patterns" (ibid.: 380).

Proposing a broader theoretical and methodological research framework for alternative media, Atton (2002a) distinguishes between alternative media as a *product* and as a *process*. On the product side, he highlights politically and/or socially/culturally radical content and news values, alternative aesthetics and form (graphics and visualization) and reprographic innovations and adaptations (ibid.: 27). And on the process side, he stresses alternative sites and networks for distribution and an anti-copyright culture, collective organization, de-professionalization and transformed social relations, roles and responsibilities. Alternative media are radicalizing journalistic practices with their progressive sourcing strategies, "native reporters," the significance of "active witnessing" and a consideration of "social movement news" in mainstream media culture (ibid 2002b: 491, Atton & Wickenden 2005). Further, alternative media ideally offer counter-hegemonic representations and discourses that differ from those in their mainstream counterparts; there is an emphasis on self-representation and a diversity of voices, as well as diverse news formats and news genres (Bailey et al. 2008: 31). Moreover, the process of alternative media transforms the communication process and establishes horizontal linkages and networks (Rauch 2007: 996).

In conceptualizing alternative media, it is crucial to investigate the relationship between media and representation because the primary aim of radical media is to give a voice to the voiceless and to under- and misrepresented ideologies, as well as to provide a platform for activists and 'ordinary people' that they can use on their own terms (Atton 2002b, Bailey et al. 2008). Alternative media are often linked to social movements and networks, but the social movement dimension, important as it is, must not diminish our understanding of alternative media (Downing 2001: 31). During periods of political contest and/or military conflict, creative media strategies have become an integral part of the resistance of rebel movements. Among the classic examples are the Algerian rebel radio station, *Voice of Fighting Algeria,* which gradually mobilized against French colonial rule during the Algerian war (1956–62) (Fanon 1968 in Downing 2001), the strategic use of illegal revolutionary audiocassettes to distribute the exiled Ayatollah Khomeini's sermons to the Iranian people in the build-up to the overthrow of the Shaw in Iran in 1979 (Sreberny-Mohammadi & Mohammadi 1994) and the transnational Internet activism of the Zapatista movement in their struggle against the Mexican authorities in the mid-1990s (Ford & Gil 2001). More recently, the strategic use of new media (cell phones, blogs and social network sites) to mobilize demonstrations against the manipulation of the presidential election in Iran 2009 (Sreberny & Khiabany 2010), and in the organization and mobilization of the current popular uprising across the Arab World, has demonstrated the role of media and information in contemporary political, popular movements (see chapters 1 and 8, this volume, for discussion).

Among the alternative news media, the Inter Press Service (IPS) is a rare example of global outlook and ambition and thus arguably represents the most relevant parallel to Al Jazeera English. This independent news agency was founded in 1964 and headquartered in Rome to provide news content with a southern perspective (Rauch 2003). The IPS was launched to report on events and processes affecting the economic, social and political development of people and nations, with particular emphasis on the global South. Its aim was to be a news agency with an alternative, process-oriented, southern (Third World) news agenda that challenged the style of conventional news agency journalism. The IPS mission statement was *giving a voice to the voiceless:* "Acting as a communication channel that privileges the voices and the concerns of the poorest and creates a climate of understanding, accountability and participation around development, promoting a new international information order between the South and the North" (IPS 2013).[2] Although researchers agree that the IPS has reported global events from an alternative, southern perspective,[3] they also make note of the agency's limited resources (Boyd-Barrett & Thussu 1992, Giffard 1998, Rauch 2003). The news agency has struggled to establish a sizeable market with limited financial resources, few correspondents, and scattered coverage of international news, and it has become more of a niche news agency for the UN and NGOs than a real competitor to the major mainstream agencies (ibid.).

The IPS case demonstrates the profound challenges for ambitious alternative media projects. The low political priority usually given to the 'marginal' is a fundamental challenge for alternative media. As noted by Atton and Wickenden (2005: 351), the "absence of professionalism in alternative news media does not prevent them from being subject to pressures similar to those in mainstream media." The alternative media are not free and liberated from the everyday structural limitations of news production, such as deadlines, tight budgets, limited staff resources and organizational pressure (Atton 2002a: 154–156). Moreover, since they are small-scale, independent and horizontally structured organizations, most alternative media suffer from lack of financial and organizational stability.[4] Even though the language, technology and staff may change, the very existence of counter-hegemonic journalism in alternative media demonstrates in practice that there are alternative perspectives on the world to those provided by the mainstream media (Harcup 2003: 372). In particular, radical television, such as public access television, has struggled to gain influence despite problems of legal and regulatory status and public relations, the concentration of broadcasting frequencies, the capital-intensive requirements of equipment, the demand for highly specialized professional staff and the lack of supporting structural links to larger political communities and institutions (Stein 2001).

Another characteristic of alternative media is their systematic critique of mainstream media and journalists. Journalists rely heavily on each other for ideas, and this reliance constitutes an important organizational routine. Zelizer's (1993) and Berkewitz and Terkeust's (1999) analyses of journalists as an 'interpretative community'—with shared definitions, metaphors, memories and understandings of their practice—provided insights into the ways in which journalists and media professionals define their own profession. The "interpretive community" is "a cultural site where meanings are constructed, shared, and reconstructed by members of social groups in the course of everyday life" (Berkowitz & TerKeurst 1999: 125). Interpretive groups are "composed of people engaged in common activities and common purposes who employ a common frame of reference for interpreting their social settings" (ibid. 127).

For those involved in alternative media, the mainstream media are corrupted by, dependent on and uncritical of the establishment. According to Atton's (2002b: 499) interviews with alternative media activists, these activists do not distinguish between different mainstream media, but regard the mainstream as one dominant bloc. Distancing themselves from the mainstream media, the radical reporters primarily identify with the protest movement itself and the grass roots as their 'interpretive community' and concur with the activists' criticism of their mainstream counterparts. In contrast to most alternative media, which consist mainly of small-scale, marginal, niche publications, Al Jazeera English has become a major, global news channel aiming to adapt alternative production strategies to the international television news format. This process has raised editorial dilemmas and conflicts in the newsroom as channel staff have struggled to find the right balance between these two standards.

EDITORIAL AGENDA AND PRODUCTION STRATEGIES

The channel's editorial ambitions have been both ambitious and lofty. In promotional presentations, AJE' mission is described as to provide "independent, impartial news for an international audience and to provide a voice of diversity of perspectives from under-reported regions" (AJN 2009a: 4). "In addition," the promotional text continues, "the channel aims to balance the information flow between the South and the North. The channel of reference for the Middle East and Africa, AJE has unique access to some of the world's most troubled and controversial locations. AJE's determination and ability to accurately reflect the truth on the ground in regions torn by conflict and poverty has set our content apart" (ibid.). Along the same lines, AJE has been portrayed on the official channel website (AJN 2010a) as "balancing the current typical information flow by reporting from the developing world back to the West and from the southern to the northern hemisphere." Moreover, the channel aims "to give voice to untold stories, promote debate, and challenge established perceptions" (ibid.) and to "set the news agenda, bridging cultures and providing a unique grass-roots perspective from under-reported regions around the world to a potential global audience of over one billion English speakers" (ibid). According to the channel website, AJE's spirit of reporting is "honest, courageous and distinctive" (AJN 2013b).

Analyzing AJE's editorial agenda and strategies, it is imperative to stress that the channel's unique model of funding largely shields it from commercial pressures, a funding model that has both positive and negative impacts on its editorial freedoms and quality, as discussed in chapters 2 and 8 of this volume. Its financial weight has given it confidence and ambitious plans, but also risks creating organizational inefficiency and indecisiveness (Lawson 2011). One illustrative example concerns the channel's understanding of a target audience, as audience segmentation and ratings increasingly influence editorial practices and priorities in international foreign news (Mody 2012). Informants see AJE as an exception to the domestication/marketization trends in international news, as the channel can afford to have a broad idea of who its target audiences are. In written internal editorial guidelines, the audience is described broadly as "worldwide, English speakers." The fact that AJE does not have a 'home audience' is frequently highlighted as a unique advantage, but other AJE informants express confusion and insecurity because they do not have a clear definition of who their (home) audience is, and consequently who they talk to and how they should frame their news. Moreover, Al Jazeera English's actual audience and distribution has been problematized in numerous academic publications in recent years (see, among others, Amin 2012, Arsenault 2012, Kugelman 2012 and Youmans 2012 for analysis), but according to top management informants, the channel has not commissioned any audience research and therefore does not know who and how many people are actually watching it. This is a new (and perhaps overwhelming) situation for many of the editorial staff coming from mainstream news media who are used to a situation in which audience numbers are seen as a concrete, frequently updated measurement of success and failure. AJE's editorial freedom not to think about its audience gives the channel a unique potential in global news coverage but this freedom can also potentially weaken its product, which can sometimes be unfocused and vague (see Lawson 2011 for a critique of its coverage of the death of Osama bin Laden).

During the channel's first years on the air, several efforts were made to articulate an editorial vision for AJE. The channel's editorial line has been broad, vague and comprehensive. After the initial channel launch period, the top management set out to refocus and tighten the vision. They strove to establish practical systems and routines to ensure that the vision was communicated in the channel branding and properly incorporated into editorial practices and operational decisions and news/programming.[5] In the first phase of the AJE renewal project (2008–9), the below six core values, or vision clusters, were selected by the top management[6] to communicate the editorial vision. To operationalize the editorial vision, the management gave examples of editorial strategies and practices, the things AJE would and would not do (not listed in priority order). Even though the process to articulate and clarify the editorial vision was not finalized at the time of the report, the clusters and examples are worth citing in detail to elucidate the ideas, concepts and language underlying the channel's editorial decisions in its first years on air. It is worth noting the ways in which the core values (particularly three through six) bear close resemblance to the editorial agenda of alternative media projects: giving a voice to the voiceless, being where others are not, having a southern news perspective and letting the word report on itself. This aim to adapt production strategies from alternative media implies a critique of the ethics, norms and routines of professional journalism (Atton 2009: 273). The repeated negative reference to 'agency' material is also noteworthy as it shows how the channel distances itself from the mainstream Western media and the global power elites:

1) *Journalism of Depth:* going behind the headlines, avoiding the wire service approach to story selection and treatment, providing context and background, showing original enterprise, and conducting investigative journalism. Would Do: more historical documentaries to provide context, more investigative journalism, and longer pieces. Would Not Do: too many talk shows, follow the news agenda of others, or dumb it down.

2) *Every Angle, Every Side:* challenging received wisdom and conventional assumptions, presenting an alternative view, exploring the magic of opposites, and not being aligned to any one country, region or political point of view (explicit or implicit). Would Do: speak to everyone and give them all a hard time (!), use hard-hitting presenters and correspondents, and invite a broader range of guests. Would Not Do: follow a predictable left-liberal agenda, go to the usual suspects, air live press conferences by politicians, or be conscious of ratios of airtime to sound bites.

3) *Voice of the Voiceless:* focus attention on the margins, not just the corridors of power, tell truth to power, be skeptical of authority, be against the system, and explore people's connection to power. Would Do: encourage interaction through New Media, invite guests who are outside the power structure, invite guests from non-mainstream NGOs, and remember that those who are 'voiceless' changes often.

Would Not Do: assume that interviews give authentic voice, or slip into activism or advocacy.

4) *Being Where Others Aren't:* telling the stories other channels don't tell, and/or telling them in a different way, focusing on the unreported and/or under-reported world, keeping away from the press pack, being on the ground in more places, and staying there in between the 'big' stories. Would Do: open more bureaus, and plan better so as to identify AJE stories and deploy. Would Not Do: Use agency pictures, deploy mid-range stories when the agency will do, or be somewhere just for the sake of being there.

5) *The Southern Perspective:* broadcast a much higher proportion of stories from the developing world, consider the impact of any story on the developing world, avoid conventional 'western' political and cultural attitudes and assumptions, adopt an indigenous perspective rather than a post-colonial one, and focus on the '3 Fs'—Food, Fuel and Finance—and their impact on the developing world. Would Do: focus reporting on Southern Hemisphere topics, open African and/or Latin American BC [Broadcasting Centre], and combine local and external perspectives. Would Not Do: ignore the rest of the world, highlight [The Economic Forum in Davos] rather than the World Social Forum, or replace news reports with features.

6) *Letting the World Report on Itself:* telling the story from the point of view of the people and places that are the subject of the story, putting human beings at the heart of the story, covering ordinary people's lives, using correspondents who have deep roots in their regions, and encouraging audience input and interaction. Would Do: use technology to get 'real people' on screen, give cameras to non-professionals, and do more 'first-persons' [news format where selected people on the ground are invited to present their own story/life]. Would Not Do: run unmediated citizen input, or over-use the first-person format.

In general, the renewal report found that most AJE staff share these core values, but informants interpret them differently and disagree about how to put them into practice. To balance, report back and challenge mainstream Western international news, AJE has employed a set of ambitious production strategies. Three of these production strategies will be analyzed in greater depth in the following sections.

A SOUTHERN PRESENCE

International media organizations spread themselves thinly or thickly across the globe. For AJE, the editorial core values are reflected in the channel's strategy of establishing a broad presence on the ground. Today, AJE has four broadcasting centers (Doha, London, Washington D.C. and Kuala Lumpur), over 1000 employees and over 70 bureaus worldwide (press office informa-tion request, May 2013)[7]—a complex, decentralized production structure that has helped the channel develop a distinctive news profile in the global news ecology. According to management informants in the Doha headquar-ters, there are concrete plans to expand the number of bureaus and to add a Latin American and/or African broadcasting center. Other sources question whether the expensive decentralized structure is the most productive model. By comparison, the BBC had 50 international television news bureaus, 250 correspondents and 2,000 journalists in 2010 (BBC 2010), and CNN has 42 news bureaus and 1,000 affiliates worldwide (CNN 2013). These com-parative figures document that AJE has a decentralized production structure compared to its mainstream competitors.

Furthermore, it is to be expected that the differences between AJE and its competitors will only increase if the current location trends in global news continue (see Hamilton 2010 and Müller & Schröder 2010 for insights). The changing economics of foreign reporting, accentuated by the current global recession, the combination of declining media stock prices, ebbing profit rates, lack of reader/viewer interest and shrinking numbers of newsroom staff has caused major mainstream Western news organizations to reduce their global networks of correspondents and analysts to warn against a "decline of foreign news" (Cooper 2011, Ginsberg 2002, Hamilton & Jenner 2004, Hamilton 2010, Hannerz 2004, 2007, Hawkins 2011, Livingston & Asmolov 2010, Moeller 1999, Müller & Schröder 2010, Palmer & Fontan 2007, Ricchiardi 2006, 2008a/b, Utley 1997).[8] In contrast, AJE has an extensive network of bureaus and correspondents around the world. Espe-cially in the Global South, where its competitors are much more scarcely represented, AJE has put much of its newsgathering capacity. During the first five years after its launch (from 2006 to early 2011), this priority was further accentuated by a decentralized headquarters structure that mani-fested itself structurally in the establishment of four headquarters in Kuala Lumpur, Doha, London and Washington D.C., respectively.

Further, in contrast to most international media that are primarily located in 'media hubs,'—places where a fair number of newsworthy events occur, from which other potential news sites can be reached fairly quickly and conve-niently and where communication facilities are satisfactory (Hannerz 2004: 40)—Al Jazeera has a truly global presence. As international mainstream media reduce their global news networks, they increasingly flock to (a) the global media and finance hubs (such as London, New York, and increasingly also the new Asian hubs Tokyo, Beijing and Delhi) and (b) to the interna-tional conflict zones where the West is involved directly or indirectly in the "war on terror" (in Iraq, Afghanistan and Israel-Palestine) (Bahador 2011, Hahn & Lönnendonker 2009, Hamilton 2010, Hannerz 2004, Hawkins 2011). Although AJE has broadcasting centers in global media hubs like London and Washington D.C., the channel has an extensive network of bureaus and correspondents in the South. In the global news landscape,

AJE's southern presence and perspective is an anomaly, which is arguably reflected in its news coverage (see chapters 3–7, this volume, for a comprehensive discussion).

Maintaining a number of foreign bureaus throughout the world, which entails relatively high regular salaries and compensation for foreign posting, housing, managing and travel costs, is a resource-intensive strategy. Consequently, media organizations try to find cost-effective substitutes for fully employed, permanent staff correspondents, such as freelancers, stringers, or regional correspondents (regional 'specialists' based at the main headquarters), local-national correspondents (Bunce 2011) and non-journalists (Cooper 2011, Otto & Meyer 2012).[9] Acknowledging the high costs, AJE informants still argue that a broad global presence is a key strategy for maintaining the channel's editorial distinctiveness. A manager based in Doha explained why it is imperative for AJE to actively go to places that are difficult to reach:

> So, we have a team in Zimbabwe, no one else has that [. . .] It's not easy, it's very tricky to get the permission in the first place, tricky to keep it, but worthwhile and it's similar in other parts of the world. We have five teams in Africa; I don't think anyone else has that level of commitment. We have four or five [teams] in Latin America. Again in the Middle East we are very well represented. So, it's partly through placing people in these regions, it's partly through the people you put there, and then it's just making sure that when we think about a story we think hard about the angles that we look at it from a variety of perspectives. (Interview with author, Doha, 3 October 2007)

Political economy/global dominance scholars and global public sphere scholars have interpreted the demise of foreign correspondence quite differently (Cottle 2009: 36). In the political economy approach, the decreasing number of foreign correspondents is seen as a symbol of the ongoing changes in the news economy and thus as a trend toward more parochial mainstream news (Ginsberg 2002, Moeller 1999, Ricchiardi 2006, 2008a/b, Utley 1997). Considering the demise of foreign correspondence from the global public sphere approach, Hamilton and Jenner (2004: 313–4) find that the alarmed accounts of shrinking news networks are based on a static and outdated understanding of what may be defined as foreign reporting, proposing a new typology of foreign correspondents to reflect the new complexity of foreign reporting.[10] Further, Archetti (2012) challenges the idea that the foreign correspondent is redundant in today's media-saturated environment. She underlines that advances in technology and the new economic realities have made the correspondents become redefined as 'sense makers,' providing contextualization, explanation and analysis of the huge tide of information available to audiences worldwide (Archetti 2012: 853–4).

In contrast to the global public sphere discourse, AJE informants frequently argue for the significance of being on the ground and criticize their Anglo-American competitors for reducing their global presence. By being on the ground in more places and over longer periods of time, they argue, the channel generates news stories that help define the channel's editorial line. A London-based manager elaborated:

> Resources always drive your news agenda. You got a correspondent in Buenos Aires, or Caracas, you'll get loads of stories out of Buenos Aires and Caracas, whether you like it or not, because they're there. So, as soon as you make that decision where to put people, that drives what the news agenda is. And if you put all your resources into Europe, and not into South America and Africa, or the Middle East or the Far East, then you'll get stories out of those places constantly. It's very easy to operate there, there are loads of satellite dishes, there are loads of stories to do, but your agenda is always driven by your resourcing and where your resources are placed. (Interview with author, London, 5 September 2008)

Being on the ground in the right place at the right time has been a fundamental success strategy for AJE's predecessor and sister channel Al Jazeera Arabic (AJA). In their organizational study of the Al Jazeera Network,[11] Zayani and Sahraoui (2007: 35–42) highlighted AJA's instinct for breaking news, its dynamic production practices, its individual freedom and the channel's wide-ranging presence on the ground, with a special concentration of bureaus and correspondents in the Arab and Muslim world. Based on a comparative case study analysis, Lawson (2011: 44), however, questions the rhetoric that AJE's broad plurality of geographical locations is an editorial advantage in itself and stresses that it has to be followed up by a conscious and focused editorial policy. The international news media's location of its international staff and bureaus is not only practically and economically motivated, but also a political decision. A primary example of the consequences of the politics of location is the fact that the mainstream international media's Middle East correspondents are stationed almost exclusively in West-Jerusalem, Israel. The international correspondents have their families and daily lives in Israel, their access to the occupied territories is restricted by the Israeli military, and financial constraints limit their travel to and presence within the Palestinian territories, where the practical journalistic obstacles are many (Deprez & Raeymaeckers 2010, Ibrahim 2003, Hannerz 2004: 61–62, Philo & Berry 2004). The principal argument here is not just that Al Jazeera has more correspondents on the ground compared to most international media: the channel has also had an active policy of countering the location practices of the Western news media. The network locates teams and bureaus in areas of importance for the Arab/Muslim (AJA) and southern (AJE) audience in contrast to most international media, which target the Northern and/or Western audiences. Al Jazeera's politics of location has been a crucial condition for the network's journalistic breakthroughs in the coverage of the Palestinian Intifada (2000–), the war in Afghanistan (2001–), and the war in Iraq (2003–). More recently, AJE's exclusive reports from inside the Burmese insurrection (2007) and the Malaysian political protest (2007), on the Kenyan election violence (2007–8), the Zimbabwean elections (2008) and on the war in Gaza (2008–9) have demonstrated how presence on the ground is a decisive editorial strategy for AJE (see chapters 6 and 7, this volume, for analysis). Moreover, Al Jazeera's politics of location has also been controversial. The channel's reports from inside the territories controlled by the 'enemies' of the West (controversial dictators, social and military movements and rogue states) have induced its critics to question the network's editorial ties and agenda.

LOCAL CORRESPONDENTS

Another interrelated vital editorial strategy to achieve AJE's ambitious editorial agenda is to cover global events with *local correspondents*, particularly in the Global South. There is a widely shared belief within the channel that local correspondents are better equipped to grasp and convey the realities on the ground than international (foreign) correspondents. A Doha-based presenter/correspondent explained the strengths of the local (southern) correspondent vis-à-vis the international (northern) correspondent in conveying the channel's core values with the following example from the Israeli-Palestinian conflict:

> I remember a story [on an Anglo-American channel], which a reporter did, and they gave the story like two or three minutes to talk about some songs that had come out—popular songs, describing some of the Israeli practices against Palestinians as 'Nazi practices.' Some of the restrictions and stuff had resembled some of the measures, which the Nazis had imposed upon the Jews, and this reporter tackled it from the perspective of 'how dare somebody . . . even suggest that!' [. . .] That's a very kind of 'northern,' to me, Northern Hemispheric kind of take on things. Instead of looking at why these people are complaining about these measures, you are complaining about why they are complaining. So I think that makes a difference when you have someone who's a middle, upper class, white American, Protestant reporter, and he's been landed in this part of the world, that's the way he sees, you know what is the most important story to him is that there are these songs coming out. It's a huge deal to him. For somebody else, I think, who is more from that part of the world, he'd have a different take what life is. (Interview with author, Doha, 2 October 2007)

According to AJE sources, local correspondents 'who have lived the story' are better qualified to communicate the channel's editorial core values. The local correspondent speaks the local language(s); knows the culture, religion and way of life; has personal experience with and a deep understanding of the challenges of the community; navigates the system and knows how to deal with local authorities; has more extensive and alternative source networks; respects local sensitivities and strives to give a fair representation of the local point of view. Moreover, since local correspondents are permanently based in the field, they have a better understanding of the context and complexities of a running news story. Local correspondents are perceived as better resourced to develop new, independent news stories and news angles. Furthermore, in the case of a breaking news story within their area, they will be quicker than their competitors, who most often have to travel from their headquarters in Europe or the US.[12] There is a broad literature critically examining the professional values, practices and challenges met by Western European or North American foreign correspondents and international correspondents working in the Global North (Archetti 2012, Boudana 2010, Hannerz 2004, 2007, Kester 2010, Markham 2011, Willnat & Weaver 2003). More recently, studies also critically investigate the "new foreign correspondents"—the local-national stringers in international news reporting (Bunce 2011) and correspondent-fixer-relations in war and conflict zones (Bishara 2006, Murrell 2010, Palmer & Fontan 2007).

When AJE informants argue for the local correspondent, they often contrast the benefits of a local correspondent to the limits of Western-centric 'parachute reporting.' A 'parachute journalist' is primarily an expert in crisis reporting more than the actual crisis who chases the most 'newsworthy' breaking news stories across the globe (Palmer & Fontan 2007: 21). Mappings of foreign correspondents have found that they are primarily white, middle-aged men, with extensive journalistic careers (Willnat & Weaver 2003), although more recent studies find that there are gradually more female correspondents and correspondents are younger than before (Archetti 2012, Markham 2011). AJE's strategy is contrasted with the stereotype that traditional Western correspondents are bigger stars than the news and people they cover, fly in from far away, spend very limited time in the field, simplify matters on the ground, and report from a Western-centric worldview to their domestic audience back home. Among international correspondents, parachuting tales are a vital, defining part of the professional identity and community: how they got into hotspots of war or natural disasters, witnessed events, the struggle to file the story, the camaraderie and how they got out (Hannerz 2004: 42–3). In their critical view of (the caricature of) the international correspondent, AJE informants distance themselves from the community of Western international correspondents, who for many of the informants were their former colleagues and friends. For many informants, their growing disillusionment with developments in editorial agendas and the practices of the major Western news organizations contributed to their decision to join AJE. This critique of mainstream media and journalists echoes the alternative media movement's one-dimensional criticism of the mainstream media as one dominant bloc (Atton 2002b: 499).

Using the example of a dramatic, sensational story about East-African albinos killed for their body parts, a presenter/correspondent based in London emphasized the benefits of the strategy by contrasting AJE's practice with that of BBC veterans:

> It makes such a big difference having a correspondent who is African— Yvonne Ndege[13] born in Nairobi in Kenya. It makes a huge difference having her telling that story compared with [BBC World Affairs Editor] John Simpson, who's never really been there before, trudging around saying look at all the crazy Africans [. . .] A degree of it is cosmetic, there's more credibility if an African person is reporting a story [. . .], but it's not just cosmetic. It's the very important cultural understanding; it's the language that's used. (Interview with author, London, July 16 2008)

The 'insider position' of the idealized local AJE correspondent shares some characteristics with the 'native reporters' in alternative media projects. Native reporters use their role as activists in order to represent from the inside (Atton 2002b: 495). Atton (2002a: 112–7) contended that 'native reporting' is a practice that emphasizes the first person eyewitness accounts, a sort of inclusive, egalitarian, radical form of civic journalism where people become reporters of their own experiences, struggles and lives. The broader aim of the native narrative is to provide relevant and meaningful news for the members of the community and for a wider audience. The strategy tends to emphasize the reporter's political position more than his/her journalistic professionalism, although a more professional form of native reporting has emerged in more mainstream media and publications (Atton 2002b: 497). In contrast to the native reporters of alternative media, who are themselves activists who primarily identify with the protest movement and/or the grass roots as their 'interpretive community,' AJE's local correspondents are first and foremost professional media workers (correspondents, producers or photographers). The distinction between activism and journalism is emphasized in the channel's editorial core values, outlined in the beginning of this chapter.

The extant research on international reporting, the international news media and the AJE staffers interviewed for this book all overlook the role of local, national editorial staff. International news today is not produced solely by the white foreign correspondent from whom AJE interviewees distance themselves, it is most often produced with essential contribution from local nationals working as freelancers, stringers or local staff for the international newswires (Bunce 2011) and news media (Bishara 2006), particularly when it comes to comes to visual reporting (Neumann & Fahmy 2012: 195). This development has been particularly evident in the South, as an indirect result of the shrinking news networks and decreasing number of permanent, full-time, international correspondents described above. This gradual transition to local media professionals is not primarily framed as a progressive, editorial strategy to capture the realities on the ground, but rather as a (negative) side-effect of tighter budgets, security concerns and more domesticated news (see Archetti 2012 and Hamilton & Jenner 2004 for alternative analyses). Local, national editorial staff, especially when from the southern hemisphere, have often been perceived to be biased, nationalist members of static cultures (Bishara 2006: 21), and, particularly in the Israel-Palestine conflict, debates over the professionalism vs. national commitment have dominated public discussions of Palestinian journalists' role in international news (ibid.: 24). Studying local-national Sudanese correspondents reporting on their own country for international media, Bunce (2011) documents that the local-nationals worked in greater fear of the authorities, that their relative absence of "watchdog journalism" norms made them less likely to search wider perspectives, and their local language skills made them more able to access regime sources (ibid.: 24), which again dominated their coverage (ibid.: 30–31). Related to this, studies from war and conflict zones problematize how dependent rotating foreign parachute correspondents are on their local fixers and how the fixers (who are not professional journalists) potentially 'influence' the reporters' view of the conflict (Murrell 2010, Palmer & Fontan 2007). Whereas AJE's local correspondents work full-time for the channel as permanent staff hired because of their local insights, the local reporters and photographers working for mainstream international media are mostly freelancers and/or stringers in a very competitive media market, and there are examples of their credibility being questioned and their reporting being treated with caution because they are local, partisan voices and/or witnesses. One recent example of this kind of skepticism to local stringers was demonstrated during the war in Gaza, where Palestinian media produced the vast majority of images of the war, thereby prompting the international media to use them more cautiously (Reporters Without Borders 2009c).

AJE's local correspondents represent one approach to the professionalized native reporter and of the inbuilt tensions between 'the native' and 'the professional' in these editorial practices. When explicitly asked about the more problematic aspects of the local correspondent strategy, AJE informants reported that the local staff may be socialized into the culture to the extent that they do not see the news stories from within their own community, that they emphasize the local cultural and religious sensitivities over newsworthiness and /or that they practice self-censorship. In other words, the local staff can be *too* native and/or locally oriented for an international news channel like AJE, too partisan for a professional reporter. These views concur with Hannerz' (2004: 80) study of foreign correspondents, where he found that most news organizations are inclined to want to have foreign correspondents 'securely domesticated' before they send them abroad; or, if they hire a new correspondent from abroad, to bring her back to the headquarters for in-house socialization: to learn the craft, absorb organizational culture and establish face-to-face relations between foreign reporters and the home desk and/or editorial management (ibid.). For these reasons, some media organizations routinely bring their correspondents back to the headquarters to remind them about the editorial and cultural values at home. Most of the AJE informants expressed similar concern about the professionalism of local correspondents and stressed the need to provide training and, when possible, to team up local correspondents with more experienced international producers (and vice versa) (AJN 2009b).

The permanent position of local AJE correspondents, and through this their tighter integration and socialization into the network, set them apart from the majority of local-national stringers who largely works independently and alone (Bunce 2011: 19–23). A member of the management team in Doha explains:

> In a country we'll usually have a team of three people: a cameraman, a producer, and a correspondent. So if we hired a locally-based correspondent, we will often try and put a producer who has international experience with him, so they can work as a team, they can learn from each other. We have a coach here, we bring people in for training here regularly, we send people from here to Egypt, for example, to work with our guy there for a month. So we don't leave them in isolation. We show them the style we want and the techniques we want them to use. Training is quite a crucial part of what we do because we want everybody to reach a similar standard. It would be easy to go to the West and hire 25 very experienced correspondents and disperse them across the world, but that isn't what AJE is about. (Interview with author, Doha, 3 October 2007)

Many of the informants highlight the rapid development—the bold, warm, in-depth reporting—of two young female local correspondents, Nour Odeh (Gaza) and Haru Mutasa (Zimbabwe)[14] as successful representatives of AJE's local correspondent strategy. At the same time, management informants acknowledge the challenges of the strategy, for it is difficult to find correspondents who have the right combination of international potential and local insight. Management informants explain that some of the recruitment has been wrong, and some training processes are more complicated than others (interviews 2007–9). In the words of one member of the middle management in Doha:

> We've had some great successes and we have had some failures. But I think it is an important thing to persist at and I think that over time, we will get that stable and we will continue to develop the talents. [. . .] The more difficult ones they take consistent time and effort; they are particularly the ones that have been doing it for a long time . . . for local news.

You've really got to break a lot of lifetime habits to kind of re-teach them to think more internationally, to step back from it a bit and wonder what does it look like from back here and to change the methods they have been using. (Interview with author, Doha, 6 December 2007)

His statement demonstrates one of the main challenges with the editorial strategy: the management team seeks local insights, but the local professional practices are not adequate for an international broadcaster. To benefit from local knowledge, the field correspondent must be trained to communicate these insights to a global audience. In essence, the local perspective is being globalized and mediated in the production process.

During the 2008–9 renewal project, an internal working group with the task of articulating and implementing the editorial vision argued that correspondents should be given more freedom to contribute to editorial issues (ibid.). They found that several reporters and producers in the field were critical of the way in which the channel framed stories and argued that the end product was often too mainstream, missing the news frames most relevant to the 'voiceless' or the 'people of the South.' Furthermore, they emphasized the need to listen more to correspondents in the field in order to ensure that the channel is ahead of its competitors instead of following the international media. According to the working group, the teams in the field sometimes have a better knowledge and understanding of issues than some levels of editorial management that are supposed to supervise the local production teams in the field. All in all, the working group called for a more egalitarian production process in which the local field correspondents have greater influence. Implicit in these demands was a criticism of the current production structure, perceived as hierarchical and top-down, which tends to undermine the channel's progressive editorial agenda and production strategies. The internal critics contended that, in practice, the local initiatives and voices that constitute a key editorial strategy for the channel have been trumped by the management (ibid.).

THE AL JAZEERA 'FAMILY'

AJE's inheritance, as part of the Al Jazeera Network, is often highlighted in marketing presentations of the channel. In order to cover the *other opinion* in international news, in other words those diverging, oppositional, controversial views and voices that are not regularly invited on mainstream news media, a third editorial strategy for AJE emphasizes taking advantage of being part of the Al Jazeera *Network*. On the channel website, to take one example, the legacy of the network is emphasized in the following way: "Building on the Al Jazeera Arabic channel's groundbreaking developments in the Arab and Muslim world, which have changed the face of news within the Middle East, AJE is part of a growing network that is now expanding this fresh perspective from regional to global through accurate, impartial and objective reporting" (AJN 2010a). The process of making Al Jazeera Arabic accessible to an international audience has been long and difficult, from the first talks of translating (subtitles and dubbing) AJA for an international audience in late 2002, to the launch of the AJE four years later (see Powers 2012 for a compelling overview). The first half-hearted attempt, the English-language website launched right before the war in Iraq 2003, failed as a result of internal conflicts and controversy over its staff, vague editorial guidelines and lack of talented, professional editorial staff and was starting to harm the network's brand internationally (ibid.: 18). As a result, the Al Jazeera management and Qatari authorities decided to build up a new, global English-language channel (ibid.).

Especially in the coverage of the Arab and the Muslim world, AJE has a comparative advantage over its English-language Western competitors from AJA's staff on the ground, network of sources and contacts, and regional experience and expertise. AJA in turn benefits from AJE's more extensive southern presence (particularly in Africa and Latin America). In the words of a presenter/correspondent based in Doha:

> The Arabic channel, they have some good reporters and they have access to some key people that they have built up over the years, and that's something obviously we would be foolish to ignore and try and operate on our own. There is a bit of sharing. There have been occasions where they have got an important player or guest and we'll coordinate so that we both get to interview this person. One of my colleagues recently did an interview with one of the key members of one of the key groups that are fighting the U.S. troops in Iraq, for example. And that was something that was coordinated between both networks so that we make sure that [they] know, and vice versa. There will be times when in Africa, for example, one of our bureau chiefs got access to the President of Eritrea, an interview with the president. He has been there for a long time and he has got contacts and then we will share that also with our colleagues in the AJA channel. So there is a bit of resource sharing and coordination between the networks going on. I think as time goes on, that will be more efficient. (Interview with author, Doha, 2 October 2007)

AJE's Middle East coverage is a focal point when it comes to utilizing the editorial advantages of the extended Al Jazeera family. The creation of the Middle East desk in the main newsroom, headed by a Middle East editor together with consultants, producers and correspondents, demonstrates that this editorial strategy has a regional emphasis. Employees from the Middle East desk attend AJA's editorial meetings on a daily basis, coordinate the regional coverage and aim to bridge the gap between the two channels. A senior member of the Middle East desk explained:

[W]hen the channel launched, it was very determined to distance itself from the Arabic channel and it seems it went too far to distance itself from the Arabic channel [. . .] To some extent the controversy that is caused by the Arabic channel, you know the Arabic channel made headlines all over the world during the Iraq war, the Afghan war, the Bin Laden tapes etc, etc, and it angered a lot of regimes, governments, countries and people, specifically the American administration. So this channel, when it launched, it did not want to do the same obviously, it didn't want to anger people, but also it didn't want to be a translation or a mirror of the Arabic channel, so it distanced itself too much and relied too much on following BBC World, and CNN or Sky News and in so doing it lost the balance a little bit. So they came up with this idea, the owners of the channel to try and bring the balance back by increasing, maybe try increasing a little bit, the Arabic input. (Interview with author, Doha, 21 November 2007)

On the network level, the top management made 2008 a year for network integration, with emphasis on making cooperation between AJA and AJE more productive and starting the process of integrating the two channels' field bureaus (many of which are run separately from each other at present). One of the members of the top management based in Doha gave an overview of the formal integration process and highlighted the Gaza bureau as a primary example of the ways in which the editorial strategy is put into practice (see also chapters 6 and 7, this volume, for a comprehensive analysis of the Gaza coverage):

[I]n 2008 we did integrate officially three bureaus, we have Afghanistan, Nairobi, and South Africa, [. . .] financially and administratively they are one bureau and they are in one place and they talk to each other. Other bureaus they are integrated by default, maybe they depend on personal relationship and cooperation. In Gaza it is one team. During the war and after and before the war, by default they were one team, used to work in one room, in one office. Of course not all AJE staff in Gaza and West Bank are Arabs, Palestinians, or Egyptians, or whatever, so they are part of the culture and the team. There is no need to bridge because they talk to each other every day. They go out with each other, they exchange cameras and footage. There are other examples of other bureaus, who are already integrated without having the official decision to integrate. (Interview with author, Doha, 15 March 2009)

From interviews with editorial staff, it becomes clear that although there are major administrative and practical benefits from a closer coordination of the two channels, the relationship between AJE and its Arabic sister channel, Al Jazeera Arabic (AJA), was another issue of concern for employees. Although the comparative advantages of being part of the Al Jazeera

Network are emphasized as an important editorial strategy, informants often struggle to identify and cooperate with their Arab colleagues. AJA has come to represent the dissident, the maverick, the anti-establishment, the eccentric and the risk-taking (Zayani & Sahraoui 2007: 25), both regionally and in the global media sphere. In a recent survey, authors Pintak and Ginges (2008, 2009) find that Arab journalists see their mission primarily as driving political and social change in the Middle East, while fulfilling a secondary role of defending the Arab/Muslim people against outside interferences (ibid. 2008: 218). Another characteristic shows the community's improved confidence vis-à-vis mainstream Western media: Arab journalists, believing they outperformed their Western colleagues in the coverage of the "war on terror," have become increasingly tired of Western media lecturing and criticizing them (ibid. 2009: 174), and these beliefs were echoed among the AJA editors interviewed for this book. Similarly, Mellor's (2011: 116) analysis of Arab war correspondents' chronicles about their performance covering the Iraq War, finds that the reporters emphasize the shortcomings of the Western media and promote their own institutions and personal capacity as analysts. Whether journalists from pan-Arab media form an interpretive community, as argued by Mellor (2008, 2012), or competing schools of Arab journalism, as documented by Sakr (2007a), the most important issue here is the key position held by AJA employees as pioneers, defining pan-Arab satellite news both regionally and globally.

Due to miscommunication, most AJA editorial staff originally believed that the English-language channel would be a translation of the Arabic news channel, intended to broadcast their Arab perspective on world news to an international audience (interview by author, Doha, 17 December 2007). In interviews conducted in Doha 2007, informants from both AJE and AJA underline that particularly before the launch of AJE and during the first launch phase, the relationship between the two sister channels was tense. The underlying causes for the tensions have to do with ownership of the Al Jazeera project.[15] First, key AJA editorial management informants explain that they were disappointed by the network management's decision to launch a broader "southern" international channel, rather than "translating" their news and current affairs programs. Second, AJA employees were critical towards the new British management and disillusioned because their (Western) colleagues in the English-language channel secured better contracts (higher salaries and better production equipment and technology). Third, because the Western AJE managers were under much pressure from the mainstream media to legitimize their new project, they often tended to distance AJE from its Arabic sister channel, underlining that, although they were part of the same network, they were two independent channels. Fourth, AJA employees express their concern that the editorial strategies of the new English-language channel will weaken the Al Jazeera brand that AJA journalists have paid for in many instances with their lives and freedom.

Addressing these conflicts, the network management restructured all of Al Jazeera's channels into the Al Jazeera Network with Wadah Khanfar (then Director of AJA), Director General of the entire network (Powers 2012: 21). Moreover, the management appointed former Editor in Chief of AJA, Ibrahim Helal, as Deputy Managing Director of AJE to reunite the two factions months before the launch in May 2006. Furthermore, the network management stressed the need for integration between the two channels by making 2008 "the year of integration" and appointing former London Bureau Chief, Sue Phillips, as Director of Foreign Bureau and Development (head of the integration process). As demonstrated here, in AJE's first years, there were some initial miscommunications, misunderstandings and controversies between the two sister channels. Internally, these conflicts have been characterized as a 'wall' between the two channels, creating an 'us' and 'them' mentality that hinders cross-channel collaboration (AJN 2009b). Taking maximum advantage of the network resources, such as talent, content, contacts and facilities, has perhaps been the most challenging editorial strategy to implement fully in the production processes in the AJE newsroom. In internal efforts to renew and professionalize the channel in 2008–2009, the integration was characterized as unsystematic and over-dependent on personal initiative (ibid.). Consequently, there was a call for more re-versioning of content and increased sharing of planning, pictures, archives and information, and greater coordination of benefits, budgets, editorial practices and codes of conduct (ibid.). A key question in the network integration process was whether AJE, which is perceived by some informants as too mainstream and Western, should be more loyal to the editorial agenda of AJA.

EDITORIAL CHALLENGES

In putting the ambitious editorial agenda and production strategies into journalistic practice, Al Jazeera English staff has faced a number of editorial dilemmas and challenges. In the first years on air, AJE interviewees identified several challenges that hindered the channel from translating these ideals into journalistic practice (see Figenschou 2012 for in-depth discussion and examples). In the following, I will outline three structural challenges AJE faced.

First, sources identified a lack of guidelines and training of editorial staff coming from very different professional backgrounds. For the majority of the editorial staff and management interviewed, with impressive professional backgrounds from international, mainstream TV newsrooms, this implied a struggle to put aside their 'Western' journalistic values, framing, terminology and in-built routines. These informants gained their training in Anglo-American news channels, predominantly from British ITN and the BBC, or American CNN, ABC and CNBC, but most of them expressed disillusionment with the developments in mainstream international TV news. In interviews, informants with long careers in mainstream newsrooms expressed particular concern over what they characterized as the increasing domestication of foreign reporting, the reduction of foreign bureaus and correspondents, the 'parachute reporting' and the turn towards celebrity and entertainment journalism.

Informants underlined how they made an extra effort in putting aside their mainstream journalistic framing, terminology and worldview, a task that has been particularly challenging in the London and Washington D.C. headquarters. A London-based editor stressed the extent of this transformation:

> I'm quite certain as well that you would have seen that while we try and look at things from a certain perspective, there aren't very many southern people here working, are there? They're more like us. I think people like me . . . middle-class, white guys trying to do our best. [. . .] For a lot of people, as you can imagine, it's been an extraordinarily sharp load. (Interview with author, London, 24 April 2008)

Also, those employees of non-Western ethnic backgrounds that have worked with Anglo-American news channels emphasize the necessity of unlearning the practices and perspectives adopted from mainstream newsrooms, as explains one Doha-based presenter/correspondent:

> I think it starts really with just thinking out of the box. That's the biggest challenge. It's just thinking differently, because if you are a journalist who has worked all your life in international or the mainstream news media, it becomes part of your culture to think in a certain way. And you need to constantly change yourself, say 'Okay', and find that moment when you take a stop, and say 'Okay, am I looking at this differently? Am I speaking to the grassroots on this story?' I think, once you make that first step, then really, the rest is—[I] can't say it's easy, but it comes. It is achievable. (Interview with author, Doha, 2 October 2007)

News journalism is known to build on implicit and unquestioned conventions rather than explicitly stated principles (Cook 1998). Newsroom routines tend to be regarded as self-evident, given, natural and therefore not the object of deliberation among the editorial staff. In its formative years, the young, diverse and global AJE newsroom struggled to establish these conventions. The broad, unarticulated editorial vision *and* the inconsistent implementation of the vision in practice were identified as a problem by AJE sources. Informants at all levels of the organization underline the lack of a coherent editorial agenda, described by one of the younger London-based producers as "a lack of understanding of who we are and where we are going" (interview by author, London, 24 April 2008). These views were supported in the renewal report (AJN 2009b), where the lack of meaningful professional development processes was identified as a major concern.

Second, the staffing profile, or more precisely the issue of staff diversity, emerged as a recurrent issue in the interviews. Although all informants highlight the diversity in the AJE newsroom, there is a call for more diversity in the top management (from executive producers and up). Initially, most of the management was recruited from the British channel ITV or ITN News (labeled the "ITN crowd" in interviews). Members of the management team explain the recruitment policy with the need to establish a tight team of professionals who know and trust each other during the intense pressure of launching a global news network. Although AJE informants broadly acknowledge the technical, logistical and journalistic expertise of the management group, informants are concerned that the homogenous management group represents 'the North' rather than 'the South.' A Doha-based correspondent explains why he believes the management cannot fully capture the South:

> I have worked with them and I know they have good intentions. I know that it is just a matter of exposure and a matter of experience and a matter of understanding, because you can't relate to a story if you don't understand it. You could relate it anyway, but you will relate it the way it was conceived in a certain part of the world. Now that you are here, now that you are in Al Jazeera, I think you have to see the story the way it is on the ground, not the way it was described to you when you were thousands of miles away. (Interview with author, Doha, 29 November 2007)

AJE sources point to the paradox that, although hiring local correspondents was one of the key editorial strategies of the channel, the channel has a global presence and a multinational staff; in the channel's formative years, the executive producers were the same professional elite (middle-aged white men) that run mainstream, global newsrooms. As explained by a producer in Doha:

> There were a lot of people hired by AJE, but all the really good people that they hired, that could bring that perspective of the South, are in lower positions. And the people that are in real gatekeeping positions, the real management positions of editorial control, hiring decisions control, control over what's the top story, control over all of that stuff—those people are all British. White, British. White, British, men! All of them [. . .] [W]hen I raised this with one of my colleagues, he said: 'What are you talking about? This is the most diverse channel in the world.' And I said: 'Yeah, up until the point where you get to the people who have power.' There is no diversity there. (Interview with author, Doha, 1 December 2007)

Third, the relationship between AJE and its Arabic sister channel, Al Jazeera Arabic (AJA), emerged as another issue of concern for employees.

Although the comparative advantages of being part of the Al Jazeera Network are emphasized as an important editorial strategy, informants often struggled to identify and cooperate with their Arab colleagues. The tensions within the network highlight some of the in-built contradictions in the set up of AJE. Most importantly, the internal struggle over ownership of the Al Jazeera project, the homogenous management in AJE and the lack of integration within the network represent organizational obstacles that prevented the network from making the most of its potential comparative advantages in its early years.

In essence, journalism can be described as transforming an abundance of information into a few selected news stories. To AJE employees, the editorial agenda, strategies and freedoms that characterize the channel represent a return to what they value as "good, truly global journalism"—free from pressure towards domestication and the cost-reduction and commercial imperatives that increasingly govern foreign reporting and international news. In practice, however, alternative projects like AJE are not exempt from the hard reality of journalistic selection. On the contrary, like their competitors in mainstream news media, AJE sources must frame the news and legitimize their editorial priorities, but unlike their mainstream competitors and (former) colleagues, they do not have the established framework to facilitate the process.

In interviews, AJE interviewees distanced themselves from both their former Western colleagues and from their new Arab colleagues within the Al Jazeera Network. By this, they have left the 'interpretative community' of Western foreign correspondents that many of them had belonged to for years: they follow different beats, interview other sources, chose alternative news stories and criticize the values and practices of 'parachuters.' In interviews, the editorial staff and management often make use of ideal types to contrast their current editorial agenda and strategies with that of their previous outlets, to clarify and exemplify how the Al Jazeera project was different and to legitimize the dramatic move many of them had made. It should be emphasized that joining AJE before it launched and during its early years was a high-risk career move for those informants who had high-ranking positions in mainstream Anglo-American newsrooms. At the time, the Al Jazeera Network was perceived as a maverick, a rebel on the global news scene—for many Western media, widely associated with graphic images, terrorists and extremists (see the next chapter in this volume for a more detailed discussion on how the Al Jazeera Network has been perceived by Western news media). Although senior Western AJE staff was compensated with high salaries, luxurious lifestyles and generous news budgets, the professional and personal risks they took should not be underestimated.

AJE journalists are relatively freer than their peers in established international media—they are journalistic outsiders who position themselves against the dominant values and practices of foreign correspondence. In interviews, AJE informants distance themselves from a negative caricature of the Western foreign correspondent and the decline of foreign correspondence. By providing examples of hazardous practices and suspect values and motivations, interviewees indirectly outline what the AJE correspondent is supposed to be, although the presentation of the 'local' correspondent remains somewhat idealized. In contrast to most international media that depend more and more on local staff because it is safer, more practical and cheaper, AJE's hiring of local correspondents seems to be editorially and politically motivated. In contrast to most international media that obscure and downplay their growing dependence on local editorial staff (Bishara 2006), AJE highlights its local staff, particularly those with backgrounds from the Global South, as it dovetails nicely with its 'southern' editorial agenda. Local correspondents working for international media outlets occupy ambiguous positions between their local society and the outside world (Bishara 2006: 34). As outlined in this chapter, hiring local correspondents poses challenges for international news organizations, including AJE, and the delicate balancing act between local and global, southern and international is amplified by the channel's staffing policy and the lack of editorial guidelines and routines.

4   Reversing the News Flow?

News Geography on Al Jazeera English

In one of Al Jazeera English's marketing campaigns, the channel's editorial objective is presented in a historical context that places the channel as a challenger of dominant news and information flows. "Historically," the channel writes, "the flow of information has run from North to South, from rich countries to poor. Al Jazeera English (AJE) aims to balance the information flow between the South and the North" (AJN 2010a). Why is it imperative for AJE to balance the information flow between the South and the North? What characterizes the northern information flow that AJE sets out to balance? Why has global information historically been unbalanced and one-directional? To understand and contextualize AJE's editorial objective, it is essential to review the contributions from the political, academic and industry debate over news flows and contra-flows.

The term 'flow' has been a favorite term for characterizing key features of media content. The idea of flow is considered valuable because it combines verb and noun and unites issues of carriage and content. As explained by Moran (2009: 13):

> Flow may be thought of as a movement, as the activity that pushes an entity from one place to another, creating or using a channel or stream. Flow may also be imagined as an object, as an entity or content that undergoes such a displacement. In other words, the idea of television flow can be seen to join the notion of transportation with that of communication.

The following chapter aims to systematize and synthesize the academic literature on media flows and contra-flows. To contextualize the academic debate I will start by outlining the politicization of the news flow debate in international organizations in the period 1960–1980 and the theoretical literature that was mutually constitutive of calls for changes in the composition of global media power. Looking at this period of literature from a historical perspective, three successive intellectual paradigms in media studies have introduced divergent understandings of international news flows: 1) communication and development, 2) cultural imperialism and 3) globalization and cultural pluralism (Golding & Harris 1997, Sreberny-Mohammadi 1991).

Researchers (e.g., Chang et al. 1987, Kim & Barnett 1996, Wallis & Baran 1990) have pointed out that different concepts and methods in the various news flow studies, and the lack of theoretical and methodological linkage between them, constitute a major problem in news flow research. In light of this view, the present chapter distinguishes between what can be characterized as the three main academic subdisciplines of media-flow research. First, the news geography approach, analyzing the *content* of media flows—the amount, nature and type of foreign news disseminated across national boundaries. Second, the news determinants approach, exploring wider *structural* factors that facilitate or obstruct media flows. Third, the television program flow approach, *mapping the export, import and adaptation* of television flows. In reviewing these three approaches, it aims to further clarify the issues at stake in debates around news flows and contra-flows.

Contemporary academic contributions to international news flows, such as studies of localization and contra-flows, will be integrated into the broader media-flow debate,[1] and the conceptual and empirical limitations of current news flow and contra-flow scholarship is assessed. In the final section of this chapter, the extent to which Al Jazeera English meets its ambition to reverse the news flow is discussed based on a quantitative mapping of its news geography.

THE POLITICIZATION OF THE NEWS FLOW DEBATE

Concerns about inequality in the international news flow date back to the 'news agency cartel' (1840s–1930s), when the largest international news agencies (British Reuters, French Havas and German Wolff) controlled international news (Boyd-Barrett & Thussu 1992). The cartel itself was formally dismantled in the 1930s, but the question of whether the expansion of international media flow is a mechanism of both economic *and* ideological domination, specifically by the Western powers, is still strongly contested in academic circles (Bielby & Harrington 2008, Chalaby 2006). After the Second World War, the debate on international news flow has been highly politicized. The 'free flow of information' concept was first formulated in the US and other Western nations near the end of the war (MacBride & Roach 1993). As viewed by its supporters, the unhampered flow of information would be a means of promoting peace and understanding, as well as spreading technical advances. At first, the idea of a *free flow of information* was embraced globally as people everywhere were tired of the propaganda and censorship that were part of the war (Carlsson 2005).

The concept of free flow won support in the United Nations (Hafez 2007), and in the 1950s UNESCO (the United Nations Educational, Scientific and Cultural Organization) became the main forum in which information and communication issues were debated in the postwar period. From the 1950s onward, UNESCO initiated influential studies of international news (see discussion below), organized conferences and summits on the international news system, and encouraged bilateral information exchanges among developing countries. Reflecting the political emphasis on free information flow, international communication research was dominated by the communication and development school from the late 1950s onward. The period was influenced by a strong belief in the role of media and communications as powerful agents of change and modernization. The modernization school of development should be considered in the Cold War framework, and both the industry and the research community in the US[2] were largely serving the US foreign policy agenda (Mody & Lee 2002: 384). The communication-for-development school was later criticized for its ethnocentrism, its ahistoricity and its linearity (Boyd-Barrett 2002: 330, McDowell 2002: 298, Sreberny-Mohammadi 1991: 120).

Starting in the late 1960s, critics argued that the free flow doctrine served the most powerful nations by helping them achieve economic and cultural domination over the less powerful ones. A rewording of the doctrine was urged by nonaligned spokespersons, calling for a free *and balanced* flow of information (MacBride & Roach 1993). Masmoudi (1979) was one of the strongest advocates of Third World rights, and his statements in many ways became the intellectual driving force behind the demand for changing the global information order.[3] In his call for this new order, he emphasized self-reliance and horizontal cooperation among developing countries (South-South flows) to balance the flows from the developed world (North-South flows) (ibid.: 185). The call for a New World Information and Communication Order (NWICO) was rooted in the historical changes in global power. These were reflected in three dimensions of the developing world's protest against the Western domination of the international system: the political dimension (decolonization, nonalignment and postcolonialism), the economic dimension (epitomized in the call for a New International Economic Order [NIEO]), and the sociocultural dimension (the aforementioned NWICO) (Boyd-Barrett & Thussu 1992, Carlsson 2005). The cornerstones of the NWICO movement in turn can be summarized with the 'four Ds': decolonization, development, democratization and demonopolization (Nordenstreng 1995 in Boyd-Barrett 2002). NWICO signifies a transition between world orders influenced by the weakening of the US from its failure in Vietnam, the newfound strength of OPEC, the persistence of communism in the Soviet Union and China, and Japan's economic miracle (Boyd-Barrett 2002: 326). The NWICO debate has most often been reduced to a West-versus-Rest debate, but this dichotomy glosses over the complexities of the debate. There were three distinct power blocs in this debate: the Soviet Union, the West and the Third World (which was generally closer to the Soviet than to the Western position but distinct) (ibid.: 333). *Furthermore,* the call for a fair and balanced flow was advocated by both Western democracies (among them France and Canada) and developing countries (Kraidy 2005: 16).

Furthermore, mirroring the political influences of the time, the cultural imperialism school largely dominated international communication research, and this theory provided one of the major conceptual thrusts behind the NWICO movement. This school of thought, most prominently represented by Schiller's influential book *Communication and Cultural Domination* (1976), argued that the UN was utilized and manipulated into making the free flow of information one of its major concerns so as to serve US public diplomacy, foreign policy and capitalist interests (Schiller 1976: 31–8). In addition, Schiller claimed that international flows of information contributed to a strengthened one-way dependency between developed and developing countries and prevented true development. Schiller (1976: 9) defined *cultural imperialism* as "the sum of processes by which a society is brought into the modern world system and how its dominating stratum is attracted, pressured, forced, and sometimes bribed into shaping social institutions to correspond to, or even promote, the values and structures of the dominating center of the system." With a more narrow focus, Boyd-Barrett (1977: 117) defined *media imperialism* as "the process whereby the ownership, structure, distribution or content of the media in any one country are singly or together subject to substantial external pressures from the media interests of any country or countries *without proportionate reciprocation* of influence by the country so affected" (emphasis added).

The media imperialism concept had a number of merits. First, it offered a macro-level analysis informed by a political and economical analysis of a world system. Second, it acknowledged the uneven nature of this process by pointing out that some societies have a scarcity of resources compared to others. Third, and this is the most contested point, it argued that the uneven relationship has an effect on less developed cultures and societies (Rantanen 2005: 77). Among media imperialism scholars, new media technologies such as satellite technology, were expected to intensify the dependency structures (Masmoudi 1979).

The establishment of the International Commission for the Study of Communication Problems, popularly known as the MacBride Commission, was announced in late 1977. The polarization of the international news debate culminated in the publication of the MacBride report. *Many Voices, One World* (1980) largely served as an intellectual justification for the call for a new world information and communication order (NWICO) and made it an important part of the global agenda (Boyd-Barrett & Thussu 1992, Carlsson 2005). The report devoted one chapter to the flaws of information flows (MacBride et al. 1980: 137–54). It criticized the major Western news media for inadequate coverage of the developing world, emphasizing every nation's right to self-representation in the media. It concluded that international communication was a one-way flow, "basically a reflection of the world's dominant political and economic structures, which tend to maintain and reinforce the dependence of poorer nations on the richer" (ibid.: 148). Furthermore, the report stated that in order to be truly free, information flows had to be *two-way* (ibid.: 140), thereby intensifying the criticism of the concept of free flow. One of the recommendations of the MacBride report was to stimulate a change from vertical (North-South) to horizontal (South-South) communication exchange.[4]

Overall, outcomes of NWICO have been modest, as the movement became a "victim of the very imbalances it critiqued and was the target of a counter-reaction from threatened interests" (Boyd-Barrett 2002: 335). Powerful players, particularly the United States' and the United Kingdom's governments and news organizations, opposed NWICO because the concept was seen as fundamentally in conflict with liberal Western values, such as the free flow of information. The Western interests tended to use a narrow definition of the call for a NWICO, focusing on dealing with the journalist's right to report freely without obstructions, and in the West the call for a NWICO was largely interpreted in a Cold War context. The NWICO concept lost influence toward the end of the 1980s (Gerbner et al. 1993), although some analysts argued for a comeback and a reintroduction of the NWICO debates in the 1990s (Kleinwatcher 1993).

Just as modernization and development theories had been largely replaced by the language and demands of media imperialism scholars, in the late 1980s and the 1990s, the media imperialism tenets were criticized and reformulated to reflect an increasingly global media ecology (see, for instance, Boyd-Barrett 1998, Golding & Harris 1997, Tomlinson 1991). In short, the theory came under fire for assuming that nation states were the main actors in global media and thus ignoring inequalities within nations, extra-media powers and changes in international media flows. Furthermore, critics argued that the media imperialism doctrine ignored the question of the audience, assuming that 'imperialist media' have a direct manipulative effect on cultures they gain access to and argued that it was a generic term that had never been empirically applied to a comprehensive extent. Another key objection to the media imperialism literature argued that it was embedded in a radical, Latin American dependency discourse against the US (ibid.).

The cultural pluralism school has studied how people *use* the media rather than the politics and economics of the media institutions (Rantanen 2005). In short, they argue that globalization leads to heterogenization, differentiation or hybridization, not to homogenization as argued by the media imperialists, because of the active, critical and selective nature of the media habits and practices of audiences. Critics of the media pluralism school have argued that it overemphasizes the power gained by the audience by neglecting the structural inequality of audience access to media and communications and exaggerating the size and/or amount of localized media production. Moreover, the cultural pluralism argument has been accused of a naïve understanding of indigenization because much of the so-called local and/or indigenous production is created by large corporations, and the big US media companies still dominate global media and cultural flows (see Kraidy 2005, Rantanen 2005).

To summarize, while the heated political debate around the potential for a NWICO has largely waned, the problems raised in that debate have remained important for research on international media, as the disagreement between the North and the South seems to have remained (Wu 2003). Academically, the debate about NWICO had an immense impact on the field of international communication, with an ever-growing number of research studies investigating the flow of international news (Hanusch & Obijiofor 2008: 10). As can be seen in the debates outlined above, in their reviews of each other, the individual research paradigms and traditions in the field of international communication have largely been polemic and inadequate (see Mody & Lee 2002: 393–5 for discussion). Drawing on the academic side of the NWICO debate, Boyd-Barrett (2002: 340) calls attention to some important lessons for communication research. He writes: "In international communication research, a strong ethnographic and empirical base of information concerning peripheral countries is as important as the case of the core countries. Special care should be taken when the subject under investigation is also high on political agendas. Advocacy is best left to politicians." Recently, scholars have called for a less caricatured and more nuanced debate on international media flow (Bielby & Harrington 2008, Chalaby 2006, Hanusch & Obijiofor 2008, Kraidy 2005).

THREE APPROACHES TO NEWS FLOW

I) The News Geography Approach: Mapping International News Output

One aspect of the news flow debate has been news geography, or more precisely, the ways in which the world is reflected in the news media. Story location, news topics and news sources have usually been the primary emphasis of these studies. One point of departure is UNESCO's *One Week's News* study (Kayser 1953). Even though the study preceded news flows research surveying news geographies per se, it was significant as an early attempt to extend comparative studies of newspaper content to the international field. Overall, Kayser found that home news tends to be prioritized over foreign news, though in some of the newspapers the two were fairly evenly balanced (ibid.: 92). Further aggravating the relative scarcity of foreign news, newspapers did not allocate the resources to maintain a network of foreign correspondents and relied heavily on news agencies for their foreign news (ibid.: 93). That same year, The International Press Institute published a pioneering study of international news flows and foreign news coverage in the US, Western Europe and India (IPI 1953). They, too, concluded that newspapers in all three areas relied chiefly on news agencies (ibid.: 101). In addition, the IPI found that agency coverage (and thus foreign coverage in general) was focused heavily on a few major countries—the US, the UK, Germany, France and the international organizations with which these were associated (the UN, NATO, etc) (ibid.: 8). Moreover, the study found that official news, such as stories about politics, foreign relations and wars, dominated foreign reporting. The stories from the news agencies were mostly headline news or spot news that were edited down to very brief news items, "leaving the cumulative picture sketchy, episodic and not very enlightening" (ibid.: 9).

During and immediately after the NWICO debate (from the 1960s to the mid-1980s), the number of empirical news flow studies increased significantly. Moreover, the research field was considerably broadened with new media and new regions and countries added in more complex, comparative analyses (Wilke 1987: 150). A point of reference in the news geography studies continues to be the UNESCO/IAMCR-sponsored *Foreign News in the Media* project (Sreberny-Mohammadi et al. 1985). In this ambitious project, 13 research teams (recruited from the International Association for Media and Communication Research (IAMCR)) conducted a comparative analysis of two weeks of news coverage by press, radio and television in 29 media systems worldwide. One overall finding was the prominence of regionalism in media systems around the world. The extensive study documented that geographical and cultural proximity is the dominant orientation for determining newsworthiness worldwide (ibid.: 52). Second, in addition to the regional emphasis, another pattern was that Western Europe and North America have been prioritized and covered worldwide. With the exception of the Middle East, which has received considerable coverage, much of the developing world remained invisible in international news. There was little evidence of a broader "Third World perspective" and flows between developing states were minimal (ibid.). In particular, Africa and Latin America received less attention than other regions (Larson 1984: 146). Third, across all regions, politics (domestic affairs in other countries or international relations) dominated the foreign news coverage (Sreberny-Mohammadi 1984: 126–7). Also pertinent to this, newsmakers were government officials, while the activities of ordinary citizens were ignored in all parts of the world (Sreberny-Mohammadi et al. 1985: 57).

The *Foreign News* project received considerable criticism for its methodological approach, for not fulfilling its aims and objectives and for a lack of contextualization (e.g., from Nordenstreng 1984, Stevenson 1984). Nonetheless, the major characteristics of the international landscape identified in the *Foreign News* project have been (re)confirmed, nuanced and bolstered with time by numerous complementary studies (e.g., Larson 1984, Stevenson & Cole 1984, Wallis & Baran 1990, Wilke 1987) and remain a key reference in debates on international news.

II)   International News (Flow) Determinants

A related analytical approach is the effort to theorize the factors influencing international news flows. The theoretical thinking about these issues can be grouped into two categories: context-oriented and event-oriented (Chang et al. 1987: 400). Within this field, the most widely cited and critiqued study is most probably Galtung and Ruge's (1965) article *The Structure of Foreign News*. In the study, they propose four factors that influence international news flows. They discuss the extent to which elite nations, elite people, personification and negative events (crisis news) influence the determination of which stories become news and which stories are ignored. By applying their experimental design to three crises, they conclude with a set of hypotheses.[5] They argue that news from nations that are culturally distant and have a low international status will have to personify and preferably be negative and unexpected, but nevertheless conform to a pattern that is consistent with an audience's 'mental pre-image' in order to qualify as newsworthy (Galtung & Ruge 1965: 84). As a consequence, they found that news from more distant (peripheral/ southern) nations had to be event-based and simple and provide the audience with something with which it could identify. Thus, over a period of time, it would facilitate an image of these nations as "dangerous, ruled by capricious elites, as unchanging in their basic characteristics, as existing for the benefit of the topdog nations and in terms of their links to those nations" (ibid.).

Reviewing the academic debate about the model, Harcup and O'Neill (2001: 264) find that the study is still regarded as *the* news study, providing a seminal framework for numerous researchers testing, investigating or replicating their arguments. Nonetheless, a number of shortcomings have been identified, and there have been numerous alternative, but essentially similar, lists of news determinants (see Harcup & O'Neill 2001 and O'Neill & Harcup 2009 for a more thorough discussion). Primary objections have been that the model's limited focus on crisis news ignores the day-to-day coverage of 'regular news' and that it appears to assume that there is a given reality out there that media professionals may choose from. In addition, critics have questioned the ideological implications behind the news values and argued that the news values are too broad to elucidate the news gathering processes (Harcup & O'Neill 2001, O'Neill & Harcup 2009). Furthermore, Rosengren (1974) and others argue that the construction of this theory as a whole has made it almost impossible to falsify and that attempts to test the theory empirically have therefore been far from satisfactory, even though some of the factors are amenable to empirical tests. Hjarvard (1995, 2002) notes the discrepancy between empirical data and methodology and results, calling attention to the fact that the theory examined the content of newspapers but drew more general conclusions about news selection processes.

The determinants of international news flows have been systematized, theorized and tested empirically in a rich body of literature (Wu 1998). Tsang et al. (1988) found that as many as 150 research papers mapped international news flows in the years between 1970 and 1986. In his meta-analysis of these contributions, Wu (1998) divided the hypothesized and/or discovered determinants of international news flows into two broader categories: (1) the gatekeeper perspective (predominantly focusing on the social psychology of the news professionals and how these characteristics affect news output) and (2) the logistical perspective (mapping the socio-economic components and physical logic of international news flows). Wu's meta-analysis (1998) identifies a number of gatekeeper factors, including traditional newsworthiness, sociocultural structure and organizational constraints, as well as the agenda-setting impact of the international news services. The presence and operation of news agencies and content-sharing agreements between television networks is considered vital for the volume of international news coming out of that country (Clausen 2003, Gasher & Gabriele 2004, Larson 1984, Meyer 1989, Paterson 2011, Wu 2007). The role of the television news agencies is so crucial for global news flows that they have been labeled "visual flow regulators" (Paterson 2011: 15) and "visual gatekeepers" (Fahmy & Neumann 2012: 8). Paterson (2011) finds that the two dominant television news agencies, Reuters and the Associated Press, the most important gatekeepers in international news, are themselves accommodating to the economic priorities of the major Western powers and the presumed interests of the Western media (ibid.: 29). The result is a limited menu of news stories and news frames from a small group of elite nations (ibid.).

These gatekeeping mechanisms influence news flow in combination with a number of logistical factors, such as the GNP of each nation, the volume of trade, regionalization, population, geographic size, geographic proximity, the political and/or economic interests of the host countries, 'eliteness,' communication resources and infrastructure, and cultural affinity (Wu 1998: 507). Wu concludes his overview by discussing how international news is selected, sifted, edited and mostly discarded through a number of complex professional practices. He writes: "With these various factors mediating the channels of international news, one cannot help but realize that the everyday representation of the world via the media is far from a direct reflection of global realities" (ibid.: 507). Overall, a complex set of factors determines international news coverage, and the more factors that are involved, the greater the chances of attracting media attention (Hawkins 2011: 62). Underlining the economic power of nations worldwide in the post-Cold War world, Wu's (2003: 19) systematization of the most covered nations in the media in 44 countries worldwide finds that economic interaction, population, the presence of international news agencies and geographic proximity are positive factors for gaining news coverage in other countries. Furthermore, the study documents the 'superstar' status of the US in international media and argues that economic interest has become the universal dominant factor in international news flow (ibid.: 19–20). In his news flow study of online news media, Wu (2007) finds that the online media (CNN.com and nytimes.com) have not amounted to an innovative, truly global medium independent of the structures and systematic barriers of traditional news, but rather reflect their traditional media counterparts in their overall picture of the world. On the contrary, the power of the news agencies seems to have resurged on the news websites studied (ibid.: 549).

III) Television Program Flows

Since the early 1970s, 'flow' has been a key concept in studies of television program scheduling (Moran 2009), and it has been a core concept in both cultural studies and the political economy school approach to media studies (White 2003).[6] The political economy approach to television flow, which attempts to survey the ways news, information and entertainment are distributed globally, is more relevant for this study. The analysis of international television flows (export/import) was pioneered by Nordenstreng and Varis' classic study *Television traffic—a one-way street?* (1974). By surveying the international flow of television material, the UNESCO-initiated study seeks to identify barriers and obstacles to the "free flow of information." They classify television programs as domestic or foreign on the basis of the picture, video or film; hence, foreign programming with subtitles or domestic narration or dubbing were all classified as imported.[7] Overall, the authors found that the US and China were highly self-supporting television markets, only importing a small percentage of their programming. In addition, Japan and the Soviet Union largely used their own programming. By contrast, Latin America and Africa (excluding Egypt) imported roughly half of their programs. Furthermore, Europe imported approximately one third of its programs, while Asia (excluding China and Japan) imported between one half and one third (ibid.: 12). The study identifies two trends in international television flows: "(1) a one-way traffic from the big exporting countries to the rest of the world, and (2) dominance of entertainment material in the flow. These aspects together represent what might be called a tendency towards concentration" (ibid.: 40). Moreover, the colonial ties of the Western European countries were reflected in program distribution from Western Europe. In addition, Western European productions took a larger share of the Eastern European market than the other way around (ibid.). In a follow-up study conducted in 1983, Varis (1984, 1986) confirmed that a few exporting countries and entertainment programming dominated the international television flows, concurring with the one-way flow documented in the first study. Nonetheless, in the 1983 study, he emphasized that despite persistently unequal television flows, there were also important regional developments in various parts of the world (ibid.: 248). More importantly, he found that the increase in regional exchange was particularly notable among Arab countries (where approximately one-third of the imported programs came from within the region) and within Latin-America (10 percent of the inter-regional imports) (ibid. 1986: 151).

A more dynamic regionalist approach acknowledging the television exports and television cultures of the more 'peripheral' regions was proposed by Sinclair, Jacka and Cunningham (Sinclair et al. 1996). They argued that the image of a 'patchwork quilt' was more precise than Nordenstreng and Varis's (1974) "one-way street" metaphor. The "geolinguistic media regions" each have their own internal dynamics as well as their global ties; they are primarily based on geographic realities, but are also defined by common cultural, linguistic and historical connections that transcend physical space. Starting in the early 1990s, strong audiovisual production centers became key exporters within their respective regions, such as Mexico and Brazil for Latin America, Egypt for the Arab world, Hong Kong and Taiwan for the Chinese-speaking populations of Asia, and India for the Indian populations in Africa and Asia (Sinclair et al. 1996: 5–8). A key point for Sinclair et al. was that although some of these regions appeared to have been victims of cultural imperialism in the past, in terms of their heavy importation of US television programs, they have simultaneously been strong regional exporters. Thus, they argued that the resulting situation was not the passive homogenization feared by cultural imperialism scholars, but rather a trend towards heterogenization (ibid.: 13). These regional flows were not so much displacing US production as finding their own intermediate level (ibid.: 14).

Surveying television flows in 24 countries, representing all geo-linguistic regions from the 1950s to today, Straubhaar (2007: 164–6) found a greater proportion of nationally produced television programming over time, particularly in prime time. He argued that the broadcasting of national programming in prime time strengthened cultural proximity because national programming was prioritized when most people were watching and when concern for audience satisfaction was the highest (ibid.: 165). Furthermore, Straubhaar argued that most national television systems were far from being overwhelmed by global imports, and many of the countries surveyed were increasingly producing for other markets. By so doing, they competed with the traditional US and European exporters, most often within the broad geo-linguistic Spanish, Arabic or Chinese markets (ibid.: 171). Nonetheless, he also documented that it has proven difficult for non-US exporters to sustain a truly global export over time (ibid.: 172). In a broad overview, Tunstall (2008: 449) concluded that the world audience outside the US devoted 10 percent of its time to US media, 10 percent of its time to other imported media (primarily from within the region or language area), and 80 percent of its time to domestic, national media. In contrast to his classic contribution, *The Media Are American* (1977), in which he emphasized the American media empire, Tunstall (2008: 245–246) now emphasizes regional variety, in which numerous national and regional blocs dominate the different world regions.[8] Notwithstanding these developments, he also finds that the US and Europe remain the most important exporters globally (ibid.: 250).

EMERGING CONTRA-FLOWS

The complex contemporary global media ecology outlined in the introduction of this work is characterized by an increasing plurality of media outlets: a multilayered, complex, multidirectional media landscape. In addition, the academic shift from global dominance (media imperialism) to local resistance (cultural pluralism) has increased the academic interest in peripheral media flows and contra-flows. Essentially, *contra-flows* (Boyd-Barrett & Thussu 1992) are flows of media products that counter the historical dominance of the Western media flows: from the less economically and politically powerful to the powerful, from the South to the North, or as horizontal South-South flows. The overall flow is still asymmetric, but there is now an interpenetration of cultures, both through increased circulation of people through migration and through a greater availability of transnational and international media. In short, the dominant flow is still from the developed North to the developing South, but there is a growing flow back as well (Straubhaar 2007: 24).

In his edited volume on contra-flows, Thussu (2007b) proposes a typology to divide the main media flows into three broad categories: 1) global flows, 2) transnational flows and 3) geocultural flows. In general, the US-led Western media are global in their reach and influence, given the political and economical power of the US. The second layer of international media players include both private and state-sponsored transnational flows that operate in a commercial environment, such as for instance the Indian film industry (Bollywood) and Latin American telenovelas (daily drama/soap operas). Thussu emphasizes that although these transnational flows, such as Al Jazeera Channel, Telesûr, Russia Today and CCTV-9, have a strong regional presence, they are also aimed at audiences outside their primary constituencies. He therefore categorizes them as representing "subaltern flows." The last of Thussu's categories includes the media that cater to specific cultural-linguistic audiences, such as diaspora groups, which may be scattered around the world (ibid.). Geocultural contra-flows illustrate the elusiveness of the contra-flow concept since these media flows can erase the boundaries between dominant flows and contra-flows in both the original and the host cultures and can be redefined by the particularities of production, distribution and consumption contexts. Thus, many of the above-mentioned contra-flows are dominant flows in their country/region of production, and only become contra-flows when they are accessed by diaspora groups or the general public elsewhere. As a consequence, it is crucial to conceptualize contra-flows empirically within their media context and to keep in mind that dominant flows and contra-flows are perceived differently in different contexts.[9]

According to Thussu (2007a), the strengthening of non-Western media could potentially reduce inequalities in media access, contribute to a more cosmopolitan culture, and perhaps also affect national, regional and even international political dynamics in the long run. In addition, media and communication contra-flows can shape cultural identities, energize disempowered groups and help create political coalitions and new transnational private and public spheres (Thussu 2007a: 4). For many scholars, international entertainment successes, such as Latin American soap operas, Japanese animation and the Indian film industry, represent the potential of cultural industries in the developing world for resistance, alternatives and contra-flows. Corporate media interests have sought to reformulate the popular rhetoric of contra-flow as a pro-globalization and anti-protectionist argument (global flows in Thussu's typology), encouraging cultural fluidity as a means of increasing their own profit—what Kraidy (2005: 76–96) labels 'corporate transculturalism.'

New regional media capitals are challenging the traditional regional media powers: in South America, Venezuela and Argentina are challenging the Mexican and Brazilian dominance; in the Arab world, Qatar and the UAE are challenging Egypt and Saudi Arabia; and in East Asia, Singapore is challenging Taiwan (Curtin 2003, Rai & Cottle 2007: 74). To capture the emerging complex, multilayered, multidirectional media flows, researchers are employing a more complex, variegated and regionalist perspective on international news flows (Cottle 2009: 32). Current academic debates on television flows and contra-flows have tended to focus more on *entertainment* flows, in contrast to the earlier debates on *news* flows. There has been particular interest in the Latin American soap opera serials, the *telenovelas* (Bielby & Harrington 2008, Biltereyst & Meers 2000, Moran 2009, Straubhaar 2007), and more recently in Arab adaptations of international entertainment and reality television formats (Kraidy 2010, Thomas 2010).

The growth of non-Western regional satellite news channels has encouraged the use of the concept of news contra-flows, but the scope of the phenomenon remains rather limited, as illustrated by the literature on Al Jazeera Channel (Arabic). In contrast to the media interest in the Al Jazeera phenomenon and the body of literature stating that the Al Jazeera

Channel is an important contra-flow in global news (see, among others, El-Nawawy & Iskandar 2002, Miles 2005, Samuel-Azran 2008, Seib 2005, Thussu 2007a/b, Volkmer 2002), there has been a striking lack of systematic, empirical research on *why* Al Jazeera constitutes a contra-flow of news and *how* different or alternative the channel has been. The contributions of Iskandar (2006, 2007) and Sakr (2007b) represent rare efforts to investigate whether AJA could be characterized as an alternative news channel and thus a counter-hegemonic contra-flow. Iskandar (2006) concluded that in its approach and programming, AJA increasingly embodies a mainstream Arab satellite style. Sakr (2007b: 129) found that AJA was not launched with the intention of being counter-hegemonic, but was simply based on a widely accepted model of pluralistic reporting governed by newsworthiness (such as in the BBC). After the polarization of world politics in the aftermath of 9/11 and the war in Iraq, the channel was gradually perceived as representing the alternative media and threatening Western interests (ibid.).

Problematizing the contra-flow concept in the Arab context, Sakr (2007b: 116–7) argued that a "contra-flow in the full sense, would seem to imply not just reversed or alternative media flows, but a flow that is also counter-hegemonic. Theories of hegemony suggest that counter-hegemonic media practices are liable to either be incorporated into dominant structures or marginalized in a way that neutralizes the threat they pose to status quo" (media hegemony approaches are explored and criticized in more detail in chapter 5, this volume). There are many examples that show that *the very existence* of an Arab perspective on the international conflicts in Afghanistan (2001) and Iraq (2003) has frequently been portrayed as a challenge to major Western media (El-Nawawy & Iskandar 2002, Figenschou 2005, Miles 2005, Thussu 2007a/b). Still, there has been a lack of research on *the ways* in which these channels have influenced the global public sphere, and the ways in which the Arab perspectives have influenced Western media and potentially challenged hegemonic practices and discourses.

There are a few notable exceptions worth citing in some detail because they nuance and discuss the most optimistic accounts of news contra-flows. Examining how major Western news channels framed and represented the regional Arab news networks, Samuel-Azran (2010) and Wessler and Adolphsen (2008) find that the Western media, particularly the US television news networks, were restrictive in their rebroadcasting of available Al Jazeera material from inside the conflict zone during the 2003 war in Iraq. Tracking news and footage produced by the Al Jazeera Channel, the Al Arabiya Channel and Abu Dhabi TV, Wessler and Adolphsen (2008) conclude that although CNN, BBC World and Deutsche Welle used footage from Arab networks, the Western media tended to distance themselves from the editorial decisions of their Arab colleagues when the Arab satellite coverage was addressed directly. In his comprehensive study of US television coverage of Al Jazeera from 2001–4, Samuel-Azran (2010) argues that the US mainstream media aired Al Jazeera footage of US military actions and statements by terrorists and insurgents, but largely filtered out graphic images of civilian suffering (ibid.: 43–4). Overall, the Arab media has been perceived and framed by both Western authorities and media, in the US more so than in Europe, as the *enemy* (King & Zayani 2008, Zayani 2011). During the "war on terror," the US media gradually adopted the US administration's interpretation of the Al Jazeera Channel as a deviant source (Samuel-Azran 2010: 55) and discredited both the message of a 'dirty war' and the messenger by framing Al Jazeera as 'biased' (ibid.: 77–86). Likewise, Fahmy & Johnson's (2009) survey study among embedded reporters in Iraq find that they largely adopted the US Administration's antipathy towards the Al Jazeera Network and largely believed the terrorist charges against AJA's high-profiled correspondent Tayseer Alouni. The studies show that during the war on terror, the existence of a contra-flow from the Arab world was recognized by the Western media, although its incorporation into Western newscasts was both limited and often (re)interpreted to fit hegemonic news narratives.[10]

THE LIMITS OF THE NEWS FLOW LITERATURE

The news flow literature reviewed above is informed by some key intellectual works. The seminal works within the three subdisciplines of news flow research emphasized above (most importantly: Sreberny-Mohammadi et al. 1985, Galtung & Ruge 1965, and Varis & Nordenstreng 1974) all originated within the broader media imperialism paradigm. Operating on the macro level, the research aim was to develop general propositions about the structure of news, with little attention devoted to looking for differences and variations. Generally, the aim has been to find all-encompassing characteristics for the news structures on an international level (Hjarvard 1995). For the empirically grounded news flow studies, the point of departure has been news selection—something is added to, removed from or changed in the international flow, depending on the countries and actors involved (ibid). However, when these empirical news flow patterns were theorized and explained, Hjarvard (1995, 2002) found that the news flow literature depended on concepts borrowed from media and cultural imperialism, political economy or dependency theory. Consequently, most of the news flow studies, and particularly the UNESCO-initiated studies, were predicated on the underlying normative conception of the need to balance news flows. Thus, contra-flows (South-North) or horizontal flows (South-South) were regarded as essentially positive developments in international news, and there has been little critical investigation of such flows (see below). Thus, many of the principal objections to the media imperialism paradigm were therefore valid in the case of the news flow studies as well.

The methodology employed in most of the research on foreign news coverage conducted in the 1970s and the 1980s was predominantly based on content analyses of foreign news reports. This preoccupation with content analysis procedures may also have blurred the importance of investigating the underlying reasons why foreign news editors and reporters select and report news the way they do (Hanusch & Obijiofor 2008). Content-analysis-based studies do not take into account the many different steps in the news flow process and the different actors involved that influence the final output. Concurring with Hjarvard (1995, 2002) and Clausen (2003), I find that by largely ignoring the middle level of analysis, the news flow literature has left the *process* of news flow unexplained.[11] In addition, the consumption of foreign TV news by audiences worldwide has been outside the scope of news flow analysis both theoretically and empirically (ibid.).

Another characteristic of the news flow literature is its focus on nation states, national media systems and flows of communication between them. The majority of the news flow studies have mapped news flows between nation states, with particular emphasis on national US elite media. Although media-flow scholars acknowledge the new transnational media, such as satellite broadcasting (see, for example, Varis 1986), media flows have continued to be measured, compared and understood in terms of constituted nation-states (White 1995). The national media flows are still important, but the national prism is arguably insufficient to capture the contemporary multidirectional, multilevel news flows (see Braman 2002 for further discussion). Furthermore, the studies have emphasized 'dominance' over resistance and adaptations although regionalism and peripheral flows have been included in the literature from the 1990s onward. The contemporary contra-flow literature, on the other hand, has included the micro and middle levels of analysis, but pays less attention to the macro structures and the fact that the majority of the truly global media organizations are still the dominant Western flows (see chapter 1, this volume). The contra-flow literature has mainly analyzed entertainment contra-flows such as Latin American telenovelas, Bollywood movies and Japanese manga. Moreover, by grouping the Arab satellite news channels together with all media flows emerging outside the Anglo-American media in a *contra-flow* category, the concept has become too vague and imprecise to maintain its explanatory value.

In contrast to the widespread assumption among researchers and television executives in the early 1990s that news travels especially "easily across borders and is less culturally rooted than other television genres"

(Rai & Cottle 2007: 64), news flows today are more consistently one-way than in flows of entertainment programs and formats (Straubhaar 2007: 25). By not distinguishing between entertainment contra-flows, which have become increasingly commercialized and export-oriented since the 1990s, and the news contra-flows, which have become increasingly regionalized and domesticated, we may overemphasize the news contra-flow phenomenon. More recently, the news flow concept has been criticized for overestimating the fluidity of the media and for treating all notions of mobility and hybridity as if they were inherently progressive (Bielby & Harrington 2008, Morley 2001, White 2003).

Paradoxically, although there has been an unprecedented boom in satellite news channels in the last 10–15 years, most of the scholarly work on news flows and contra-flows has continued to concentrate on national media. There is an acute lack of empirical studies of both the dominant satellite news flows (CNN and the BBC) and the emerging contra-flows. Although there has been an overwhelming interest in satellite news contra-flows as a phenomenon, we know little about what characterizes these channels, aside from their not being Anglo-American. Furthermore, due to the limited number of empirical studies of the dominant channels, we also lack insight into what their 'contra' nature consists of. Related to this, there has been strikingly little scholarly attention devoted to the back players of international news, the international news agencies and television news agencies (Paterson 2011 is an honorable exception).

Moreover, the (re)entrance of strategic actors with political aims in the satellite news landscape in contrast to the commercial news organizations must be properly investigated and theorized. The role of the state has grown in salience in international communication research (Curran & Park 2000, Kraidy 2005), and a critical study of state actors is pertinent in the study of transnational satellite news and mediated public diplomacy, particularly in the Arab world (see chapters 1, 2 and 8, this volume, for discussion). The increasing salience of the state demonstrates that although the media-imperialism school had severe limitations and blind spots (see above), its critical emphasis on structural power remains relevant in international communication processes (Kraidy 2005).

The news flow literature originated within a much more overseeable international media system, where a group of Western national and international media was the main exporters, and the remaining nations were primarily importing news. The directionality of news flows has become largely irrelevant in today's complex satellite news landscape: technological developments, the plurality of news outlets, new patterns of global ownership, new global media institutions, and new financial hubs and emerging media centers blur the traditional dichotomy between dominant flows and contra-flows. Furthermore, adaptation and coproduction trends and the multi-located news production processes in international news have made the origin of news flows largely untraceable. As outlined in the introduction of this book, the traditional dominant satellite channels such as CNN and the BBC have localized their broadcasts. There is no global version of CNN today, only local/regional versions, and this blurs the strict dichotomies between dominant flows and local flows.

In the following section Al Jazeera English's news output will be discussed with reference to this debate on news flow and contra-flows.

NEWS GEOGRAPHY ON AJE: THE GLOBAL SOUTH

With the geographical South as a point of departure, AJE informants emphasize that the 'the South' encompasses more than just the Southern Hemisphere, though there is an overlap between the two. Informants use notions like "philosophical South" (London, 16 May 2008), "South with a capital S" (London, 24 April 2008) or "political South" (Doha, 15 December 2007).

A Doha-based news anchor gave the following illustration of his understanding of the South:

If a husband is the North, his wife is the South. If the politician is the North, his driver is the South. If I am the North in this office, the coffee guy in a yellow jumpsuit, the one who come in to pick up my coffee cup and take it from me—he is the South [. . .] For me that is possibly the closest that I can imagine. If you were to define the voice of the South in a studio, you've got someone from the North and someone from the South. Give that person from the South more time [. . .] because most of the time, those with wealth or those with political power, or those who are celebrities get free reign and make headlines. (Interview with author, Doha, 1 December 2007)

A senior producer in Doha argued that the South is a state of mind and not just a geographical entity:

You can find the South in the North. You can find the South as individual people who feel not really represented by the system, or groups of people who feel the same, or areas and countries which feel the same [. . .] So, it's not a geographical thing, but it is based on geography because the biggest bulk of people who are disenfranchised and in disenchantment, are in the South. But that's why geographically, if you have a camera and you have to work somewhere, that's where you will go. Of course, you will have to go to the North as well. It's for the world; this is a channel for the world. (Interview with author, Doha, 4 December 2007)

Although these quotes illustrates an understanding of 'the South' that addresses patterns of power, wealth, development and privilege across and within regions, most AJE editorial staff interviewed for this book seemed almost hesitant and uncomfortable explicating their understanding of the concept. Some interviewees, particularly among those based in the London headquarters, seemed insecure about a definition of 'a southern news perspective' claiming that they did not know the term, that they did not have a proper definition and that they were not sure if their definition fulfilled the initial ideas of the top management. Other London-based sources signaled that the 'southern perspective' was a cliché, a lofty ambition by the top management rather than an active convention in their day-to-day work. Among the AJE staff that expressed a conscious, clear idea about the 'southern perspective,' the majority had a professional background from non-Western newsrooms or personal background from the non-Western world. There are several plausible explanations for these variations: First, the concept of 'the South' may seem more distant and irrelevant for Europe-based staff covering Europe than from the Middle East. Second, since the top channel management was based in Doha, in the same building as the regular staff, their influence may have been stronger on the Doha staff than the London newsroom. And, third, the fact that the concept of a southern news perspective was not fully internalized among the editorial staff confirms the lack of defined editorial guidelines and editorial challenges discussed in the previous chapter.

REVERSING THE NEWS FLOW?

The vague definitions of a 'southern news perspective' notwithstanding—to what extent did AJE emphasize the Global South in their daily news coverage? In the following, this question will be answered quantitatively, in which AJE's southern perspective (the philosophical, political and symbolic South) is operationalized in terms of news geography (the geographical South). This was done primarily to relate the findings to the existing news flow and contra-flow literature. Notwithstanding its limitations outlined above, the news flow literature served as a point of departure for the analysis of the news geography of AJE. First of all, numerous studies of the ways in which the world is reflected in the news media from the 1950s till today document the prominence of regionalism in media systems throughout the world. They also show a systematic emphasis on the Global North (Western Europe and North America) worldwide. The key features of the news geography studies are largely confirmed and theorized by the international news determinant research.

News flow studies have documented that the international flow of information has been overwhelmingly one way, a geographical pattern that AJE aims to reverse. Given the channel's intended southern perspective, a key question in this book is whether the channel covers the South more extensively than the North. Studies of the Al Jazeera English news geography have documented that the channel emphasizes the Global South (Africa, Asia, the Middle East and Latin America) over the Global North (Europe and North America) (Al-Najjar 2009, Figenschou 2010a, Painter 2008, Uysal 2011).[12] The point of departure here is the most comprehensive of these quantitative studies at the time of writing, analyzing two months of AJE newscasts from October–December 2007 and May–July 2008 (1,324 news items altogether) (see Figenschou 2010a for details and discussion). First and foremost, it documents that the South was covered more frequently than the North (61 percent to 38 percent). Second, breaking the numbers down by region, Europe and Asia were the most covered regions, closely followed by the Middle East, with each of these regions accounting for about one-fifth of all locations. Third, AJE covered the South with in-depth news formats (offering reflection, discussion and background information) more frequently than it did the North. Fourth, by considering the world region in which news items originate, regional variations in news formats became apparent as Europe, North America and Latin America were covered in briefer formats, whereas Asia and the Middle East were reported in greater detail. Finally, the channel had a greater presence on the ground in the South than in the North. In total, Al Jazeera English correspondents were present on the ground in 38 percent of the 1,324 news items in the sample. The channel has a greater presence on the ground in the South than in the North. In the *NewsHour* coverage of the South, Al Jazeera English correspondents were present where the events unfold in 45 percent of all the news items. In their news stories

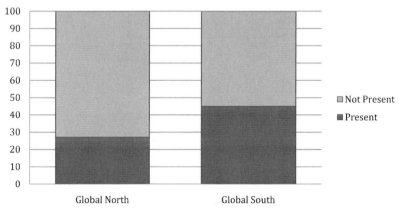

Figure 4.1 Percentage of news items covered with an Al Jazeera English reporter or anchor present on the ground (N:1324) (Figenschou 2010a).

from the North, the channel is present on the ground in 27 percent of the stories (see Figure 4.1).

The study largely corresponds with Painter's (2008) comparative analysis of one week of AJE, CNN and BBC news in November–December 2007. He found that AJE had significantly more coverage of the developing world than the BBC and CNN, with 81 percent, 47 percent and 53 percent, respectively (Painter included Russia and Turkey in the 'developing world' category, which may explain why his percentages were higher than those mentioned in the preceding paragraph). Also Al-Najjer's (2009) comparative analysis of four weeks of Al Jazeera English news, spread over six months from the channel launch in November 2006 to April 2007, documents a geographical emphasis on the Global South in 65 percent of the news items. Although, he does not employ a North-South perspective, Uysal's (2011: 11) mapping of AJE's news geography shows that over 73 percent of the news items are from the Global South. Taken together, these findings reveal that AJE's geographical emphasis is on the Global South (see Figure 4.2 below).[13]

The southern emphasis in AJE's newscasts dovetails nicely with the editorial core values discussed in the previous chapter. This is particularly true for AJE's emphasis on the unreported and/or underreported world away from the press pack, which entails being on the ground in more places and staying there in between the 'big' stories ("Being where others aren't"). In addition, the channel's 'southern perspective' reflects the channel's editorial values and thus its concept of newsworthiness through a higher

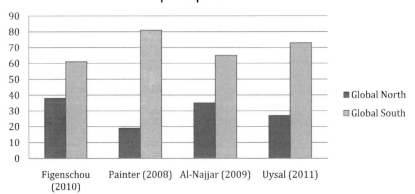

Figure 4.2   The Southern perspective is documented throughout several studies of Al Jazeera English's news geography (percentage of news items from the Global South/Global North).

proportion of stories from the developing world. Furthermore, the quantitative findings show how the editorial strategy to establish a southern presence contributes to a higher number of news stories from the South. Employing the news determinant terminology outlined above, these findings give more weight to gatekeeper factors than to logistical factors. AJE's southern emphasis is a result of the channel's definition of newsworthiness as broadly articulated in its editorial core values. Moreover, it is a result of its organizational structure, demonstrated in the previous chapter through its extensive news network in the South, its local correspondents and its cooperation with the other channels in the Al Jazeera Network. These progressive production strategies seem to have somewhat counteracted the logistical factors that traditionally determine international news, such as a nation's GNP, volume of trade, population, geographic size, regionalization, elite domination, communication resources and infrastructure, and cultural affinity.

Studies have criticized the typical news story from the South for highlighting political coups and crises, natural disasters and violent conflicts (MacBride 1980, Sreberny-Mohammadi et al. 1985). Al Jazeera English aims to challenge traditional perception and biases, and it is therefore relevant to ask whether news items on crisis and conflict are more prominent in the channel's coverage of the South than its reports from the North. When mapping Al Jazeera English's news focus (see Figenschou 2010a), the first finding is that AJE laid most emphasis on politics, which was the main topic in over one-third of all the news items. A closer examination of the kinds of political news that are reported from the different regions demonstrates that internal political crisis is the most frequent political news story to originate in the South, while political processes such as election coverage and results are covered more frequently from the North than the South.[14] Armed conflict is the second most covered news topic on the *NewsHour* as the primary topic in one-fifth of all news items. In this category, there are noticeable differences between the South and the North. Stories about armed conflict constitute over one quarter of all news items out of Asia, the Middle East, Africa and Latin America. In contrast, in the stories from Europe and North America, armed conflict were the main topic in 12 percent of the total coverage.[15] These differences may reflect the situation on the ground, and, arguably, if Al Jazeera English had not covered these stories, it would not have fulfilled its mission as an international news channel. To some extent, however, these tendencies may signal that Al Jazeera English maintains the mainstream news criteria they aim to counter.

The remaining categories covered were legal affairs (13 percent of coverage), the economy (9 percent), ecology (7 percent), and aid and social affairs (3 percent). Other categories, such as culture, science and religion, topics that could provide nuance and extend hard world news,[16] received minimal coverage in the *NewsHour*. Al Jazeera English's coverage of global affairs seems to be an answer to the repetitive critique of mainstream international news as both inadequate and superficial (Sreberny & Paterson 2004). Thussu (2008), among others, argues that international satellite news is increasingly presented in an entertaining manner, as "global infotainment" (2008: 8). In contrast, AJE emphasizes hard, political news and ignores the global celebrity culture (celebrity stories comprise less than 0.5 percent of the total stories, see Figenschou 2010a).

IS AL JAZEERA ENGLISH AN ARAB CHANNEL?

Regionalism has been a defining feature of international news since the first news geography studies in the 1950s. It is thus relevant to discuss the extent to which AJE reflects its geographical home region or counters the localization trend in international news. As underlined by Al-Najjar (2009), Al Jazeera English is funded by Qatari authorities; it is headquartered in Doha (Qatar), an Arab, Muslim country; and the channel broadcasts half its daily airtime from Doha. AJE's sister channel, Al Jazeera Arabic (AJA), has been a primary example of the regional second-generation satellite news channels and its Arab orientation—an Arab channel broadcasting from the Arab and Muslim world in Arabic to an Arab audience—was highlighted in Zayani and Sahraoui's (2007: 64–8) analysis of AJA's success factors. Whether AJE should be first and foremost an Arab channel or an international/global channel has been contested within the Al Jazeera Network, as demonstrated in the previous chapter. Although most AJE informants interviewed for this book repeatedly stressed that the channel does not primarily have an Arab news perspective, it has a stated aim of being the channel of reference for the Middle East and Africa (AJN 2009a).

The Middle East was among the most covered world regions on AJE, together with Asia and Europe (Figenschou 2010b).[17] First, the Middle East was overemphasized relative to its geographical size, population size and GDP per capita (ibid.: 115–18). Second, it was covered in more analytical news formats. Among the three most covered regions, Asia and the Middle East were reported in greater detail, and the Middle East in particular was covered in analytical news formats, indicating that AJE put special emphasis on its home region. These findings provided initial evidence of regionalism in the coverage, although the documented regionalism was not as evident as in Painter's (2008: 29) analysis, which identified a stronger regionalism in AJE's coverage. In Painter's survey, AJE had significantly more coverage of the Middle East than the BBC (which had more coverage of Europe) and CNN (which had more coverage of the US). Moreover, compared with its competitors in the global satellite news ecology, AJE had a stronger presence in the Middle East region than in other parts of the world (ibid.). Comparing the geographical emphasis on Al Jazeera English (AJE) and Al Jazeera Arabic (AJA) to test how Arab the English channel is, Al-Najjar (2009) finds that the Middle East and North Africa was the most extensively covered region on both channels, with 42 percent and 55 percent of the total news respectively, but that AJE devoted more time to the region than AJA altogether by reporting longer stories (ibid.). Finding that both channels cover the Middle East more than any other region, Uysal (2011) finds that AJA has a markedly stronger regional emphasis than AJE, with 78 percent of the news items compared to the English channel's 39 percent. Al Jazeera English's regional emphasis and competitive advantage will be explored more in depth in relation to regional conflicts and uprisings, primarily in the comparative analysis of the channel's coverage of the 2009 Gaza War (chapters 6 and 7, this volume) and the discussion about the channel's coverage of the Arab Spring (chapters 1 and 8, this volume).

5 A Voice of the Voiceless
Al Jazeera English's Source Hierarchies

"I was joking that 'the voice of the voiceless' is the voices of our male anchors," former AJE Director General Tony Burman remarked drily after he was confronted with the elite-domination in the news sources interviewed on the channel. He elaborated on the challenge in finding and putting alternative voices on air:

> The decisions that affect the world are made on kind of a stage and that up until now that stage has been dominated by certain elites coming from certain countries, and that by exclusion, they have had the opportunity to make decisions that not only affect their lives, but the lives of everyone. So essentially what we are committed to is making sure that others are able to join that stage on an equal basis and that means both that they are allowed to, they are helped to find the stage, but also that the others who are on the stage basically leave it. And if you imagine our coverage as trying to achieve that, then it's a question of articulating, helping others articulate their positions, empowering people. (Interview with author, 19 March 2009)

AJE management and staff aim to redress the elite domination in international news by consciously redirecting attention from the "corridors of power" to the margins. When the channel promotes its editorial distinctiveness, AJE is characterized as *different* from established, mainstream international news organizations. The website states, "The channel aims to give voice to untold stories, promote debate, and challenge established perceptions. With broadcasting centers in Doha, Kuala Lumpur, London and Washington DC and supporting bureaus worldwide, the channel will set the news agenda, bridging cultures and providing a unique grass-roots perspective from under-reported regions around the world" (AJN 2010a). The channel's editorial priorities emphasize the perspective of the marginalized and the deviant and distance the channel from international power elites and mainstream media. This perspective is also underlined in the editorial core values outlined in chapter 3 (this volume), in which the channel management reiterates that AJE aims to go behind the headlines, challenge conventional wisdom, give a voice to the voiceless, focus on underreported stories and regions, and cover the world with a southern news perspective. AJE's aim to be systematically critical towards authority and elites, invite all sides of the story into the studio, including "the other opinion" that is denied access to mainstream news, signals an ambition to challenge the established elite domination in global news. How does the editorial staff perceive these alternative sourcing strategies?

In the Arab context, Al Jazeera Arabic has stood out with its emphasis on inviting alternative voices on air, reflected in the channel motto "the opinion and the other opinion." Inviting oppositional forces, including the Islamist opposition, to participate in televised debates and being interviewed in the news, AJA broke powerful, long-time taboos in the region and challenged the regional Saudi Arabian and Egyptian superpowers' 'control' over Arab television (Alterman 1998: 46–7). The channel's sourcing strategy has resulted in practically every Arab government filing formal complaints, sanction the network or its owner, the Qatari government.[1] On the international level, the Arabic channel's sourcing strategy in the regional conflicts in Afghanistan (from 2001) and Iraq (from 2003), foregrounding local sources including Al-Qaeda, Taliban and Baath officials, stirred massive criticism from US and Coalition officials (see Figenschou 2005 for analysis).

Informants, particularly those with a professional background from Arab or other southern news channels, expressed concern that the channel has been too cautious and unwilling to move outside what they see as a Western oriented narrative or worldview, and consequently that controversial voices are denied access on AJE (see Figenschou 2012 for discussion). They often illustrate the problem with examples from the channel's coverage of political leaders or projects that have been severely criticized by Western leaders and international organizations, such as the governments in Sudan, Zimbabwe, the Democratic Republic of Congo and Venezuela. Although informants underline that these controversial international political leaders and systems should be examined thoroughly and critically in the channel's coverage, they believe that it is important to give a platform to 'The Other' to try to understand their position.

Internal critics within the AJE newsroom argue that the channel has not been open to try to explain these 'enemies of the West,' present the world from their perspective, or invite them on the air. A Doha-based producer illustrates her point with the example of Zimbabwe:

> Our Zimbabwe coverage, at least up until now, has been dominated by a British perspective, which is almost kind of like a revenge. Let's get revenge on Mugabe. So that every single story, it's like the network has been for the last year obsessed with Zimbabwe, obsessed with proving that Zimbabwe is a dysfunctional idiotic country with an idiotic leader who needs to be brought down immediately. I mean it is a campaigning

kind of coverage [. . .] I don't think that is the view of the South. I just don't. (Interview with author, Doha, 1 December 2007)

Informants argue that the channel has not been bold and brave enough when it comes to providing a platform for the other opinion hostile to the West. Informants critical of the channel's sourcing practices argue that the channel only exposes the other opinion and oppositional voices if they agree with the 'West,' while silencing those critical voices that are threatening them. A Doha-based correspondent, who articulates this point of view, is worth quoting in some detail. He demonstrates his point through the reactions to an interview with Ahmad Muhammad Harun, former Minister for the Interior within the Sudanese Government, who was summoned before the International Criminal Court in February 2007. He says:

> You tell people what they don't know otherwise you are not making any news—you are not really. [. . .] In The Hague he is a war criminal against humanity, in Khartoum he is a Minister of Humanitarian Affairs. It's a nice story; we focused on that. And we filmed in a meeting where he was hailed, cheered by crowds, and his colleagues in the Ministry of Defense defending him and saying: 'He's a hero. He's our hero. We will not hand him to the enemy' and so on. We focused on that. Our colleagues were not very pleased with that. They said: 'How can you do propaganda for this criminal?' My objection was that for me he is not a criminal. For me he is a human being. Yes, he is suspected by the United Nations, but I am not a judge to issue a verdict on him. And even the judges they have not yet issued a verdict, they said he is a suspect. That is just one of the things that, one of the problems, that results from the conflict of perceptions, the conflict of backgrounds. (Interview with author, Doha, 29 November 2007)

The quote illustrates that there are conflicting views on whether these controversial voices should be covered on AJE. These cases illustrate that although there is a shared understanding across AJE that the channel needs to be bolder and a broad agreement to voice "the other opinion," there are opposing interpretations of what this means in journalistic practice.

COUNTER-HEGEMONIC NEWS

In accordance with the progressive AJE rhetoric, academic works on Al Jazeera Arabic and Al Jazeera English have frequently organized the analysis around the concept of *counter-hegemonic* contra-flows (Samuel-Azran 2008, Painter 2008, Seib 2005). What is striking in most of the analysis of Al Jazeera as a counter-hegemonic challenger in the global news landscape, noted in the previous chapter is the lack of theoretization, problematization and operationalization of media *hegemony* and *counter-hegemony*. All in all, the perception of the Anglo-American media as dominant and hegemonic is generally implicit in the discussions as a context for the analysis of the Al Jazeera phenomenon, but rarely discussed explicitly. Thus, the Gramscian notion of hegemony serves as a point of departure for the following discussion of satellite news media and power. In his work on media power, Curran (2002: 142) argued that the elusiveness of the hegemony concept made the media hegemony tradition something of a "blank check," meaning very different things for different people (ibid.). The concept of counter-hegemonic media must be clarified to avoid the conceptual hollowness associated with media hegemony. This chapter explores different theories that examine whether the media serves the agenda of the established elite or the people, a question that has been a perennial subject of investigation in the general field of political communication. It analyzes how elite sources can access, influence and control the media, and how protest movements or other outsider groups are marginalized as a consequence. In the concluding sections, these theoretical insights from the media–elite debate are employed to analyze to what extent Al Jazeera English's self-declared bottom-up perspective is reflected in its the sourcing strategies, practices and hierarchies.

Gramsci's *Prison Notebooks* (1971) were written in a fragmented and ambiguous style that allowed for numerous interpretations of his work. This book does not engage in an in-depth theoretical, Marxist analysis of Gramsci's concepts and terminology, but it problematizes the ways in which the concepts of hegemony and counter-hegemony have been employed in the analysis of Arab satellite news and develops a framework for analyzing satellite news contra-flows. In contrast to models equating power imbalances with explicit force and coercion, Gramsci saw hegemony as the process of cultural and political leadership attained through the (semi)conscious consent of those dominated. The two major superstructural levels—the civil society and the political society/the state—"correspond on the one hand to the function of 'hegemony,' which the dominant group exercises throughout society and on the other hand to that of 'direct domination' or command exercised through the State and 'juridical' government" (1971: 12). He defines hegemony as "[t]he 'spontaneous' consent given by the great masses of the population to the general direction imposed on social life by the dominant fundamental group; this consent is 'historically' caused by the prestige (and consequent confidence) which the dominant group enjoys because of its position and function in the world of production" (ibid.). The hegemonic group thus maintains its dominance through the negotiated construction of a political and ideological consensus, which incorporates both dominant and dominated groups. Hegemony positions multiple groups with varying and different degrees of power in dialectical relationships that result in control through negotiation and accommodation (Evans 2002: 313). Moreover, Gramsci argued for the need to challenge and replace the hegemony of the ruling classes with a coherent and convincing alternative structure of society

(Downing 2001: 14). Some forms of leadership, which Gramsci labels 'the organic intellectual,' are crucial to coordinating the challenge to hegemonic practices and establishing a credible alternative program and perspectives. In contrast to traditional intellectuals, who are unaware that they are incorporated in the dominant, hegemonic culture, the organic intellectuals recognize their place in the dominant ideology and use their position to challenge it from within.

Thus, hegemony is therefore not mechanical or constant, but the political outcome of the leadership's ability to win the consent of those whom it rules. Gramsci argued that, once in power, the dominant coalition of elites cannot expect to take their dominant position for granted. They must continually reinforce their position by making their own values and interests appear commensurate with the values, cultural expressions and needs of the masses and oppositional groups in order to incorporate the challenges from below. Gramsci emphasized that hegemony is based on *continuous* negotiations between dominant and subordinate social classes. As such, capitalist cultural hegemony is unstable and may be subject to serious intermittent crises; though, for the most part, it enjoys a rarely questioned normalcy over long periods of time (ibid.: 16). The mainstream media play a crucial role in naturalizing these dominant forms of 'common sense,' although subordinated groups exercise their power to contest hegemonic meanings through a discursive practice of resistance, such as posing nonconformist and sometimes counter-hegemonic representations of the views of those who are marginalized, misrepresented and underrepresented in the public sphere (Bailey et al. 2008: 17).

Numerous works have employed the concepts of *counter-hegemony* or the *counter-hegemonic* to categorize attempts to challenge dominant ideological frameworks and supplant them with radical, alternative visions, though Gramsci himself never used the term. Alternative media are one of the many available sites that provide activist groups (and others) with the opportunity to produce nonconformist and counter-hegemonic representations (Bailey et al. 2008, Cox 1993, Downing 2001: 15). Contemporary accounts of hegemony focus primarily on political and ideological contestations, both on the national and on the wider global level[2] (Marmura 2008: 6).

HEGEMONY ANALYSIS IN MEDIA AND COMMUNICATION STUDIES

For journalism studies, hegemony proved a compelling frame for linking journalism to its broader institutional environment (Zelizer 2004: 73). Cultural hegemony analysis has investigated the ways in which particular media, technologies or institutions have contributed to a broader sociopolitical domination by forces such as fascism, communism or market capitalism (Kellner & Durham 2001: 8). Furthermore, a Gramscian theory has emphasized the ways in which counter-hegemonic forces always contest the hegemonic social order, and the ways in which more liberal hegemonic groups compromise with the dominant conservative forces (ibid.).

In media studies, there are at least two contemporary developments of Gramsci's hegemony concept. The first tradition I label the 'capitalist hegemony approach.' According to this tradition, the capitalist media serve as a tool for elite domination, best exemplified by Herman & Chomsky's (1988: 1–35) influential 'propaganda model.' The propaganda model represents a set of news filters that secure the elite domination of the media and the marginalization of dissidents globally. The first filter is the size, concentrated owner wealth, and profit orientation of the dominant mass media firms; the second filter is the dependency on advertising in the mass media; the third filter stresses the mass media's dependency on corporate and political elite experts as news sources and the influence of these groups on the media; the fourth filter highlights systematic criticism ('flak') as a means of disciplining the media; and the fifth filter involves 'anticommunism' as an ideology ('national religion') and control mechanism. According to the model, the five filters interact and reinforce each other, narrow down the range of news that end up in the media and can become big news, and determine the stories that are found 'worthy' and 'unworthy' of media coverage (ibid.: 31). Moreover, the authors found that "the mass media of the US are effective and powerful ideological institutions that carry out a system-supportive propaganda function through reliance on market forces, internalized assumptions, and self-censorship without any significant overt coercion" (ibid.: 306). It should be added, however, that they acknowledge that the propaganda system is not all-powerful, particularly with the growth of new media outlets such as cable and satellite communications (ibid.: 307). More recent contributions on corporate hegemony continue the emphasis on what they see as the hegemony of global corporate media, ownership concentration, privatization, mass entertainment and consumerism (Artz & Kamalipour 2003). To these scholars, the global culture of corporate media features two complementary representations—homogeneity and hybridity—and hybridization processes are understood to be part of the incorporation process in successful media hegemony, rather than resistance to the hegemonic structures (Artz 2003, Kraidy 2005).

The second tradition represents what I call the 'media consensus' approach. In contrast to the instrumentalist tradition above, it emphasizes the dynamics and complexity of hegemony (Hall 1977, Kellner 1990, Williams 1973) and the contest over meaning in the media. One point of departure is Williams' (1973) essay on cultural theory, in which he calls attention to the extensiveness of hegemony, arguing that hegemony constitutes the limit of common sense for most people under its sway (Williams 1973: 8). He emphasizes the complexity of hegemony: it is not singular; its own internal structures are complex and have to be renewed, recreated and defended, and by the same token, they can be continually challenged and, in certain respects, modified (ibid.). Within a particular effective and dominant culture, alternative meanings, values, opinions and attitudes can be accommodated and tolerated as long as they remain within the limits of the central effective and dominant definitions (ibid.: 10). Literature, the visual arts, music, film and broadcasting contribute to the effective dominant culture and are a central articulation of it (ibid.: 14).

In his classic contribution on the ideological effects of the media, Hall (1977) elaborated on Gramsci by emphasizing the non-coercive aspects of domination. To begin with, Hall emphasized the mass media's role in the structuring and reshaping of consent and consensus (ibid.: 340). Furthermore, he discussed the ways in which media discourses become systematically penetrated and infected by dominant ideologies. According to Hall, the media must encode events to make them intelligible, and there are significantly different ways in which events can be coded (ibid.: 343). Particularly problematic or troubling events that break with the normal, common sense or threaten the status quo will be encoded within the repertoire of the dominant ideologies. In mainstream media, he argued, the tendency to systematically draw on a very limited ideological or explanatory repertoire will have the overall effect of giving things 'meaning' within the sphere of the dominant ideology. The selection and encoding process, he argued, is part of professional journalistic ideology:

> [T]hose practical-technological routinization of practice (news values, news sense, lively presentation, 'exiting pictures,' good stories, hot news etc.) which, at the phenomenal level, structure everyday practices of encoding, and set the encoder within the bracket of a professional-technical neutrality which, in any case, distances him effectively from the ideological content of the material he is handling and inflexions of the codes he is employing. (Hall 1977: 343)

The audience, Hall acknowledged, will not automatically decode the media according to the encoders' intentions. The great range of decodings will tend to be negotiations within the dominant codes, rather than systematic decodings of a counter-hegemonic nature (ibid.). The complex processes of constructing consensus involve systematic inclusions (the definitions of a situation that legitimately structure controversial topics) and exclusions (those groups, interpretations, positions and aspects of the reality that are regularly ruled out as 'extremist,' 'irrational,' 'meaningless,' 'utopian,' 'impractical,' etc.). A final point by Hall is the argument that the media's classifications of our world within the discourses of the dominant ideologies are not necessarily conscious work. Moreover, the media's work of ideological reproduction is, by definition, work in which counteracting tendencies will constantly be manifested. Consequently, it is a systematic tendency in the media to reproduce the ideological field of a society in such a way as to reproduce its structure of domination (ibid.).

The first empirical investigations of media consensus focus on the media coverage of social protest. In his pioneering study of the media coverage of the New Left in the 1960s, Gitlin (1980) argued that simply by doing their jobs, journalists tend to serve the political and economic elite definitions of reality (ibid.: 12). Gitlin employed an active notion of hegemony—"hegemony operating through a complex web of social activities and institutional procedures" (ibid.: 10). In modern capitalist societies, he argued, the media are only granted independence as long as they do not violate core hegemonic values or contribute too heavily to radical critique or social unrest (ibid.: 12). If the media cross the red lines defined by the economic and political elites, journalism itself becomes contested.

In his discussion of the media's framing of the leftist opposition and protest movement in the US in the 1960s, Gitlin concluded: "Even when there are conflicts of policy between reporters and sources, or reporters and editors, or editors and publishers, these conflicts are played out within a field of terms and premises which do not overstep the hegemonic boundary" (ibid.: 263). For Gitlin, mainstream news values in the US media serve to secure the boundary: news emphasizes the new rather than the underlying, the person rather than the group and the visible conflict rather than the deep consensus (ibid.). The work of hegemony, he argued, consists of imposing standardized framings of events, where problems are solved by authoritative agencies, and those who threaten stability are stereotyped (ibid.: 264–9). These mechanisms are largely confirmed in Hallin's (1989) analysis of the Vietnam protests in the US mainstream media. He found that, although the media themselves grew increasingly critical of the war, they routinely marginalized the antiwar movement by emphasizing its deviant role and by focusing on the most radical and militant factions of the movement (Hallin 1989: 194). Moreover, coverage of the antiwar movement focused primarily on the movement itself as an issue, rather than on its more substantial opinions about the war (ibid.: 199–201).

The protest movement and the global media ecology have changed substantially since the pioneering studies of the media and social protest movements documented the ways in which the media covered protests through a dominant law and (dis)order frame (Cottle 2008: 855). More recent works on mediated global activism suggest a more complicated relationship among radical grass-roots activism, semi-institutionalized activism by large, well-resourced NGOs (formally structured nongovernmental organizations) and the mainstream media than the aforementioned critical literature (Cottle 2008, Jong et al. 2005: 5, Shaw 2005). Politically marginal groups employ alternative strategies to communicate their agenda or alternative media (Coyer 2005: 169),[3] and social activists have become increasingly conditioned by their pursuit of media attention (ibid.). Radical voices may learn from the experience with alternative media and with time improve their ability to get their message through in the mainstream media as well (Harcup 2003); but all in all, access for activists to radical and mainstream media remains stratified (Atton 2002b: 503).

CRITIQUE OF THE MEDIA HEGEMONY APPROACH

In the literature on Al Jazeera Network, the ideas of hegemony and counter-hegemony have remained influential categories, but as a research tradition, the media hegemony approach has come under continuous criticism. First, research on media hegemony has been accused of vagueness and has been under criticism for its highly abstract, theoretical nature and its failure to successfully operationalize the concept so that hegemony becomes a label that substitutes for explanation rather providing it (Carragee & Roefs 2006: 222, Curran 2002: 142, Gamson 1985: 114). Conceptually, the vague and abstract idea of hegemony makes it difficult to distinguish between the two models of the media: one hegemonic, the other critical; one incorporated, the other counter-hegemonic. Contributions, "which seem to be alternative and oppositional may still operate within a specific ideology, and may be limited, neutralized, and incorporated by it. By the same token, what may be labeled hegemonic at first glance may yet supply us with alternative readings 'between the lines' " (Liebes 1997: 2).

Related to this, another set of criticisms have questioned the empirical adequacy of media hegemony. The idea that hegemony perpetuates the status quo represents another methodological challenge to the hegemony thesis—the fundamental problem of empirically demonstrating that the powerful, hegemonic media are causing an absence of change. Altheide (1984: 479), among others, argued that hegemony is treated both as an attribute and as an effect and is therefore almost impossible to falsify. As an *attribute* of a late capitalist order, he wrote, hegemony defines any activity or process as a product of the ideological and economic context from which it emerges. As an *effect* of the efforts by the dominant class to keep its control and to legitimize itself, hegemony is incorporated into the news reports sustaining the pervasive ideology (ibid). For hegemony scholars, all kinds of news, even news stories explicitly critical of powerful economic groups, is liable to be interpreted as maintaining ideology. Furthermore, hegemony scholars have been criticized for a selective reading of empirical findings and for ignoring the processes and effects of social change (ibid.: 486). In accordance with this argument, Gamson et al. (1992) pointed out that the notion of *hegemony* has lost its more specific reference to the world of common sense and seems to mean no more in most cases than "the dominant message in some domain of discourse—in particular, the message of a powerful state and corporate actors" (ibid.: 381).

Moreover, Manning (2001) argued that the hegemony school neglects the agency and role of individual media professionals and has been challenged in many of the same areas as the media imperialism school, primarily for its simplistic model of the relationship between news media and audiences and its emphasis on instrumental connections between journalists and powerful governments or business personnel (see Manning 2001: 39–40). The global ambitions of the contemporary media proprietors, most often exemplified by Murdoch's News Corporation, are indeed worth studying, but it is imperative to acknowledge that power exists within the political and economic environment of news production in complex ways in which each case must be contextualized and studied empirically (ibid.: 88).

THEORIZING THE LIMITS OF MEDIATED DEBATES

Although the more instrumental readings of the media hegemony thesis have clear limitations as demonstrated above, the media consensus approach provides a fundamental elucidation of the power relationships between political elites, media elites and marginalized groups. The media consensus approach to hegemony has been refined, modified and operationalized into more nuanced models of analysis, such as the three-sphere-model (Hallin 1989), indexing theory (Bennett 1990) and framing contests (Gamson et al. 1992, Entman 2004). Though some of these approaches have challenged the instrumental hegemony thesis, they do not profoundly contradict the fundamental contributions of the media consensus approach.

For marginal or deviant groups, media accommodation and news media access do not automatically change the power relationships. Related to this, more powerful news sources can usually deploy more media resources over time and are thus able to secure their own access. One approach to detecting elite domination over the media has been studies of the ways in which elite sources access, influence and control the media. Studies of these source-media relations, what Zelizer has labeled the "smallest interactional setting of journalism," (Zelizer 2004: 150) consider journalism in the context of other institutions. The media are sites of struggle in which the powerful seek to secure their positions, but within these struggles, the subordinates may also offer resistance, and oppositional interpretations may surface (Manning 2001: 40). Key works in this body of literature have emphasized television as a "terrain in an ever-shifting and evolving hegemony in which consensus is forged around competing ruling-class political positions, values and views of the world" (Kellner 1990: 16).

A rich body of literature has found that official sources, associated with the government and the state, enjoy crucial advantages in the competition for news access (see Manning 2001: 140 for a comprehensive overview). Pioneering efforts to systematize media access were usually dichotomous, distinguishing 'insider groups' from 'outsider groups' (Grant 1989)[4] and 'primary definers' from 'those groups without access to the media' (Hall et al. 1978). In particular, the notion of *primary interpretation* and *primary definers* has been influential in source studies.[5] Hall et al. (1978) argued that in the structured reciprocal relationship between the media and primary definers (elite sources), the media reproduce the primary definitions of the power elites. The notion of primary definition has been criticized for not distinguishing between the potentially very different messages coming from the group of primary definers, nor does it take into consideration the varying degrees of legitimacy accorded different sources by the media (Hansen et al. 1998: 109). Nonetheless, it offered imperative insights into the literature on journalistic sources and made it apparent that some sources are accorded greater credibility and authority than others.

All in all, the relations between the political establishment and the media are highly complex sets of interactions and negotiations, and the process may be reciprocal. An important premise for a nuanced debate about elites and the media is that political elites can very rarely control (promote and restrict) information flows entirely at their own convenience because political elites are confronted by both external competition and internal conflict (Manning 2001: 148–9). As exemplified in Hallin's (1989) groundbreaking study of the US media coverage of the Vietnam War, the media relied primarily on official sources and military sources in the field throughout the war (ibid.: 10). In contrast to the conventional interpretation of 'US television losing the war with its bloody graphic field reports,' he found that the US media continued to rely on these same sources and that critical media coverage was largely a result of growing internal disagreement and dissension within the political and military establishment, whereas the antiwar movement and Vietnamese sources remained marginalized (ibid.).[6]

Media scholars have made use of different terminology to explore the struggle over the issues, discourses, frames and actors that get to dominate the media. From his Vietnam study, Hallin (ibid.: 116–18) argued that media professionals distinguish between three spheres of contest, where each sphere has internal gradations and the boundaries between them are often fuzzy. The first one, the sphere of consensus, encompasses those social objects not regarded as controversial by the media or most of the society. Journalists do not feel compelled to balance issues within this sphere with opposing views or to remain disinterested observers; they regard their role here as to serve as advocates or celebrants of consensus values. Second, the sphere of legitimate concern includes the field of election contests and legislative debates of issues recognized as such by the political establishment. Within this sphere, objectivity and balance are supreme journalistic norms, as exemplified by the US coverage of the internal elite dissent over Vietnam. In short, the weaker the consensus, the stronger the emphasis on the journalistic principle of balance. Hallin (ibid.: 208) found that during political crises, "the media in such periods typically distance themselves from incumbent officials and their policies, moving in the direction of an 'adversary' conception of their role. But they do not make the 'system'—or its core beliefs—an issue, and if questioned, usually rise to their beliefs." Beyond the sphere of legitimate controversy is the sphere of deviance, the realm of those political actors and views that the media and the political mainstream reject as unworthy of being heard. Which of these three spheres prevail depends on the political climate and on the editorial line of the various media (ibid.: 118).

The three-sphere model has been extended and nuanced by media scholars theorizing about media–elite relations by investigating the issues that are opened up for debate in the media, the regulation and framework of these debates, and the parties who are excluded and marginalized (Bennett 1990, Entman 2004, Karim 2003). Bennett's (1990) indexing hypothesis addressed the ways in which official views are processed and synthesized by reporters. Indexing holds variation in elite consensus as the centerpiece of variation in news content, and among the areas in which indexing can be expected to operate most consistently are military decisions, foreign affairs, trade and macroeconomic policy (ibid.: 122).[7] According to indexing, controversy and debate on media output conform to the framing of debate among political elites whom journalists regard as crucial to the outcome of the issues in the news. Moreover, the indexing hypothesis predicts different standards for sourcing with regard to views that challenge the official consensus. Whereas official sources are generally afforded high credibility and receive little scrutiny, dissenting voices are questioned and critically examined (Hamilton et al. 2010: 86).

FRAMING CONTESTS AND FRAME SPONSORSHIP

Introducing the concept of framing contests, Gamson et al. (1992: 382) suggested emphasizing the distinction between two media discourses. One realm is uncontested: the social constructions are rarely seen as such by the viewer, and the producers are also largely unaware of their role as image producer. Through their examination of the realm of contest, Gamson et al. (1992) argued for the advantage of focusing attention on movements and negotiations between the realms; i.e., developments over time as public controversies die and re-emerge in the public arena. Over time, naturalized meanings are contested, and issues that were once contested are naturalized. What is uncontested now may be difficult or impossible to detect without contrasting it with another culture or another discourse where such matters are controversial and matters of contested meaning (ibid.: 384).

Gamson and Modigliani (1987) defined a frame as "a central organizing idea or story line that provides meaning to an unfolding strip of events, weaving a connection between them" (ibid.: 143). A frame generally implies a policy direction or implicit answer to what should be done about the issue, and a concrete policy position is often formulated as a *package* of positions rather than a single one (ibid.). Furthermore, in the media and public debates over policy issues, packages are usually displayed through signature elements that imply the core frame and invoke it with condensing symbols (ibid.), such as metaphors, exemplars, catchphrases, depictions, visual images, roots, consequences or appeals to principles. Gamson and Modigliani (ibid.: 165) have made significant contributions to the analysis of frame contests, frame sponsorship and journalistic counter-strategies.

Emphasizing the active role of media professionals, Entman (1993, 2004) argued that both the hegemony and indexing approach "perceive the media as too subservient to government" (Entman 2004: 4). He noted that although the media rely mainly on elite sources, media professionals influence the public discourse with their framing of events. To frame, according to Entman, is to "select some aspects of a perceived reality and make them more salient in a communicating text, in such a way as to promote a particular problem definition, causal definition, moral evaluation, and/or treatment recommendation for the problem described" (Entman 1993: 52). Moreover, Entman regarded the indexing theory as rooted in a Cold War context and thus outdated in today's political climate (2004). Entman's cascading networks model (ibid.: 9–22) elucidated the ways in which a frame extends down from the political establishment through the rest of the system and specified the characteristics of the frames that were most likely to eventually win the framing contests. The model includes the cascading flow of influences linking each level of the system: the administration, other elites, news organizations, the texts they produce and the public. Furthermore, he argued, the cascade metaphor was selected to emphasize "that the ability to promote the spread of frames is stratified; some actors have more power than others to push ideas along to the news and then to the public" (ibid.: 9). For the administration to influence the framing of a news story, it must package frames so that they conform to the media's institutional and individual motivations. All in all, the frames that are culturally congruent will cascade more effectively through the different levels of the framing process than more ambiguous matters and issues incongruent with the political consensus and habitual schemas (ibid.: 14–15).

Concurring with most of the literature on elite-media relations, Entman's study of framing contests over US foreign policy found that a network of elite sources largely shapes the news, forming an elite public sphere (ibid.: 164–8). More recently, a rich body of research has documented the ways in which American elite journalists and publications had to admit that their coverage of the build-up to the invasion of Iraq reflected the US Administration's rush to military action, that they neither systematically tested or verified the veracity of administration claims, nor countered them with opposing information, and that that they were aware of competing viewpoints, but relegated them to the back pages (Hamilton et al. 2010, Reese & Lewis 2009). As a result of the increased visibility, visual framing has gained importance in the management of political information and framing analysis of international news, particularly the role of photojournalists in the framing of US foreign policy (see chapter 7, this volume) (Kennedy 2008, Griffin 2004). Framing analysis has been employed in a vast array of contexts and issues, to the extent that is has been characterized as "a victim of its own success," and the theory is currently being clarified and criticized (see Entman et al. 2009 for an in-depth discussion).

MEDIA–ELITE RELATIONS REVISITED

So far, this chapter has problematized the media hegemony literature, an approach that is often employed in studies of Al Jazeera but rarely discussed explicitly. I find that the media consensus approach is a compelling point of departure for critical investigations of media power, but that it is a difficult set of concepts to operationalize for empirical analysis. The fundamentally critical view of the media consensus school is maintained in the literature that theorizes the power struggle between news media and political elites synthesized in this chapter. These approaches, although different, all aim to elucidate the relationships between mediated political consensus, legitimate elite dissensus, and the views and issues that are systematically marginalized by the media. These insights provide a valuable basis for the empirical analysis of AJE's sourcing practices, which examine whether AJE challenges consensus expands the sphere of legitimate debate and gives a voice to the marginalized.

Most of the studies surveyed in this chapter have been conducted on national media-government relations, primarily on the mainstream, elite, American media's coverage of American foreign policy and their relations with the US government and administration. In contrast, this book aims to discuss AJE as an alternative, transnational contra-flow within the global news ecology. Being a transnational channel, AJE's position on the mainstream-alternative-continuum may vary with the context because it can cross boundaries between mainstream and alternative media in both the original (sending) country and in whatever country it is received. Globally, AJE has different relations with different political elites,[8] and it can be redefined by the particularities of its production, distribution and consumption contexts. Consequently, to transfer the theoretical insights to a study of AJE's position as a contra-flow in the global satellite news ecology, it is imperative to contextualize, operationalize and adapt these theories to the AJE case. Due to the vagueness and elusiveness of the notion of *counterhegemony*, the refined approaches to the media–elite relations described above will replace this concept in the book. At the same time, the aim is to follow up on hegemony theory's fundamentally critical perspective of the media.

The literature on alternative media (see chapter 3, this volume) demonstrates the increased media competence and new media professionalism among marginalized groups. It is imperative to expand the empirical analysis of news sources to reflect the rapid expansion of alternative media outlets and the plurality of interest groups competing for media coverage. In the following analysis of the ways in which different groups in society access the media to promote their interests, it is important to also balance two ideas (Manning 2001: 148–9). First, it is imperative to move away from the instrumental understanding of the domination of media elites and acknowledge that power relations between the media and the political establishment are complex and dynamic. Second, just as the groups that contest, challenge and counter the established elites for media access must be included in the analysis, so must the structural inequalities in the distribution of material and symbolic resources (ibid.).

AL JAZEERA ENGLISH'S SOURCING STRATEGIES

AJE management and staff aim to redress the elite domination of international news by consciously redirecting attention from the 'corridors of power' to the margins was elaborated in chapter 3 of this volume. This has two potential influences on the sourcing strategy. First, the channel aims to be systematically critical of authorities and elites and to invite all sides of the story into the studio. Second, it aims to invite ordinary people who are touched by the story to express their views and experiences. A senior AJE correspondent described the channel's sourcing strategy in the following words:

> This is a channel that will give a voice to those that have not been heard for whatever reason; be it geographical, be it political oppression, whatever the reason; you should go out of your way to liberate those voices. So certainly, that's a very strong editorial position. No, I don't think its Arab, and it's not very much an underdog thing. You know, some of the voices that we are giving voices to are not underdogs; that's patronizing and actually simply that they have been cut out of the news flow which being run by northern, western interests for decades. And there has not been an international forum where those voices can be heard unless what they do impacts someone of those [Northern] countries. (Interview with author, Doha, 3 October 2007)

For AJE informants, the sourcing strategy requires extra resources and effort. A Doha-based manager explains the challenges of finding and recruiting outside the established elites:

> So, I'll say, 'voice of the voiceless' is probably the most useful way of describing what we are attempting to do, not exclude any opinion, any valid opinion should be able to be aired on AJE. Not just the people who

shout the loudest, speak the best English or have the best PR machine. We'll go further and seek out people who have not gotten their message across. (Interview with author, Doha, 2 October 2007)

Other AJE informants go further and argue that giving a voice to marginalized groups means going beyond the balancing norm in mainstream journalism, toward alternative sourcing strategies. A Doha-based news anchor argued for more progressive sourcing in the following way: "I believe that we need to give more voice to the voiceless and back the underdog. I am against the idea of giving equal airtime to both sides in a conflict if one is occupying the other, if one has invaded the other, if one has the bottle on the other's neck" (interview with author, Doha, 1 December 2007).

Informants further emphasize the challenges of interviewing ordinary people on television and particularly the linguistic barrier that favors elite sources. An interview producer with experience from both Doha and London explicated this dilemma:

The big issue is more often than not language, and it's unavoidable. Like, we cannot put someone on air who speaks bad English. Immediately it limits our guests, it limits the number of alternative views we can put out. That's just the limit of the language we broadcast in, and there is nothing we can do about it. We cannot put someone with broken English on to the screen if someone in Jamaica or someone in Kuala Lumpur is not going to understand what they are saying. It has to be balanced. One of the jobs as an interview producer is to judge someone's English and their accent when we talk to them, and we let the editor know if it is suitable for air or not. A lot of times I have to say 'I'm sorry. I understood about 50 percent of what you said, although the 50 percent I did understand sounded great.' (Interview with author, London, 24 April 2008)

AL JAZEERA ENGLISH'S SOURCING PRACTICES: ALTERNATIVE ELITE HIERARCHIES

How do these sourcing strategies influence AJE's sourcing patterns in its day-to-day newscasts? In an extensive quantitative source analysis,[9] I find that Al Jazeera English, like most international media, is elite-dominated, and four out of five sources can be said to represent elite interests.

When mapping Al Jazeera English's choice of news sources, the first finding is the high number of news items that have no sources other than Al Jazeera's editorial staff (Figenschou 2010a: 100). In as many as 45 percent of the news items, no external news sources are interviewed to contribute to the story (see Figure 5.1). As a new channel, AJE affords much time and credibility in their newscasts to its correspondents on the ground. Al Jazeera correspondents report and analyze the situation in 13 percent of the total news items, while 32 percent of the items are brief anchor news from the Al Jazeera English news centers.

In the following analysis, these news items that do not include statements from external sources will be omitted.

Who then, are invited on AJE to voice their opinion? Elites are the main source in about 80 percent of the news items, while only 19 percent of the total number of news items where an external source is interviewed has ordinary people as the main source. However, the elite sources represent a broader spectrum of elites than just government. To reflect this diversity, I further differentiated the definition of 'elite sources' and divided them into two subcategories. The first category consists of 'Independent elites,' such as the political opposition, international organizations, nongovernmental organizations (NGOs), media or cultural personalities and analysts and/or academics; whereas the second category consists of 'Establishment elites,' such as government officials, diplomats and/or ambassadors, military and/or armed forces, business leaders and religious leaders, who are more obligated to defend the status quo.

Although government officials are the most frequently used news sources on Al Jazeera English and constitute the main source in over one-fourth of the total news items, independent elites as a group are more frequently used as main sources than the elite groups that represent the establishment. Independent elites are quoted in 43 percent of the news items with an external

External or internal (AJE) sources

■ External Sources   □ AJE: Anchor news   ■ AJE: Correspondent

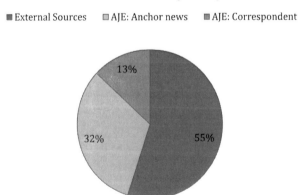

Figure 5.1   In almost half its news items (45%), Al Jazeera English uses or interviews internal editorial staff without giving airtime to external news sources (N:1324) (Figenschou 2010a).

source statement, and the establishment elite is quoted in 37 percent of the items (see Figure 5.2).

In addition, the independent elites were accorded more authority: in addition to being invited to give their opinion more often than the elites representing the establishment, they were given greater visibility on AJE; and related to this, they were invited to speak in more analytical news formats. To illustrate, the independent elite sources are most often invited into the Al Jazeera studio, more than four out of five studio guests represent independent elites, whereas the establishment are only present in the studio in less than one in five times. These independent elites are more likely to represent the 'other opinion' than establishment sources as they represent both the channel's progressive sourcing strategies and meet the realities of international English-language news. Over time, the systematic authority accorded to the independent elites gave them a platform that was not often given to ordinary people (Figenschou 2010a: 98–101).

This sourcing pattern provides an interesting parallel to the "alternative hierarchy of sources" described by Atton and Wickenden (2005). In their investigation of sourcing practices in alternative, activist media, they found that the primary sources in the activist newspapers were the groups that the editorial staff identified closely with—radical activists as well as the reporters themselves. At the bottom of the alternative sourcing hierarchy were the non-activist, non-politicized 'ordinary citizens.' On top were the activist sources involved in direct action and campaigning. These activist sources constituted a *counter-elite* of 'activist intellectuals' or 'non-established intellectuals' (Atton 2002a: 106), which are given power, legitimacy and authority in the alternative media as significant as that given to establishment elites by their mainstream competitors. This alternative hierarchy did not challenge the notions of hierarchical sourcing or sourcing relationships or even the elite notion of sourcing

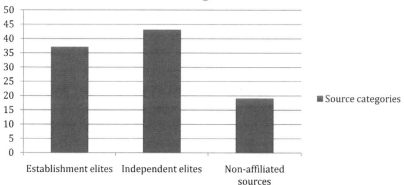

Figure 5.2 External news sources interviewed on Al Jazeera English (N: 728).

(Atton & Wickenden 2005: 357). Similarly, Al Jazeera English primarily altered the perception of *which elites* were accorded credibility in its news; it did not alter the elite-grass-roots distribution (see Figure 5.2 above).

Although gender is not explicitly mentioned in the Al Jazeera English official mission statements, it is relevant to assess the presence of female news sources compared to male news sources. On the *NewsHour*, 20 percent of the news items with an external source have women as the main source, compared to the 80 percent interpreted by men. The women that are interviewed as main sources on AJE are primarily speaking as unaffiliated individuals, so-called 'ordinary people' (39 percent), whereas women are underrepresented in all elite source categories. Among the AJE editorial staff, there is noticeably more gender equality, with around 50 percent female anchors and correspondents in the field (see Figure 5.3).

International news events have largely been interpreted and commented on by elites and government officials, while ordinary people on the ground particularly in the South—the "subaltern" (Spivak 1988)—are ignored and spoken for. In the AJE newscasts, only 19 percent of those interviewed were unaffiliated sources ('ordinary people'). Examining whether AJE chooses different sources when it reports from the South compared to reporting from the North reveals that there are more ordinary people used as main sources in the channel's stories from the South than from the North. When unaffiliated individuals are the main sources of a news item it is located in the South in 72 percent of the items and from the North 27 percent of the time. This reflects the channel's aim to be a "voice of the voiceless" (underprivileged groups in the South). In the channel's alternative source hierarchies, ordinary people are still at the bottom of the hierarchy. Independent elites

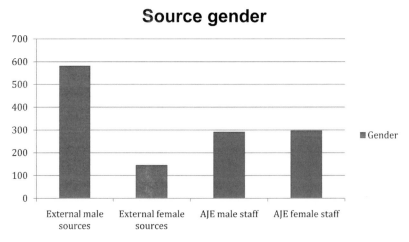

Figure 5.3   Gender equality among external news sources and internal Al Jazeera English news anchors and correspondents (N: 1324).

and AJE editorial staff hold the definition of power over official government sources. This sourcing practice illustrates how the channel's alternative agenda of providing a grass-roots perspective on world events comes into conflict with the elite orientation in international news journalism. AJE emphasizes the situation and problems of the 'subaltern woman,' but she is not invited to speak for herself. "'The voice of the voiceless,' is the voices of our male anchors," as AJE General Director Tony Burman's poignantly diagnosed from its records.

The subaltern is spoken for and represented by male, independent elites, such as oppositional politicians, representatives from international organizations and non-governmental organizations (NGOs), media or cultural personalities, analysts, academics and channel staff. Is a qualitative approach necessary to examine the extent to which these independent elites provide 'the other opinion'—alternative viewpoints and perspectives, criticism of the establishment (or sharing of their elite values) and voicing the interests of the voiceless? The answers to this question will provide new insight into the processes of silencing, 'othering' and representation in the new, non-Western international news. Some of these issues will be investigated in the following chapter analyzing Al Jazeera English's coverage of the 2009 Gaza War, a conflict that has represented a compelling example of global sourcing imbalance.

6 Challenging the Spin
The Gaza War 2008–2009

The war in Gaza, lasting from 27 December 2008 to 18 January 2009, was an asymmetric war with high numbers of civilian victims. During the three weeks of war, over 1,400 people (Amnesty International 2009)[1] were killed, almost all of them Palestinians. Israel deployed its navy, air force and army in the operation it codenamed "Operation Cast Lead," and the asymmetry between the Israeli forces (the IDF) and Hamas, the journalists' limited access to the battlefield and the political spin from Israel and Hamas represented major challenges to the international media covering the war. Aiming to be a *point of reference* in the Middle East, Al Jazeera English has an extensive network of bureaus and correspondents in the wider region and inside Israel-Palestine in particular. Since the outbreak of the second Palestinian intifada, its Arabic sister channel has devoted extensive coverage to the Palestinian cause (El Obeidi 2003, El Tounsy 2002, Lynch 2006, Maiola & Ward 2007, Sakr 2001).

For AJE, the Gaza War represented the first large-scale conflict in its home region since the channel launched in late 2006, and thus its first chance to stand out as an alternative news contra-flow. Preparing for the expansion of the Gaza War, the channel's editorial management briefed the editorial staff to keep ensuring that there was a genuine diversity of views on air and encouraged its staff to make an extra effort to find more Palestinian voices to counter the professional Israeli officials.[2] It also urged the channel staff to expose the human suffering of war on both sides, place people at the center of the story and reflect the realities of war. Furthermore, the management warned its staff about the spin and media campaigns of official spokespersons, and advised everyone involved in interviewing officials to prepare carefully to avoid becoming a vehicle for propaganda.

The present chapter analyzes the channel's coverage of the Gaza War in a quantitative, qualitative and comparative content analysis. It discusses the war coverage in relation to previous research on Al Jazeera Arabic's coverage of the "war on terror" and the extensive literature on war reporting with particular emphasis on information control and access to the war zone, news sources and reporting of civilian casualties in armed conflicts. AJE's coverage of the Israeli ground offensive (3–18 January 2009) is analyzed through a quantitative content analysis of the channel's flagship news, considering the use of news sources, location, topics and news formats. Second, it examines the channel's interviews with Israeli and Palestinian officials in a qualitative textual analysis. To put these findings in context, a one-week sample of AJE's Gaza coverage is compared to the Gaza coverage on the BBC and CNN.

The Gaza War (2008–9) was the first documentation of AJE's potential as news contra-flow and potently proves the channel's comparative advantages in the coverage of regional and international conflicts. For AJE management and editorial staff, the war coverage represented a significant breakthrough and it thus represents a milestone in the channel's formative years. The channel's presence on the ground in the war zone, its sourcing strategies, documentation of atrocities and civilian suffering, dramatic visualization from the ground (discussed in detail in the next chapter) and exposure of the official Israeli framing of the war distinguished it from its main Anglo-American competitors. In hindsight, the Gaza coverage was the first demonstration of potential of AJE's editorial strategies and comparative advantages, forcefully employed two years later in the channel's coverage of the 'Arab Spring.'

ASYMMETRICAL INFORMATION WAR: ISRAEL'S VS. HAMAS' STRATEGIC FRAMES

In all wars from the Crimean War until today, the media and the military have fought on contradictory principles: the military's need for secrecy and distribution of strategic information, against the journalists' need for facts, information and news (Knightley 2002, McLaughlin 2002, Tumber & Palmer 2003). Since the 1991 Gulf War, military information strategists have professionalized their media management strategies during armed conflicts. The military has become increasingly mediatized, striving to appeal to, reassure and elicit support from multiple audiences, primarily the internal military audience (military personnel and their families), the external political audience (international and international "opinion formers" and key decision makers) and the (domestic) public audience (see Maltby 2013 for analysis). For the military, there are mainly two principles for influencing media coverage: to control and restrict the media's access to the battle zone and to promote a coordinated, strategic core frame of events through the media (see chapter 5, this volume, for an introduction to the framing literature).

First, the military's purpose of controlling the reporters' access to the battlefield has taken various forms in the last 20 years of US-led international conflicts, from the pool system organized during the Gulf War (1991) (Fialka 1991, McLaughlin 2002) and the lack of access to Afghanistan (2001) (Hickey 2002, Thompson 2002) to greater access to and dependency on the military in the embedding system organized in Iraq (2003) (Tumber & Palmer 2003, White 2003). Controlling the media's access to both the state of Israel and the occupied Palestinian territories, the Israeli military has employed various strategies. Before the Al Aqsa intifada (also known as the second intifada (2000-)), reporter teams could operate relatively freely in both Israel and the occupied territories (Enderlin 2003). From time to time, the Israeli military would restrict certain areas for the international media, but Israeli reporters and photographers could still move around and report from the occupied Palestinian territories (ibid.). After the outbreak of the second intifada, Israeli reporter teams stopped filming inside the occupied territories due to security threats, Palestinian teams were denied working permits (Bishara 2006: 24–28) and foreign correspondents were struggling to obtain the necessary permits from Israeli information authorities (Enderlin 2003). During the most intense fighting throughout the intifada, the Israeli incursions into Jenin in 2002, the IDF closed military areas all over the West Bank (ibid.). Some journalists managed to enter the conflict zone, however, and documented the Palestinian side of the story (ibid.).

Days before the launch of operation "Cast Lead," the Israeli military banned foreign correspondents from entering Gaza and prohibited Israeli soldiers from bringing their cell phones (Ward 2009: 2). The media blackout was designed to let the Israeli government (and media) control the facts coming out of the war zone. Moreover, holding the international press corps back on the Israeli side of the border would expose them to the Hamas smuggling tunnels and rockets and thus leave them positioned to report the conflict from the Israeli point of view (ibid.). During the war, press freedom organizations strongly condemned the Israeli military's restriction of international media's access to the war zone as well as the Israeli military's attacks on local, Palestinian media inside Gaza.[3]

Second, the political-military establishment has systematically refined its strategic information campaigns (Knightley 2002, McLaughlin 2002, Tumber & Palmer 2003). Both Palestinian and Israeli authorities have realized that the struggle over international media can be as important as the battle on the ground (Sheafer & Gabay 2009, Wolfsfeld 2003). The Israeli government's strategic information campaigns have frequently been underlined in the literature on the media coverage of the Israeli–Palestinian conflict (Dunsky 2008, Hass 2007, Lowstedt & Madhoun 2003, McManus 2003, Wolfsfeld 2003). In addition to its multifaceted institutional public relations apparatus served by the IDF intelligence and officer corps, the Ministry of Foreign Affairs and the Government Press Office and its media training of military staff (Wolfsfeld 2003), Israel established a new information directorate to influence the international media and diplomats before the war in Gaza in 2009 (McGreal 2009) and stepped up its activities in social media (Ward 2009). According to Wolfsfeld (2003), the Palestinian side is more dependent on the international media as it represents one of the most important means they have of convincing the international society to intervene. But, in contrast to the well-organized, multifaceted Israeli media campaign, the Palestinian information apparatus was more unorganized, rudimentary and divided and its press cards without meaning, as much of the infrastructure in Gaza was in ruins after four decades of Israeli occupation and recent intra-Palestinian violence (Enderlin 2003, Schanzer 2008).

It is imperative to underline that there is no such thing as *one* Palestinian side and *one* Israeli side (although such a façade of unity is often stressed to serve propaganda purposes), and far from all Israeli and Palestinian citizens subscribe to the official core frames analyzed in the present chapter. Israelis are far from united: the cabinet was split during the attack on Gaza, there was resistance to the attack inside the army and the media (see Hass 2007, Liebes & Kampf 2009, Orgad 2009), and the Palestinian minority inside Israel (about 20 percent of the total population) represents important counter-publics (Jamal 2009). Palestinians are not only split, Hamas and Fatah have engaged in open warfare with each other, and there are different factions within both movements (see Schanzer 2008 for a detailed discussion). For analytical purposes, however, it is fruitful to synthesize the conflicting parties' strategic core frames in official statements given before and during the war. Based on statements from the Israeli Ministry of Foreign Affairs' Gaza website entitled *Gaza Facts: The Israeli Perspective*,[4] the Israeli government's strategic information campaign can be summed up in the following core frame:

> Hamas broke the ceasefire by firing rockets into Israel. Israel had no choice but to attack in response to the 8-year-long barrage of 12,000 Hamas rockets. Having exhausted all other options, Israel had to attack 'the infrastructure of terror' in Gaza. Israel principally targets Hamas terrorists, but Hamas operatives regularly fired rockets into Israel from within or near their own residential and public buildings, including schools, mosques and hospitals. They intentionally chose to base their operations in civilian areas not in spite of, but because of, the likelihood of harm to civilians, which could then be used as propaganda against Israel.

Although Hamas did not have a coordinated international information campaign, the strategic Gaza (Hamas) core frame[5] could be summarized in the following:

> Israel broke the ceasefire when it killed Hamas members inside Gaza in November 2008. Israel has not lifted the blockade on Gaza although this was part of the ceasefire agreement. The blockade was punishing the people of Gaza for voting Hamas into office. Hamas had no choice but to react to the blockade that was wrecking the economy and causing desperate shortages of food, fuel and medicine. Only after the

Israeli killing-machine stops the aggression, lifts the siege and opens all crossings will Hamas stop the rocket fire. Israeli occupation, oppression and aggressive military operations in Gaza continue to kill innocent civilian Palestinians.

This direct comparison of the Israeli core frame vs. the Hamas core frame illuminates how the conflicting parties hold diametrically opposite understandings of the conflict, including how they define the main problems (Hamas rockets vs. Israeli blockade), make moral judgments (terrorism vs. Israeli aggression and oppression) and support remedies (destroying the "infrastructure of terror" and ending Hamas rockets vs. stopping the Israeli aggression, lifting the siege and opening all crossings).

Having outlined the two strategic core frames, it is vital to acknowledge that the asymmetry of the Gaza War (a powerful well-organized state [Israel] vs. a state bureaucracy weakened by occupation, civil war and international boycott [Hamas]) also has a bearing on the two parties' abilities to sponsor media campaigns and influence the international coverage of the war. According to Enderlin (2003), the quality of information provided to the foreign media has been one of the main differences between the two sides. Before, during and after "Operation Cast Lead" Israeli authorities activated a wide range of strategic communication initiatives. Among the activities were advertising, speech making, public diplomacy, article- and press-package writing, media training of spokespersons and key officials, and online campaigning on popular websites (such as YouTube, Twitter, etc.) (Ward 2009). Moreover, the unequal communication resources are even more sharply defined by pressure/interest groups whose strengths and weaknesses parallel those of the parties in the conflict. In the Israeli–Palestinian conflict, the influential pro-Israeli lobby in the US pitted against the pro-Palestinian camp illustrates this structural inequality (Dunsky 2008: 10, Marmura 2008, Philo & Berry 2004: 248).

In wartime, the involved authorities strive to differentiate three distinct messages aimed at the home front (the home audience/the national media), the opponent's media field, and the international media, respectively, and the tensions between the different framings are difficult to maintain in the current global media landscape (see Blondheim & Shipman 2009, Sheafer & Shenhav 2009 for discussion of these dilemmas during the Gaza War). Historically, the literature on the national media coverage of the Israeli–Palestinian conflict since the second intifada finds that the messages aimed at the home media have been largely successful. Studies of the Israeli (Dor 2003, Korn 2004, 2007, Rinnawi 2007, Wolfsfeld 2003, Wolfsfeld et al. 2008) and Palestinian (Dajani 2003, Daragmeh 2003, Wolfsfeld et al. 2008) media coverage find that the national media were first and foremost patriotic, mobilized media—promoting conflict before reconciliation. Although there were some critical voices in the Israeli media, primarily in the quality newspaper *Haaretz*,[6] both countries' national media were highly dependent on official sources and official framing of the conflict; they portrayed 'the Other' as a threat, legitimized their own actions and delegitimized 'the Other' (see Rinnawi 2007 for a systematization of the 'delegitimization mechanisms' of the media), foregrounded and personalized their own victims and suffering while ignoring the victims on the other side, and employed a 'victim strategy' to justify military action (Dajani 2003, Daragmeh 2003, Dor 2003, Korn 2004, 2007, Rinnawi 2007, Wolfsfeld 2003). In a comparative study of Palestinian and Israeli media coverage, Wolfsfeld et al. (2008: 415) find that both the national media were ethnocentrically emphasizing their own victims ('victims mode' of reporting) and rationalized their own actions ('defensive mode' of reporting).

SYSTEMATIC SOURCE IMBALANCE: ISRAEL AND PALESTINE IN WESTERN NEWS MEDIA

Due to the complex and multifaceted nature of the conflict itself, active lobby groups and competing interests on national, regional and global stages, the media coverage of the Arab–Israeli conflict has been a matter of extreme interest and sensitivity (Gaber et al. 2009: 239, Ibrahim 2003: 88–9, Richardson & Barkho 2009, Zelizer et al. 2002: 283).[7] Academic studies of mainstream Western news media coverage of the conflict from the second intifada (2000) to today find that, while upholding conventional journalistic practices such as objectivity and balance, most news media have a tendency to systematically subscribe to the Israeli government's framing of the conflict (Barkho 2008a/b, Deprez & Raeymaeckers 2010, Dunsky 2008, Gaber et al. 2009, Ibrahim 2003, Ismail 2009, Loughborough University 2006, McManus 2003, Philo & Berry 2004, Richardson & Barkho 2009, Viser 2003, Zelizer et al. 2002). In their review of these studies, Deprez and Raeymaeckers (2011: 189) conclude that the international media coverage has been biased and imbalanced.

Various authors explore how the news production practices of international news organizations and correspondents perpetuate the observed imbalance (Deprez & Raeymaeckers 2010, Enderlin 2003, Hannerz 2007, Ibrahim 2003, Philo & Berry 2004, Richardson & Barkho 2009). Many mainstream news organizations have developed internal style guidelines on how to report the conflict and strong editorial supervision, securing a conservative coverage (see Richardson and Barkho's 2009 study of the BBC's top-down editorial control). The literature documents a linguistic, cultural and religious gap between the international correspondents covering the conflict and the Palestinian officials and people; most international correspondents are stationed in Israel; their access to the occupied territories is restricted and logistically challenged by the Israeli military; and financial constraints limit their travel to and presence inside the Palestinian territories, where practical journalistic obstacles are many (Deprez & Raeymaeckers 2010, Enderlin 2003, Hannerz 2007, Ibrahim 2003, Philo & Berry 2004). After the outbreak of the Al Aqsa intifada, foreign correspondents experienced increased hostility from the Israeli government, primarily from the Government Press Office, which strictly regulated work permits and press cards (Enderlin 2003).

Imbalances in mainstream American and European media reporting have most notably been manifested in sourcing. Although the Western television channels and newspapers studied strive towards a balanced reporting, the analyses find that there are systematic tendencies to indirectly promote the Israeli views. Overall, Israeli sources were interviewed more frequently (Deprez & Raeymaecker 2010: 105). Moreover, the Israeli viewpoints were given longer airtime and more space, and Israeli sources were interviewed in calmer and quieter surroundings than their Palestinian counterparts (Philo & Berry 2004). Palestinian sources are rarely quoted, directly, as reporters tend to narrate the Palestinian view in their own words, and when they are, they are usually not officials in positions of authority (Dunsky 2008: 147–8). Moreover, when Palestinian sources on the ground are interviewed, for instance in numerous reports from the refugee camps, they are routinely portrayed as a group that is highly emotional, angry, irrational, and preoccupied with the utopian dream of a homeland they have never seen (ibid.: 119). More importantly, Palestinian voices are systematically countered by official Israeli sources (ibid.: 68), reiterating that Israeli actions are a response or retaliation to attacks from terrorists or hostile neighbors (Philo & Berry 2004: 160).

In mainstream Western media, Israeli officials thus represent what Manning (2001: 150) has characterized as "insider groups" (given higher authority and credibility and with increased abilities to shape processes of primary definitions), whereas Palestinian sources largely represent "politically marginal groups" struggling for media access. Furthermore, independent sources and references to international law and human rights have generally been ignored (Dunsky 2008: 149). Consequently, many of the studies of Western media coverage of the conflict find that essential contextual information, crucial in order to understand the rationale of Palestinian action, such as the historical context of the conflict, direct consequences of the Israeli military occupation for Palestinian daily life and Palestinian deaths, has been largely underreported (Deprez & Raeymaeckers 2011, Dunsky 2008, McManus 2003, Richardson & Barkho 2009). After the 9/11 terrorist attacks, the Israeli–Palestinian conflict was increasingly framed as part of the broader struggle against terrorism, and the Israeli assertions of a "war against terror" was internalized and articulated by Western correspondents and anchors (Deprez & Raeymaeckers 2010: 107, Dunsky 2008: 258). On the other hand, Deprez and Raeymaeckers' (2010: 107) analysis of Flemish newspapers finds that Palestinian victims were more personalized and individualized than Israeli victims.

CONTEXTUAL OBJECTIVITY: THE PALESTINIAN
CAUSE ON THE ARAB SATELLITE CHANNELS

The Arab satellite channels' extensive coverage of the Israeli–Palestinian conflict (from 2000) and the war in Iraq (from 2003) has been vital to the regional satellite channel's rapid growth and immense popularity. Moreover, the Arab news coverage of the regional conflicts has challenged Western media narratives and representations. Competing with Abu Dhabi TV over regional audiences in the early 2000s, Al Jazeera Arabic devoted extensive airtime to Palestine, and the intifada provided a powerful indicator of the impact of Arab satellite networks in general and Al Jazeera in particular (El Obeidi 2003, Sakr 2001: 191). As outlined above, both Western and Arab news teams were in Palestinian territories during the uprising, documenting the fighting on the West Bank and in Gaza. The framing and explanations given of the violence, however, marked a clear difference between the Arab and the Western networks (Sakr 2001: 191). The Arab satellites paved the way for the advocates of Palestinian resistance, such as Hezbollah, Hamas and Jihad, as well as other proponents of the intifada, appealed to Arab nationalism, and reported nonstop on Palestinian demonstrations, casualties, wounded children, destruction, and frustration, and had an important impact on the Arab public opinion (Amin 2002, Ayish 2002, Sakr 2001, Telhami 2004).

On the pan-Arab satellite channels, regional issues of wider appeal tend to dominate issues of purely local concern—primarily Palestine, Iraq and Arab reform, and then increasingly the "war on terror," Islam and the United States (Lynch 2006: 25). The Palestine cause is central to the Arab conception of identities and interests, and Palestinian issues have always been primary to Arab public discourse. The political consciousness of the entire region has been largely defined in relation to the Arab–Israeli conflict (Telhami 2004). This editorial priority is apparent in Lynch's (2006) analysis of the main Al Jazeera Arabic talk shows where he documents that Palestine was the topic of about one-third of all talk-show debates in 2001 and 2002 (Lynch 2006: 80). Some analysts argued that the transnational media of the region could help establish peace, or at least leave a positive impact on the Middle East peace process (Amin 2002). The Arab satellite channels broke the silence and invited Israeli politicians to speak on Arab networks to present both sides of the conflict. Al Jazeera Arabic, for example, aired interviews with Ehud Barak, Shimon Peres, and their Palestinian counterparts, and at the time the channel was criticized for being pro-Israeli (Sakr 2004, 2007).

The networks also enabled different forms of interactive dialogue between individuals and groups (Amin 2002). A new openness in representing the 'Other' (Palestinian) can also be found in Israeli media (Liebes & Kampf 2009) through interviewing the enemy (Palestinian political leaders); there was also extended representation of ordinary Palestinians and the creation of Palestinian desks in the TV newsrooms (some of them managed by Palestinian citizens of Israel) (ibid.: 439–40).

Based on in-depth interviews with senior editorial staff,[8] Figenschou (2007) analyzed why regional news stories from Palestine and Iraq were top priorities in the Arab newsroom and how these priorities influenced Arab media development. According to the interviewees, the two conflicts were at the top of the Arab news agenda because there is a popular demand for complete coverage of Palestine and Iraq; the conflicts are central to Arab identity; the conflicts are long-lasting, dramatic and violent; and the channels favor covering regional affairs over national affairs. The interviewees underline that, although they are generally very satisfied with the extensive coverage of Palestine and Iraq, the immense focus on these two conflicts could undermine their credibility due to repetitive and superficial news bulletins, compromised objectivity, self-censorship practices and silencing of non-political issues.

The standards of news objectivity on the Arab satellite channels in particular have given rise to much discussion. The Palestinian issue is often highlighted as an example of compromised objectivity (Ayish 2002). Overall, the satellite networks are generally in favor of the Palestinian cause. There are several well-documented examples of how the satellite networks have mobilized their viewers in support of the Palestinian cause: All the Arab satellite channels have organized fundraising campaigns for the Palestinians. Some news anchors have announced during fundraising shows that they will donate their own salaries (El Obeidi 2003). In addition, the Al Jazeera news anchors have appealed to their viewers to rally and take to the streets to demonstrate against Israel's policy. Moreover, Al Jazeera's program *Under Siege* called upon the viewers to send petitions and objections to human rights organizations (El Tounsy 2002). El-Nawawy and Iskandar characterize the Arab satellites' coverage of the Palestinian issue as an example of what they term "contextual objectivity":

> Contextual objectivity implies that the medium reflects all sides of the story, while retaining the values, beliefs and sentiments of the target audience, and thus expresses the inherent contradiction between attaining objectivity in news coverage and appealing to a specific audience. This inherent dilemma of news reporting is never more evident than during periods of war and conflict. (El-Nawawy & Iskandar 2002: 209)

In line with this perspective, Ayish (2010: 222) distinguishes between Al Jazeera Arabic's moral point of view (condemning Israeli oppression of Palestinian victims) and its professional point of view (objective and balanced reporting). Criticizing the notion of "contextual objectivity," Hafez (2006) warns that it may justify the obvious bias of the Arab satellites' coverage of regional conflicts, a bias that will misinform the Arab public and discredit the Arab satellites in the rest of the world (Hafez 2006). Further, he argues that the Arab news and current channels try to combine factual (objective) information with culturally adapted worldviews: they only allow for objectivity in some fields that are not sensitive to Arab sentiments (ibid.). Concurring with this view, the interviewees in Figenschou's (2007) study working in Al Jazeera Arabic, the Al Arabiya Channel and Abu Dhabi TV highlight that their editorial line is based on objective and balanced reporting, they all acknowledged that the focus on the liberation from foreign occupation was more popular *and* less controversial than stories sensitive to powerful Arab nation states or inner-Arab conflicts (Figenschou 2007: 16–20).

COVERING THE GAZA WAR (2008–2009)

In the context of Al Jazeera English's aim to both compete with and challenge the Western media's coverage of international affairs and be a point of reference in the Middle East (see AJE's editorial agenda and strategies outlined in chapter 3, this volume), the channel's coverage of the 2008–9 Gaza War can serve to illuminate to what extent news on AJE is different from its Western counterparts and/or the pan-Arab satellite channels. In the following section, AJE's coverage of the Israeli ground offensive (3–18 January 2009) is examined in a quantitative, comparative content analysis. The program selected for analysis, the *NewsHour* at 18:00 GMT, is the flagship news program of the channel. What makes the *NewsHour* a particularly interesting program to analyze is that it (at the time of the broadcast analyzed) linked up the Doha headquarters with the London and Washington broadcasting centers (the Kuala Lumpur broadcasting center is not included due to the time difference). All 18:00 *NewsHour* programs during the two weeks of Israeli ground offensive, lasting from 3 January to 18 January 2009, were included in the analysis. For the comparative analysis, one week drawn from the Al Jazeera English coverage was compared to CNN International's *Your World Today* (17:00 GMT) and BBC World's *World News Today* (18:00 GMT).[9] The international versions of the channels were chosen to document the three channels' competition for audiences worldwide. The three news shows selected for analysis are directly comparable—they highlight the main news of the day, to audiences worldwide, and all three last for one hour. The news item, most often distinguished by an introductory statement from the studio, is the basic unit of analysis. As recommended by Lombard et al. (2002), multiple coders (two research assistants) coded a total of 30 hours of news and measured for intercoder reliability with satisfactory results.[10] The analysis will pay particular attention to how AJE, CNN and the BBC prioritized the war, the formats they used, where they placed their editorial teams (location), what aspects of the war they selected (news topic) and who they invited to voice their opinion on the conflict (news sources), in particular which political and government officials they interviewed and the extent that the news media challenged the strategic core frames outlined above. Where relevant, the findings will be discussed in relation to Ayish's (2010) analysis of Al Jazeera Arabic's Gaza coverage, analyzing 144 video reports accessed on the channel's YouTube website between 28 December 2008 and 18 January 2009).[11]

i) Priority: The literature on the media coverage of international conflicts has established that the Israel–Palestine conflict has been overrepresented[12] in international media from the 1990s to today (Bahador 2011: 42, Hawkins 2011: 57). From the outset of the war, it is obvious that AJE evaluated the war on Gaza as highly newsworthy. It altered its regular schedule and broadcast an extended version of *NewsHour*—90 minutes instead of 65 minutes—whereas its Anglo-American competitors kept to their fixed schedule. During the three weeks of the Israeli ground offensive, the channel broadcast as many as 305 news items on the war in its extended *NewsHour*—an average of between 17 and 18 news items per day. In the week selected for the comparative analysis, AJE aired 134 news items on the war, compared to CNN's 46 news items and the BBC's 37 items (see Figure 6.1).

Moreover, AJE labeled the story differently in their permanent visual templates: it had a striking orange banner (signaling the urgency of the story) with *WAR ON GAZA* written in capital letters throughout the period. By choosing a template stating "War *on* Gaza" instead of "War *in* Gaza" AJE underlined that it identified with the civilian, Palestinian victims of the war, not the Hamas fighters (Pintak 2009). The BBC and CNN avoided the "war" terminology altogether, labeling the military escalation as the *GAZA conflict* (BBC) and *Crisis in the Middle East* (CNN). These templates signal that

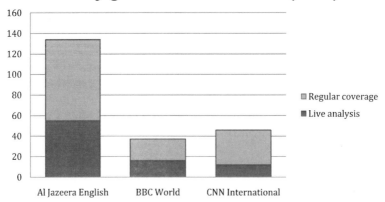

Figure 6.1   News items covering the Gaza War in one comparative week (7, 8, 9, 13, 14, 15 and 16 January 2009) on Al Jazeera English's *NewsHour* (18.00 GMT), CNN International's *Your World Today* (17:00 GMT) and the BBC World's *World News Today* (18:00 GMT) (N:217).

while AJE regards the conflict escalation as a full-scale Israeli war on Gaza, and thus a significant deterioration of the situation, the BBC and CNN frame the Gaza War as a continuation of the ongoing Middle East conflict/crisis. Furthermore, AJE's template *WAR ON GAZA* underlines that it is Gaza that is being attacked (by Israel) although Hamas continued firing rockets into Israel throughout the war. The Anglo-American templates present the war as a crisis or conflict without stressing the asymmetry between the actors. Additionally, AJE's choice of news formats (with extensive live analysis from correspondents in the field and studio guests) and diverse locations, both analyzed below, demonstrated how strongly the Al Jazeera Network prioritized the Gaza War.

ii) News format: Another indicator of how the satellite channels' prioritized the Gaza War is the extent to which they broadcast the events live and the news format that is selected to tell the story. Traditionally, live coverage of international wars and conflicts signals urgency and immediacy,[13] as live reporting is relatively expensive and involves careful planning and logistics. In AJE's coverage of the Gaza War, the channel broadcast live in around half of its total reporting (48 percent of the channel's total news items were live). Al Jazeera English aired live analysis by its correspondents from Gaza, Israel, the West Bank and other locations in the Middle East, North America and Europe. The most important locations for these live analysis/stand-ups were Gaza (30 percent), Israel (27 percent) and North America (17 percent), reflecting the channel's aim to balance perspectives from the two conflicting parties, but also how it made the most of its exclusive presence inside Gaza. The English channel also aired numerous live analyses from guests interviewed by the news anchors in the studio or on direct link. Al Jazeera English prioritized live coverage to a much higher extent than its competitors and broadcast live 55 times, compared to the BBC's 16 and CNN's 12 in the comparative sample week.

Overall, Al Jazeera English covered the war in in-depth news formats and almost half of the channel's total coverage was analysis conducted by its correspondents or studio guests. Compared to the news formats on the BBC and CNN, Al Jazeera English had relatively more live analysis than its competitors. The BBC also had an emphasis on more analytical formats, although the channel did not prioritize going live. CNN, on the other hand, had relatively more anchor reports, packages and reports from press conferences.

iii) Story location: The locations from where the news items on the Gaza War were filed were categorized as reports from Israel, Gaza, the West Bank, the Middle East, Europe, North America, and non-specific (mainly studio) locations. In the three weeks of the Israeli ground offensive, AJE reported the war from the Palestinian territories in one-third (out of Gaza in 28 percent and the West Bank in 5 percent) of the news items, almost twice as often as from Israel (18 percent of the total stories). The fact that AJE reported more frequently from the Palestinian territories than from within Israel sets it apart from the overwhelmingly Israeli-centered Western reporting out-lined above. The channel's emphasis on reporting the war from within the occupied territories reflects the prominence of the Palestinian issue for the regional media (see discussions above). Taking into account that Israeli mili-tary and political leadership did not want unilateral journalists reporting from the war zone and that working and living conditions inside Gaza were extremely hard during the ground offensive, AJE's high number of news stories filed from the ground inside Gaza is particularly significant. The BBC had a team of local stringers inside Gaza throughout the war. The Gaza team published one package from Gaza for *World News Today* daily but, for reasons unknown to the author, the channel's Gaza team was not pro-filed in the BBC coverage and not featured as authoritative internal experts, nor was their presence on the ground used extensively in the coverage. In contrast, AJE repeatedly underlined that they were "the only international news channel present in Gaza."

In the comparative analysis, AJE reported most frequently out of Gaza (25 percent of items), North America (20 percent) and Israel (16 percent), whereas the BBC reported most frequently out of Israel (35 percent), fol-lowed by Gaza (16 percent) and North America (14 percent), and CNN balanced its location between Israel and Gaza (15 percent each) and the wider Middle East (13 percent). Throughout its history CNN has striven towards being present on location when and where the action unfolds (Cush-ion 2010) and, in particular, its live reporting of global breaking news and international crises gave it an unparalleled position in international com-munication in the 1990s (Volkmer 1999, Gilboa 2005b) (see discussions of the CNN effect argument in chapter 1, this volume). In its Gaza coverage, however, CNN International had relatively fewer reporters present on the ground covering the story than the other two channels and almost half its coverage was studio/newsroom-based news items. In so far as presence on the ground and proximity in reporting is an indicator of priority, this shows that CNN gave the Gaza War lower priority than the other two.

iv) Topical emphasis: Overall, AJE primarily emphasized the political development and humanitarian consequences of the war. The international and domestic political developments in the war formed the main topic in more than one-third (36 percent) of the channel news during the three weeks of war. Second, the social aspect of the war—how the war affected the civil-ian populations in Gaza and Israel, and the emergency aid efforts to help civilian victims—was a prioritized topic in 31 percent of AJE's news items. The third most-covered topic on the channel was news on the military devel-opments of the war (17 percent) (see Figure 6.2).

The public discussions on appropriate and legitimate war practices are intensified when the atrocities are directed towards civilians (Zelizer 1998: 10), and both Israeli and Palestinian authorities strove to influence both the national and the international news media's coverage of the civilian victims of the Israeli–Palestinian conflict. For explanations summarized above, the

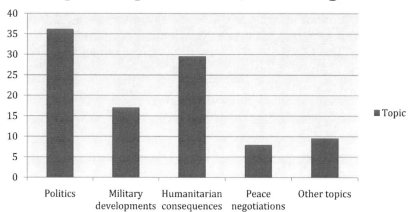

Topical emphasis on Al Jazeera English

Figure 6.2 Topical emphasis on Al Jazeera English's Gaza coverage from 3 to 19 January 2009 (N: 305). News items emphasizing the economic consequences, aid, legal affairs and cultural and religious developments in the war received minimal attention and are grouped under 'Other topics' above.

civilian victims of the conflict have been covered differently in the Israeli, Palestinian, Western and pan-Arab media. Against this background, it is particularly interesting to examine how civilian casualties and suffering were covered on AJE. A first finding is that 7 out of 10 reports on AJE of the civilian suffering were filed out of Gaza, compared to 1 out of 10 from Israel. Furthermore, the preprepared news package format was the preferred format, underlining how the civilian populations were affected (47 percent of the channel's news items on the humanitarian aspects of the war); civilian citizens were the most frequent news source in these news items (40 percent of the social stories) together with AJE correspondents (25 percent of the stories) (AJE's visualization of civilian suffering will be discussed in detail in the next chapter).

The topical emphasis on the political, military and social developments of the war is also found in the comparative study of one week of Gaza coverage, and was prioritized on all three channels. There are some minor variations in the relative importance accorded to the different topics on the three channels though, with the BBC stressing the political developments, CNN underscoring the military developments, and AJE underlining the social aspects. The political development was also the most prominent on Al Jazeera Arabic, where half the news items analyzed were official and non-state political reactions to the Gaza War (Ayish 2010: 225–6), and notably on AJA, the oppositional and popular political protests against the war were twice as prominent as the official political reactions. The international and regional popular resistance was also noticed on AJE and was the fourth most frequent topic, although ignored on both the BBC and CNN. As summarized above, the pan-Arab satellite news channels have a long tradition of underlining the regional, popular opposition to Israel, an editorial strategy employed by AJA and to some extent on AJE during the 2008–9 war. The Anglo-American news channels' muting of popular protest, on the other hand, corresponds with the systematic marginalization of protest movements by mainstream Western media discussed in chapter 5 of this volume. Further, the humanitarian aspects (28 percent) and the military strategies and developments (19 percent) were underlined on AJE's Arabic sister channel.[14]

v) News sources: AJE's substantial presence within the Palestinian territories is reflected in the channel's news sources. During the three weeks of armed conflict, 37 percent of the external main news sources invited to speak on AJE's news were Palestinian, compared to 15 percent Israeli voices (see Figure 6.3).

Furthermore, there are some noteworthy differences in the kind of sources that are interviewed from the two parties. The majority of the Israeli sources interviewed on AJE are representatives from the Israeli government and military (68 percent of the interviewed Israeli sources), whereas the Israeli civilian population and victims of the war are largely neglected. These figures were reversed for the Palestinian voices, with half of the main sources being civilians and one-third political and military officials. Although Ayish (2010) does not map news sources in his Gaza War analysis, his mapping of news actors (operationalized as those who initiate action and give statements)

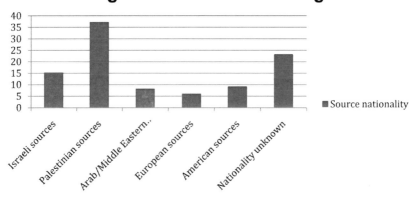

Figure 6.3   The nationality of Al Jazeera English's external news sources (only news items where external news sources voice their opinions are included here, and the 108 news items in which only AJE staff are speaking are omitted from this analysis) (N: 186).

concurs with the findings above: On AJA, the Palestinian civilian population was accorded the greatest presence in the Gaza coverage, and 21 percent of the analyzed items feature civilians as actors (ibid.: 226), while Palestinian officials were registered as actors in 12 percent of the stories. On the Arabic channel, as well as on AJE, the Israeli actors were primarily official representative (12 percent), whereas civilian Israelis received very limited attention in the war coverage.

In the comparative analysis, there were some minor variations in the source selection—the BBC had the highest percentage of Israeli main sources (32 percent) and AJE the highest number of Palestinian sources (33 percent), while CNN had more news sources from the wider Middle East region (20 percent) than the other two. Furthermore, the BBC relied most heavily on government officials, and more than half of the external news sources being interviewed on the BBC's coverage of the Gaza war (52 percent) were government representatives, compared to over one-third (35 percent) on CNN and one-fourth (26 percent) on AJE. AJE, on the other hand, had most often invited civilians on the ground to express themselves on the air (in 23 percent of the channel's news). In addition, AJE had greater source diversity than the two other channels, inviting a broader group of independent elite sources (analysts, legal experts, international organizations and international nongovernmental organizations) to provide other perspectives on the coverage.

INTERVIEWING ISRAELI AND PALESTINIAN OFFICIALS

Numerous Israeli and Palestinian officials were interviewed by Al Jazeera English's news anchors, or gave their official version of the dramatic events in press conferences and television addresses broadcast on the channel. During three weeks of ground offensive, AJE's news anchors interviewed twelve Israeli officials on the *NewsHour* and broadcast three extracts from statements and press conferences by Israeli officials. The news anchors interviewed six Palestinian officials (only one of them represented Hamas, whereas others represented Fatah, PLO or minor Palestinian groups) and broadcast nine extracts from statements and press conferences, four of them with Hamas representatives. In the analyzed newscasts, the channel thus broadcast 15 Israeli official statements and 15 Palestinian, but the studio anchors interviewed the Israelis more often than their Palestinian counterparts.

In the comparative sample week, both AJE and the BBC seem to have striven to balance Israeli and Palestinian official voices, whereas CNN interviewed solely Israeli officials who were all repeating the Israeli core frame.[15] Moreover, on CNN, the Israeli officials were given extended time to explain the Israeli official line and, on average, the five interviews/statements by Israeli officials on CNN were over five minutes long. On the BBC, Israeli and Palestinian officials were granted about the same airtime, while AJE devoted more time to the Palestinian side (Hamas and Fatah) than to the Israeli officials. This mapping of which Palestinian and Israeli officials (military or political elite actors) the three channels give airtime concurs with Sheafer and Gabay's (2009) study of the mediated public diplomacy. Measuring Israeli and Palestinian strategic communication towards US and UK news media in 2005–6, they find that although the Israeli elites were granted the highest media access in both countries, the UK media granted comparatively more access to Palestinian officials and showed a higher level of support for the Palestinian position (Sheafer & Gabay 2009: 456). Operationalizing mediated public diplomacy, Sheafer and Gabay explain these variations as cultural and political congruence (see the next chapter for elaboration on cultural and political proximity and distance), the position of foreign governments, and the strategic core frame's correspondence with news media values (2009: 463).

Overall, Hamas officials were given the least airtime on the three channels. All three channels principally used officials representing the Palestinian Authority and Fatah, headquartered in the occupied West Bank, to voice the official Palestinian view, even though Fatah has been in bitter violent conflict with Hamas since 2007 (Schanzer 2008, Tamimi 2007). For the Anglo-American channels, Hamas are more culturally and politically distant than Fatah/PA, and the limited number of interviews and statements from Hamas officials may reflect the fact that the US and the EU consider Hamas a terrorist organization and that Hamas officials thus represent a controversial source of information. Secondly, CNN and the BBC did not have any of their permanent reporter teams on the ground inside Gaza during the war, which complicated their access to Hamas' sources based inside the war zone (the BBC did have a team of local stringers). Furthermore, Hamas did not seem to have a well-organized information campaign with officials accessible to international media and may be more restrictive in giving out contact details or volunteering to give interviews because contact with Hamas personnel (even via mobile phone) could have revealed their whereabouts and invoked an Israeli air raid.

It is beyond the scope of this book to evaluate the conflicting parties' strategic core frames outlined above, and rather examines how the three news channels approached the strategic information and how the strategic core frames were represented by the news media. How did the channels' editorial staff interview the officials and to what extent were the interviewers prepared to challenge the strategic core frames? All three channels asked critical, solid, well-prepared questions addressing the situation for the civilian population. Still, this critical approach only partially challenged the official line simply because most interviewers followed the interview script closely and moved on to the next question, even though the officials frequently circumvented the critical questions. Consequently, professional high-profiled officials were able to talk around the issue rather than addressing the criticism. Overall, the officials did not offer, nor were they asked for, evidence to back up their allegations and, although their position was challenged temporarily by critical questions, they were quickly able to uphold and re-establish their strategic communication. On CNN and the BBC, the interviewers rarely followed up on the answers provided, they did not interrupt when the officials talked around the question, and they did not reformulate or reiterate the question until the officials addressed the critical issue.

Overall, the Israeli officials were interviewed more frequently than their Palestinian counterparts, and they were also more frequently invited into the studio or interviewed at greater length, most probably reflecting the availability of official Israeli spokespeople, the resources devoted to influencing the international media, and the highly professional Israeli information campaign. At the same time, the Israeli officials were also scrutinized and criticized more thoroughly, being held directly responsible for the civilian suffering on all three channels. Interestingly, none of the interviews with/ statements from Palestinian officials on the BBC and AJE explicitly questions the Palestinian, more precisely Hamas', responsibility for the large numbers of civilian Palestinian casualties. The Palestinian officials are largely questioned about regional and international politics, diplomacy and peace negotiations in the conflict, rather than to what extent they provoked the Israeli attack and whether they were able to protect their own people. As a consequence, the Hamas core frame outlined above is largely absent in the interviews with Palestinian officials—it is not communicated, nor exposed. This is most probably an indirect consequence of the fact that the Palestinian Authority or Fatah was selected to represent the Palestinian view even though they were not directly involved in the war and thus not responsible for the situation. It is a paradox for the mainstream Western news channels, represented here by CNN and the BBC, that the imbalance in sourcing, due to Hamas' terrorist status and the lack of Hamas officials on the screens, indirectly let Hamas avoid critical interrogation and led the media's critical interviews and scrutiny towards their Israeli counterparts.

The role of government officials as news sources in AJE's alternative sourcing hierarchies is crucial here (see the elaboration on AJE's sourcing strategies and practices in chapter 5, this volume). For the alternative media, it is important to invite official sources to set the terms of reference for the reporters to recontextualize these voices by criticizing them—to expose the contradictions, ignorance and spin of the establishment in power (Atton & Wickenden 2005: 353). By frequently inviting officials to give interviews and make statements, while placing the official narrative in a very critical context, continuously repeating and reformulating the same critical questions to demonstrate that the officials avoided the issue, AJE's editorial approach seemed determined to investigate and expose the perceived gap between the Israeli media campaign and the realities on the ground. This inclusive, yet critical, sourcing strategy echoed the channel's aim of inviting "every angle, every side" on air. In its Gaza coverage, AJE's systematic emphasis on the ways in which the Israeli core frame diverged

from the realities inside Gaza exposed the political spin of Israel's information campaign and distinguished the channel from its Western counterparts.
The channel's critical interviews with Israeli officials have been characterized by Gilboa (2012) as one of its three major weaknesses covering
the Gaza War, arguing that AJE presented "one-sided, highly biased, and
inflammatory accounts of what was happening on the ground," (ibid.: 152)
being highly critical towards Israel while avoiding confronting Hamas on
its policy, strategy and violence.

AL JAZEERA ENGLISH'S COMPARATIVE ADVANTAGES

The Gaza War (2008–9) was a particularly challenging war to cover, due
to the deep controversies; sensitivities and complexity that characterize the
Israeli–Palestinian conflict; the active lobby groups and competing interests
on national, regional and global stages; the asymmetry between the Israeli
forces (the IDF) and Hamas; the journalists' limited access to the battlefield
and the political spin from Israel and Hamas officials.

Al Jazeera English's editorial strategies, elucidated and problematized
in chapter 3 of this volume, arguably gave the channel a comparative
advantage over its Anglo-American competitors covering the war. First
and foremost, it was the channel's presence inside Gaza, in addition to
its extensive presence in Israel, the West Bank and throughout the region
that set the ground for a different coverage. The fact that AJE had permanent teams inside Gaza reflects the channel's emphasis on the Palestinian
story and the Middle East, as well as its extensive news net in the South.
In the global news landscape, AJE's southern presence and perspective is
an anomaly (see chapter 3, this volume). During the Gaza War, the channel's presence on the ground, after Israel closed Gaza to the international
media on 27 December 2008, gave AJE a comparative advantage over its
competitors: AJE reporters did not gain special access after the media ban
and they were already inside Gaza at the time Israel closed the borders. As
discussed in chapter 3 of this volume, it has been an editorial strategy to be
permanently present in areas that most international media are not willing
or able to prioritize, and when Israel closed the border, the channel's teams
could report first-hand on the situation inside Gaza while CNN and the
BBC were forced to cover the battlefield from Israel or through its local
stringers and Palestinian media. This journalistic scoop was frequently
stressed in AJE broadcasts and promotional texts after the war. More
importantly, it is a continuation of Al Jazeera Arabic's tradition of accessing and establishing unilateral reporter teams in dangerous, controversial
and inaccessible places and, by this, undermining the political and military
elites aiming to control and restrict media activities in the area. Second, the
AJE teams inside Gaza were Arabic speakers, some of them permanently
based in Gaza City and with extensive knowledge of Palestinian culture

and religion. The two AJE correspondents inside Gaza, American-Egyptian Ayman Mohyeldin and British-Egyptian Shirin Tadros, in addition to its most prominent news anchor throughout the war, Sami Zeidan, combine vital insights into the Palestinian cause with extensive professional backgrounds from both Arab and Anglo-American newsrooms (NBC/CNN, Al Arabiya and MSNBC, respectively). As discussed earlier, within AJE there is a widely shared belief that local correspondents are better equipped to grasp and convey the realities on the ground than international (foreign) correspondents. In the channel's Gaza War reports, the key editorial staff in the field and in the news studio all shared a Middle Eastern background. Third, the Gaza War also established that the two news channels within the Al Jazeera Network could cooperate and coordinate resources, content and staff. Although there were important differences in the tone and terminology of the two channels (Ayish 2010), they were able to benefit from having more people on the ground. Taking into consideration the conflicts and challenges that have characterized the relations between the two channels since before AJE even launched (see chapter 3, this volume) the cooperation on the ground represented a milestone within the network. In particular, AJE could benefit from the extensive source networks, knowledge and expertise of their Arabic sister channel, which has covered the Israeli–Palestinian conflict closely for over a decade.

These progressive production strategies arguably distinguished AJE's Gaza coverage. Throughout the Israeli–Palestinian conflict, the two parties have struggled over access to and influence over international media (Sheafer & Gabay 2009), and particularly the Israeli government's professional media management and strategic information campaigns have frequently been underlined in the literature. Historically, Israeli government officials have represented "the insider side" in international news, whereas Palestinian officials have been more marginalized outside the Arab public sphere. During the Gaza War, the editorial management of AJE explicitly set out to counter this asymmetry: They briefed the channel staff to acknowledge the structural inequalities between the two parties. They also made an extra effort to include Palestinian officials and voices in their coverage, even though they were not as professional, soft-spoken or accessible as the representatives of the Israeli government information apparatus (AJN 2009b). This was reflected in the channel's sourcing practices of the conflict. First, AJE had a higher number of Palestinian sources than CNN and the BBC, the fewest official government sources on all sides of the conflict and the most Palestinian officials invited to express their views in studio interviews or statements. Second, AJE had the highest proportion of civilian voices and greater source diversity than the two other channels and invited a broader group of independent elite sources (analysts, legal experts, international organizations and international nongovernmental organizations) to provide other perspectives on the coverage. And third, by frequently inviting officials to give interviews and make statements, while placing the official narrative in a very critical context, AJE's editorial approach fundamentally undermined the Israeli media campaign. By exposing the contradictions in the Israeli position, instead of ignoring the Israeli view in the same way as CNN, and to some extent the BBC, or muting the Hamas narrative, AJE repeatedly questioned whether "Operation Cast Lead" was fought in accordance with international law.

The Al Jazeera Network's comparative advantage over mainstream Western news media—most importantly its extensive presence on the ground, local correspondents, alternative source networks and exposure of official spin, as demonstrated during the war in Gaza—anticipated the network's editorial strategies covering the Arab Spring uprisings two years later. In hindsight, the topical emphasis on the popular opposition to the war on AJA (and to a certain extent also on AJE) served as a powerful forecast of the network's ability to broadcast and mobilize the "voice of the frustrated masses" (Ayish 2010: 235).

7 Suffering Up-Close
Al Jazeera English's Dramatic Visualizations

The intensification, diversity and complexity of the contemporary global news media outlined in the introduction of this book have contributed to an increased awareness of 'other' news perspectives (Liebes & Kampf 2009, Orgad 2009), what Thompson (2005) characterized as "the new visibility." In this cacophonic news landscape, researchers have found that visual framing in the media has become ever more difficult for geopolitical actors to control (Frosh & Pinchevski 2009, Kennedy 2008: 279, Roger 2013). Moreover, numerous scholars have documented that the news media tend to focus more on civilian populations as victims of conflict and war than ever before (Höijer 2004, Konstantinidou 2008, Parry 2010, Sontag 2003, Zelizer 1998), and that the understanding of armed conflicts and humanitarian catastrophes among people who have not experienced such crisis themselves is now chiefly a product of these media images (Chouliaraki 2006, Höijer 2004, Moeller 1999, Sontag 2003, Robertson 2010). Through the media, and particularly through television images, the public has become aware of the sufferings of remote others and are challenged to include these strangers in their moral conscience. Consequently, a discourse of global compassion has developed in the intersection of politics, humanitarian organizations, the media, and the audience/citizens (Höijer 2004, Manzo 2008, Moeller 2002). A paradox of contemporary Western media is the tendency toward more sanitized visualizations of international conflicts and a creeping visual conservatism (Griffin 2004, 2010, Hanusch 2010, Kennedy 2008, Kitch & Hume 2008, Robertson 2004, Silcock et al. 2008, Wells 2007, Zelizer 1998, 2005) even though there is a plethora of casualty images available.

The tradition of critical analysis of mainstream Western media is timely and important, but it has not reflected much on how other media cover civilian suffering. There has been a strong call for studies of mediated suffering on non-Western media (see, among others, Chouliaraki 2008, Hanusch 2010: 168–71, Robertson 2010: 142). Aiming to go beyond the Western-centric literature on mediation of death and suffering, this chapter explores Al Jazeera English's dramatic visualizations. Political theorists, elites and media elites all believe that powerful news images can drive journalistic perspectives, public opinion and, in some cases, foreign policy (confer the debate on images in 'the CNN effect' in chapter 1, this volume) (Domke et al. 2002, Zelizer 2005). Reflecting elite concern over critical images, some of the major controversies surrounding the Al Jazeera Network have concerned its broadcasts of 'graphic images' (Hanusch 2010, Figenschou 2005). Images of war have been of high interest to media scholars because images associated with conflict, life and death tend to draw intense public attention; it tests professional journalistic norms and practices; it reflects cultural perspectives and reproduce cultural representation; and it reveals the political, military and social influence on media representations (see Griffin 2010 for a historical overview of the photograph's position in war reporting). Moreover, images of suffering are especially contested and politicized during wartime (Manzo 2008). In this context, the present chapter analyzes AJE's dramatic visualization of suffering and death during the 2008–2009 Gaza War. First, it quantifies the channel's images of casualties and suffering during the three weeks of war and compares it to the BBC's and CNN's coverage. Second, it explores how the channel personalizes the images of civilian suffering, and third, it analyzes how the AJE's images from the ground inside the war zone profoundly and systematically counter the Israeli core frame discussed in the previous chapter. The ethical aspects of this editorial policy are discussed and problematized in the final parts of the chapter.

"REFLECTING REALITIES ON THE GROUND": THE POWER OF THE VISUAL

Images are powerful because they are generally perceived as *evidence* (Zelizer 2005). Synthesizing why images are believed to be powerful, Domke et al. (2002) list (a) that images can easily be recalled in general detail, (b) images potentially become icons or metonyms symbolizing particular events or issues, (c) images can have great aesthetic impact, (d) images have the ability to provoke emotional reactions and (e) images hold potential political power as when employed strategically by political actors.[1] The idea of the veracity of the photograph has been under strong theoretical attack (see Wells 2007), and it is widely acknowledged that images are easily manipulated. The history of war photographs, to take one illuminating example, has demonstrated that many of the most iconic images from the battlefield have been staged or manipulated in other ways. Still, news photographs are widely perceived as documentary proof (Taylor in Wells 2007: 56).

In her studies of images of atrocities and death, Zelizer (2005: 29–31) finds that there are four interest groups that have particularly invested in articulating assumptions about this special value and authority of images: First, journalists value the 'photographic verisimilitude' because photographs document that they were there to witness the news as they unfold. Second, media executives and owners value images, understanding that images compel public attention. Third, officials and politicians regard images as valuable tools for shaping public opinion and justifying policy in wartime. And, last, the public sees images as a manageable, reliable and readily understandable way to grapple with the complex realities of the world. Images of war seem to be particularly powerful and attractive because they potentially offer glimpses of life and death, dramatic events that most viewers are shielded from in their everyday existence (Griffin 2010: 8). For the news media, aiming to grab and hold audience attention, warzones, disaster areas and dangerous locales are often chosen in the hunt for potential 'high impact' pictures (ibid.: 9). The international news channels in particular emphasize wars and conflicts, as audiences tend to turn to these channels primarily in times of crisis.

For the AJE informants, it is perceived as an obligation to document the consequences of war and conflict and to expose underreported suffering. They express an ambition to document and reveal the atrocities that powerful political and military elites want to keep out of sight. Informants argue that strong images are needed to have an impact, but at the same time they argue that strong images should not be used gratuitously. A London-based senior correspondent with long experience in British news explained:

> I think it's important if war is being waged in the name of the people of this country, in America, or in whichever country it is that you see the consequences of what they support, what their government support is doing. And that will upset governments, because seeing dead bodies implies that things aren't going terribly well for them or that they've gone too far or that's there's an element of bloodshed in that. So they will always try and discredit, dissuade, or persuade people not to watch it, to look away from what they're seeing, and I think we should continue to do that [. . .] Al Jazeera is very good at it: it shines a light where many people would like to keep a little bit of dark. (Interview with author, London, 13 February 2008)

AJE's sister channel Al Jazeera Arabic has faced strong criticism for its graphic images of war and suffering (Fahmy & Johnson 2007a, Figenschou 2005, Samuel-Azran 2010). To AJA and the other Arab networks, the consequences of the "war on terror" and the civilian casualties were among the most important frames from the war. In interviews, editorial staff and management emphasized the importance of documenting the dramatic consequences of war, as explained by one member of the executive team: "People would think it's a clean war, but war is never clean, this is our disposition. We are not trying to infuriate anybody; we're just trying to reflect what's happening on the ground" (Figenschou 2005).

The interviewees reflect the dominant understanding of news photographs among media professionals—images as authentic, true and valid. Drawing on his experience with AJE and Arab satellite news channels, a Doha-based correspondent explained why it is imperative for the channel to document atrocities. He asked,

> Do you show these things or do you cover it under the pretext that it is graphic? Well, one has to weigh out the risks and benefits. [. . .] I don't want to go and cover up stories so as not to upset others. I need to show the world these things. A lot of atrocities took place in this part of the world. (Interview with author, Doha, 3 October 2007)

AJE broadcasts from Britain and is thus regulated under Ofcom, and informants emphasize that the channel aims to take a middle road, between the most sanitized Western images and the goriest images broadcast on the Arab satellite channels. As explained by a news anchor in Doha:

> We definitely have some standards and guidelines because obviously we are broadcasting to a much bigger part of the world than simply Al Jazeera Arabic. I think here, in this part of the world, the tolerance level for seeing bloody and graphic images is much higher than, for example, in the West, where people don't have much stomach for that kind of pictures on their TV. They don't want to see that. So, I think that we would be cautious about, maybe more cautious than [AJA] in showing graphic pictures. But at the same time, I think maybe we will go further than some of the western networks in what we do decide to show or not to show. I think sometimes there are other reasons involved [. . .] for why other organizations decide not to show pictures of destruction and death of civilians, properties and life, than simply that it's not something the audience wants to see. I think we would be somewhere in between. (Interview with author, Doha, 2 October 2007)

There are no formalized, widely recognized definitions of a 'graphic image,' and these issues are rarely explicitly addressed in visual ethics codes (issues that will be discussed more in detail towards the end of this chapter). Some researchers have emphasized close-ups, zooming in on a violent act or a wounded person, in contrast to long-distance shots, and the degree of physical alternation of the victim as indicators to identify 'graphic images' (Hanusch 2012, Potter & Smith 2000).[2] The elusiveness of the concept is also underlined by AJE sources interviewed for this book who argue that the criticism against the Al Jazeera Network is mainly politically motivated and that the term 'graphic images' in itself is being exploited for political purposes.

THE POLITICIZATION OF IMAGES:
IMAGES IN THE "WAR ON TERROR"

Military involvement of Western (including Israeli) troops seems to drive international media coverage, and particularly the "war on terror" has received disproportionally great attention in the current era of "shrinking foreign news" (Bahador 2011, Hawkins 2011). Photographs and TV images have become increasingly significant in news reporting (Doberning et al. 2010), and the editorial decision process over which images to publish is a highly politicized one, particularly during times of military conflict. Due to its seemingly analogical character, images are efficient pieces of evidence and legitimization strategies employed to criticize or support particular military actions (ibid.: 89). In wartime, governments aim to control, channel, limit, and /or delay image production and circulation, aiming not only to shield the public from particular images but also to promote and facilitate the preferred images (Griffin 2010: 8). One of the most enduring myths in the recent history of war journalism is the 'Vietnam syndrome,' the widespread belief that the US television was losing the war with its "bloody graphic field reports" and critical journalism (Hallin 1989: 10). Since Hallin's ground-breaking (1989) study, the idealized Vietnam 'myth' has been systematically countered by numerous studies (see Griffin, 2010, for an overview).[3] More important here, TV images and photographs of fallen soldiers, prisoners of war, battles gone badly and civilian war casualties and suffering on the 'other' side have continued to influence strategies for military and political control of the media in subsequent international conflicts (Griffin 2010). Instead, the military and political leadership aims to depict their wars and military interventions as "clean, heroic and just, with images limited to those that are consonant with prevailing sentiments about the war" (ibid.: 31).

From a military perspective, military sources argue that the media constantly emphasize negative and critical news such as tensions between coalition partners, tensions between political and military officials, the efficiency of military equipment, and military and/or civilian casualties or "mission creep" (Maltby 2013: 260). Al Jazeera Arabic, AJE's sister channel, has been in the very midst of numerous controversies concerning images of the "war on terror." During the war in Afghanistan, Al Jazeera Arabic's presence on the ground in Afghanistan gave international news outlets unprecedented access to images that the US-led Coalition aimed to stop, particularly images of civilian casualties and military casualties and action (Samuel-Azran 2010). A couple of years later in Iraq, the channel broadcast frequent images of civilian casualties and Coalition casualties, Coalition military setbacks or Coalition prisoners of war (Figenschou 2005), the kind of images that were largely absent from US news media (Griffin 2010: 30). In particular, photographic documentation of dead and wounded soldiers, most often symbolized by the US Administration's ban on photographing coffins draped in the national flag, has been controversial. From 2006, the US

Administration expanded the ban to include all images of soldiers killed in action—a ban that was lifted by the Obama Administration in 2009 (Johnson & Fahmy 2010: 46). In this context, AJA's broadcast of an Iraqi video showing bodies of at least four US soldiers lying on the ground and five US prisoners of war (POWs) who were being questioned by the Iraqi military, aired early into the US-led invasion and caused massive criticism and strong condemnation from the US Administration (see Figenschou 2005 for a detailed analysis of the March 23rd 2003 controversy in relation to the Geneva conventions). Critics argue that the Arab media highlighted every Coalition setback and Iraqi victory and, by this, misled their viewers into believing that the Iraqi forces could actually win (ibid.). Confronted with the criticism, the AJA editorial management stressed that these videos were among their most important during the first phase of the war and claim it was newsworthy, relevant and credible. Interviewed by the author, one member of the management team explained:

> If you look at these visuals of injured and dead service personnel, a man and a woman, you would find that it was newsworthy because not only [the] Arab audience was interested [in] this news, but also Western audiences and Western governments. It was relevant because it came within the context of the war, a war that some people claim to be clean, and the source was credible because we did not stage it, it was actually a reflection of what happened. So in professional terms we were very right to do that. (Interview with author, 5 October 2003)

Moreover the editorial management asserted that the accusations from the American authorities represented American double standards and hypocrisy: As they see it, Al Jazeera had broadcast pictures of dead people and prisoners of war before (from Chechnya, Bosnia Herzegovina, Palestine, Afghanistan and Iraq), but this was the first time they were criticized for doing so, and, additionally, they argued that US networks had shown humiliating pictures of Iraqi prisoners of war (Figenschou 2005).

In the years since 9/11, the global media landscape has changed fundamentally and, today, the dominant traditional, centralized and hierarchical military information is continuously challenged by instantaneous global online distribution systems and cheap, simple media production (Christensen 2008). In his book on the role of image warfare in the "war on terror," Roger (2013: 170–1) argues that images have become notoriously uncontrollable for military and political authorities. Through case studies of the Bin Laden tapes, the images of suicide terrorism (through footage of attacks and suicide wills), hostage execution clips and images of the Abu Ghraib abuse and how these images are remediated and reframed in various contexts and formats, he argues that the communication strategy of the US and UK political and military authorities, aiming to control and limit the media's access to images, is outdated and inefficient. Due to contemporary media production and distribution technologies, images released by the military and political authorities are contested and reframed, such as the iconic images of the masked, orange-clad, kneeling detainees held at Guantanamo (2002), which quickly became global symbols of resistance against the camp (van Veeren 2011). The Abu Ghraib photographs in particular documented cruel abuse and have been the subject of massive political and academic debate, although the mainstream media did not challenge the official deflection of the events (blaming a few 'bad apples') and it had little noticeable effect on the continuation or progress of the Iraq war (Bennett et al. 2006, Griffin 2010, Laustsen 2008, Rowling et al. 2011).[4] The Abu Ghraib scandal brought attention to the mushrooming of unofficial, dissenting, often disturbing video clips, blogs and photographs produced and uploaded by soldiers within the US/ Coalition forces (Christensen 2008). After the Abu Ghraib scandal, the US government sought to prevent future leaks by restricting the military's ability to take and distribute unofficial images by banning the possession of camera phones (Laustsen 2008: 135). A few years later, the Defense department removed the troops in Iraq and Afghanistan's access to video-sharing sites such as YouTube, officially because these sites took up too much bandwidth (Christensen 2008: 156).

In this context, with numerous images and videos of 'the dark side of the war' made available by professional media including news wires (see, among others, Fahmy 2005a), the involved parties, and ordinary people (user-generated content), it is rather noteworthy how rarely these images of dissent have been broadcast by the major, mainstream Western news media. In the last decade, the Western news media has moved toward more sanitized visualizations of international conflicts and a creeping visual conservatism (Griffin 2004, 2010, Hanusch 2010, Kennedy 2008, Kitch & Hume 2008, Robertson 2004, Wells 2007, Zelizer 1998, 2005). Numerous studies document that in the ongoing "war on terror," the US media have been less likely to publish graphic images than would have been the case 10, 20, or 30 years ago (Griffin 2004, Kennedy 2009, Robertson 2004, Zelizer 2005). In a comparative study, Fahmy (2005a) finds that Arabic and English language newspapers selected different images to frame the "war on terror" based on the same image pool provided by the major Western news agencies, and that only a limited percentage of the available images were used (Fahmy 2005b). More specifically, Samuel-Azran's (2010) study of which of the available Al Jazeera Arabic videos that they selected for publication by US television networks illustrate the politicization of images of war: First, the US broadcasters proactively sought and aired AJA's images of air bombings (Samuel-Azran 2010: 43). Second, the US broadcasters actively filtered out images of military failings and civilian suffering included in the original AJA reports (ibid.: 44–5). Further, Zelizer (2005: 33) finds that although there were many photographs of dead Taliban soldiers, they were rarely published. Overall, the major Western news media ended up selecting images that showed less of the war in itself and more of the official narrative of the war, and consciously or intuitively ended up "using images in ways that upheld larger strategic aims" (Zelizer 2005: 33) while avoiding the most problematic realities about the war.

In wartime, the photographic genre of 'human casualties' becomes particularly politicized. One example is the antiwar movement's strategic use of images of civilian suffering during the war in Iraq, 2003, emphasizing how the US-led Coalition harmed particular individuals and groups (see Konstantinidou 2008: 145). The mediation of war casualties will be explored in more detail in the following sections.

THE POLITICAL ECONOMY OF SUFFERING: MEDIATED DISTANCE AND PROXIMITY

"Confronting Western spectators with distant suffering is often regarded as the very essence of the power of television," writes Chouliaraki (2006: 18), thus referring to a Western-centric perspective in the literature on distant suffering. From this perspective, the literature has identified and analyzed the "economy of witnessing" (Frosh & Pinchevski 2009). Although there should be no social boundaries for qualifying as a victim worthy of help, many victims never qualify as 'worthy victims' in international politics and media (Höijer 2004: 516). The literature on mediated suffering documents culturally constructed global hierarchies of civilian suffering, as the media give preference to certain victims over others. The news media do not primarily follow a "principle of correspondence" in its coverage of casualties and crisis, as numerous studies have documented that the scale and seriousness of the humanitarian crisis do not drive media coverage (Bahador 2011, Cohen 2001, Hanusch 2008, Hawkins 2011). The criteria of selection are extrinsic to the events' seriousness, following patterns deriving from the context (geopolitical interest, ideological affiliation, social and geographical distance), the assumed newsworthiness of the event itself (ability to sympathize, simplicity, continuity and sensationalism), and logistics (staff/ resources in proximate bureaus and access to the scene) (Cohen 2001: 171, Hawkins 2011: 61–2) (see chapter 4, this volume, for a review of more studies of the determinants in international news).

Deconstructing this political economy of mediated suffering is one of the key contributions of the current literature in the field. In the 2000s, studies measuring media coverage of international conflicts have documented that only a few conflicts received massive media attention, whereas the vast, marginalized majority of stealth conflicts are virtually ignored (Hawkins 2011). In particular, military involvement by Western (including Israel) military troops seems to drive the media attention in Western media (Bahador 2011, Hawkins 2011). The restrictions and limitations on what journalists capture on camera and what editors will show to the public are constantly negotiated and news producers and photo editors make decisions every day that shore up the wavering consensus about the boundaries of 'good taste' (Sontag 2003: 61). To media professionals, sensitivity towards the local audience and advertisers constitutes an argument against publishing the most graphic images available. Also, ethical dilemmas over exposing private pain publicly, especially the pain of subjects closer to home, have made the Anglo-American media more discreet (Hanusch 2010, Robertson 2004, Sontag 2003).

All news reports are subject to a process of selection and symbolic particularization that defines whose suffering matters to the audience and highlights civilian victims who are perceived to be culturally proximate to the audience (Chouliaraki 2006: 187). In the contemporary global media landscape where the Anglo-American mainstream news media remain the most influential, this implies a systematic emphasis on Western civilians (Chouliaraki 2006, Hanusch 2008, Moeller 1999). Considering media professionals' news values in relation to nationality, it appears that home country victims and death are considered extremely important. Moreover, violent deaths, accidents and natural disasters are reported more frequently than other (slower) causes of death (Hanusch 2008: 346). Consequently, to 'qualify' as newsworthy in the major Western media, victims in the Global South have to reassert their closeness or relevance to a Western center, and/or offer a media-friendly sensational story with dramatic visualizations of suffering (Chouliaraki 2006: 144). At the same time as Western media professionals are emphasizing the ideal Western image of the victim, they are generally more cautious in their exposure of victims closer to them. Whereas the naked faces of American victims have been covered or censored throughout the history of war photography, the Western media have been more likely to publish full frontal views of the dead and dying in culturally distant and exotic places (Sontag 2003: 63). But, as Sontag reminds us (ibid.: 65), distant victims also have wives, children, parents, sisters or brothers, who may one day come across the images of their beloved husband, father, son and brother photographed in their hour of pain—a scenario that should be taken seriously in an increasingly transnational media landscape.

On a sociocultural level, children, women and elderly people are often seen as helpless in violent situations and humanitarian catastrophes (Moeller 1999: 107) Whereas the children are pure and ideal victims, there are cultural and historical variations in the victim status of women (Höijer 2004: 517), and women have largely been replaced by children as the public emblem of purity, goodness and vulnerability after the feminist movement of the 1970s (Moeller 2002: 38). Today, conflicts and disasters around the globe are often are made more comprehensible and accessible by the news media's referencing of children (Manzo 2008, Moeller 2002, Wells 2007). In a competitive news environment, children are perceived to be among the very few subjects to attract attention and, consequently, children have become proxies for all sides in a variety of media debates (Moeller 2002: 42). In sum, children often headline international events, not because their story illuminates the core of the broader story but because they attract attention (ibid.: 53). Children have an iconic status in Western imagery, writes Wells (2007: 55) because they are the embodiment of innocence, playfulness and hope for the future. Moreover, stories about children are sentimental and engaging because the most efficient way to dramatize the righteousness of a cause is to contrast the innocence of a child with the evil actions of adults in authority. When children are victims, the tragedy seems especially intense and meaningless.

Analyzing how death is visualized during wartime, Zelizer (2005) finds that the Western news media increasingly publish memorable, artistic, symbolic images instead of newsworthy, realistic documentation of actual death. Standard, easily recognized images are efficient and easy to read; they have greater currency as they can be sold and reused repeatedly across media platforms; and, if they emulate genres or icons from the history of war photography, they are more likely to be sufficiently reproduced and potentially become icons in their own right (Griffin 2010: 36). The mediation of suffering has become more hierarchical in mainstream Western media after the economic downturn accelerated ongoing changes in the news economy and domestication trends in international news, discussed in detail in chapters 1 and 3 of this volume.

CASUALTIES OF WAR: DOCUMENTING GAZA CASUALTIES ON AJE, BBC AND CNN

By widening the perspective and including the new non-Western media, the distance and closeness to the mediated suffering will change. After all, the geographical and cultural distance or proximity to the events on the ground will naturally change according to the where we are in the world. To take one plain example: US media and Arab media will have diverging perspectives on the war in Iraq and will emphasize different humanitarian stories from the conflict. The US media are likely to focus on the hardships of the US soldiers in Iraq, whereas the Arab media will concentrate more on the voices of the Iraqi civilian population. The geographical and cultural distance that characterizes both the literature on mediated suffering and the Western mainstream media coverage of suffering outside the West is not universal. There are alternative editorial strategies for covering civilian suffering, audiences outside the Western world may interpret images of suffering differently, and the Western politics of mediated suffering may be challenged in non-Western media. In the second part of this chapter, AJE's visualization of the Gaza war 2009 will be analyzed to exemplify how the channel challenges the Western hierarchy of suffering.

First, as documented in the previous chapter, civilian suffering and casualties were emphasized on all three satellite news channels—AJE, the BBC and CNN. From AJE's preparation for the war and editorial strategies we learned that war means people: people who die and people who kill. People are the center of the story, and the ugly face of war and civilian suffering ('the voiceless') should be documented in the coverage. Throughout the Israeli ground invasion, AJE aired images of Palestinian casualties in one quarter of all its news items on the Gaza War. The images of Palestinian casualties were most often included to illustrate news packages, but also frequently edited into studio interviews and live stand-ups by AJE correspondents. There were no images of Israeli casualties, reflecting the extreme asymmetry of the war.

The comparative study, where one week of AJE Gaza coverage was compared to that of the BBC and CNN, shows that none of the three aired any images of Israeli casualties (there were no images of wounded or dead Israelis available for the news media), and all three included images of Palestinian casualties in their reporting. Comparing the three channels demonstrates that the emphasis on Palestinian victims was not an AJE-specific framing of the war. AJE aired 35 news items showing images of Palestinian casualties in the comparative week, compared to CNN's 15 and the BBC's seven items. (see Figure 7.1).

If we measure the share of the three channel's total coverage that included casualty images, these images were used most frequently on CNN (depicted in one third of its news items), followed by AJE with around one-quarter and BBC with around one-fifth of its news on the war. On both AJE and CNN, casualty images were edited into various news formats, whereas the BBC only used it in its edited news packages. It must be noted that this only measures presence of casualty images within a news item and not how long, how close, or how frequent these are aired within each item, and that CNN and the BBC covered the war less extensively than AJE as discussed in the previous chapter. What it shows, however, is that all three

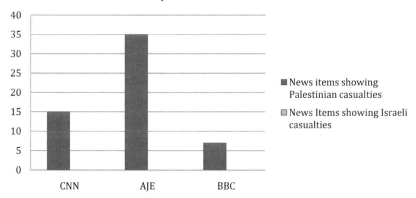

Figure 7.1 Number of news items with images of Palestinian/Israeli casualties (there were no items in the comparative week showing Israeli casualties) (N:217).

channels—AJE, which was present inside Gaza, and its competitors, which were denied access by Israeli military authorities—had access to casualty images provided by the Palestinian-based Ramattan News Agency and the international news agencies.

The availability of images of Palestinian victims in the main Western news agencies (AP, Reuters and AFP/Getty) was documented by Fahmy and Neumann's (2012: 17) study finding that almost one-third of all the analyzed agency images depicted victims of war, defined as "suffering, refugees and visuals depicting demolition" (ibid.: 11). The news agency images emphasized Palestinian victims—there are more depictions of physically harmed Palestinians (particularly Palestinian children) and the emotions of the Palestinians were almost exclusively negative, portraying sadness, anger and frustration (ibid.: 17). The images of Palestinian suffering influence how the public respond to the conflict emotionally, as demonstrated in the experimental study by Brantner et al. (2011) measuring effects of different images from the Gaza war. In the study, visual human-interest framing elicited stronger emotional effects than other images and articles without images, and those exposed to the images of Palestinian casualties found the war significantly more 'disturbing' and were more 'empathizing' (although not significantly) with the situation than others (ibid. 530–531).

The analysis of the images on AJE, CNN and the BBC shows that as the war developed it became almost impossible for the international media to balance the Israeli suffering over the Palestinian without compromising journalistic ethical standards. By this, the media coverage of the Gaza War diverged from previous Western coverage of the Israeli–Palestinian conflict (see the previous chapter) in its increased criticism of Israeli politics and greater emphasis on Palestinian suffering. To sum up, these changes mirrored the extreme asymmetry of the conflict. On another level, the emphasis on Palestinian suffering and Israeli responsibility reflects the broader developments in international news towards a greater visibility and increased global compassion and emphasis on children as 'idealized victims.' Additionally, it demonstrates how difficult it is for political and military authorities to control the flow of images in the current media landscape. In spite of the Israeli media blackout, banning international media from entering Gaza during the war, locally based stringers and photographers working for international media—the local Ramattan news agency and Al Jazeera teams from both channels—documented and distributed casualty images. Although the international media aired casualty images, they had to cover the war from a distance and were dependent on local Palestinian staff. Not being there, not being present on the ground, prevented the international media from witnessing and zooming in on the human-interest stories from the war. With two teams inside the war zone, AJE was able to both authorize and personalize the pain of Gaza, and these strategies will be explored more in detail below.

A JOURNALISM OF ATTACHMENT:
AUTHORIZING THE VICTIM'S VOICE

The literature on mediated suffering mainly focuses on the distance and detachment in mainstream Western media and thus risks ignoring those media organizations that practice what Bell (1998: 16) labels as "journalism of attachment." Bell defines this approach to crisis reporting as "a journalism that cares as well as knows; that is aware of its responsibilities; that will not stand neutrally between good and evil, right and wrong, the victim and the oppressor"(ibid.). By actively taking a position, media of attachment may give institutional authority to stories of civilian victims. Ward (2010) captures much of the same in his notion of 'humanistic journalism,' explained as combining reason and emotion in a form of journalism that "brings empathy to bear on the victims of tragedy—an empathy informed by facts and critical analysis." In AJE's Gaza coverage, the channel's interactive video wall elucidating the number of dead children epitomized how AJE extended its institutional authority to the voiceless victims of the story: the children in Gaza. The video wall design bears a resemblance to the iconic Vietnam Veterans Memorial in Washington D.C. Its somber, minimalist design, displaying the names of 210 of the more than 300 dead Gaza children written in white on a dark background, brings to the fore the extent of civilian suffering. The grand scale of this installation, together with the fact that AJE staff collected the names of 210 children killed inside Gaza during the war, demonstrates the resources the channel has devoted to telling their story. By using the installation as a studio background and integrating it into the studio design, AJE lends maximum credibility to the story. Further, by having the news anchors—the public faces of the news organization—presenting short biographies of selected deceased children makes their deaths seem more important. Secondly, by highlighting the biographical background of some of the victims, the video wall personalizes the suffering of the many. When the news anchors give short backgrounds of a handful of the names, the viewer realizes that there are similar stories behind the more than 200 remaining names on the wall. The careful concretization of where the children died ("in his mother's arms") and the mundane circumstances under which they were killed ("as they took out the rubbish near their home") brings the story closer to viewers around the world. To capture the spectators' attention, writes Boltanski, the sufferer's singularity must be projected in such a way that suffering is made concrete. The victim must be "hyper-singularised" through the accumulation of the details of suffering, conveyed as if the spectators were there in person, as if one could touch their wounds and hear their cries (Boltanski 1999: 12). At the same time, their pain must be generalizable—"it is that child there that makes us cry, but any child could have done the same" (ibid.). Although brief, the bios of the deceased children start this process: We all take out the rubbish. We have all, as children, sat on our parent's lap for protection.

This contrast between the atrocious and the mundane has remained a key narrative in mediated suffering and death, with emphasis on the ordinariness of the victims and details of their daily lives before the catastrophe. More than anything, the mundane invites the viewer to identify with the victims, because, if the victim was an ordinary person like us, then it could have been me. The introduction showing the video wall thus invites the viewers to reflect on the traumatized Gaza children as individuals, thereby preparing the viewers for the account of personalized suffering in the upcoming reports. Furthermore, by foregrounding the dead Gaza children, AJE fundamentally questions the legitimacy of the war.

ZOOMING IN ON THE IDEALIZED VICTIMS

In her book *Regarding the Pain of Others* (2003), Sontag writes about the affective power of war photography: "Look, the photographs say, *this* is what it's like. This is what war *does*. And *that*, that is what it does, too. War tears, rends. War rips open, eviscerates. War scorches. War dismembers. War *ruins*" (ibid.: 7). The ugly face of war was exposed in all its horror in AJE's reports from outside and inside Gaza's main hospital. In the following examples from one particular report, broadcast on AJE *NewsHour* 18:00 GMT on 15 January 2009 will serve as an illustration[5] of how the channel constructed the children as relevant victims and worthy of our response (Chouliaraki 2006: 11, Höijer 2004).

In the 15 January report from the Al-Shifa hospital in Gaza, the camera zooms in on the devastated faces of wounded children and we hear their childlike, straightforward explanations of how they were hit and how their relatives died. The chaotic scenes outside and inside the Gaza hospitals open with diegetic sounds of desperate shouting and crying over dramatic background music. Throughout the Gaza report we can see images of more than 20 different dead or wounded children, four of them speaking on camera. The children in the story are sufferers whose exposure affords a certain degree of individualization but only a limited, conditional form of agency. The children are given a voice and a chance to tell the distant viewers about their situation, and the camera zooms in on their faces as they do so. However, their answers are brief and we do not meet them outside the hospital or in roles other than that of idealized victims (Höijer 2004, Liebes 1997). In the news media, images of suffering children are predominantly represented as victims to be rescued (Moeller 2002: 41, Wells 2007: 59) demanding the protection and care of adults. Children as 'idealized victims' top what Moeller (2002:48) has labeled the "hierarchy of innocence": "Crowned the most innocent, the hierarchy begins with infants and then includes, in descending order, children up to the age of 12, pregnant women, teenage girls, elderly women, all other women, teenage boys, and all other men" (ibid.).

The first child talking to the camera, a boy about 10 years old, is closing his eyes in pain. Through his tears and clenched teeth he mumbles: "My brother was bleeding so much, and right in front of my eyes he died. My other brother Ismail also bled to death. My mother and my youngest brother, they are gone. Four brothers and my mother . . . dead." The report consists of a number of brief interviews with other hospitalized children, cross-edited with close-ups of infants on the operation table, dead children on the floor being covered with blankets, the hectic attempts to resuscitate a lifeless little body, desolate mute children and distressed adult relatives looking up in despair. The wounded children are eyewitnesses to gruesome atrocities against themselves and their family. A little girl with neat curls is being interviewed from her hospital bed. Appearing to be 3–4 years old, she describes, in a childish matter-of-fact narrative, how she was shot: "I saw the soldier next to the shop. I looked for my mom. Then he shot me. One bullet hit my hand and the other went through my back and out of my stomach." It is deeply disturbing to see innocent toddlers describe the atrocities they experience in such a mundane tone, and their engagement with the camera and their voice conveys a strong appeal to the audience.

Drawing partly on the aesthetics of raw documentary, the affective power of the Gaza report comes primarily from the authentic documentation of the chaos in the hospital: Images show wounded children, desperate relatives and helpless medical staff. The lack of an authoritative voiceover and elite sources puts the suffering of these children in the face of the viewers. The report is narrated from what Graddol (1994: 145) has labeled the 'naturalist' tradition of television news, inviting the viewer to directly experience the situation: "From the naturalist perspective, a news report provides vicarious experience, an image of the world as we might expect to experience if we were to stand where the reporter stands" (ibid.). The camera angles, the noise, and the children speaking directly to us, pull us into the dramatic scenes in the hospital. The naturalist perspective is considered a powerful ideological tool because it gives a closer, more subjective view of the events, in contrast to the realist perspective in news, which stresses objectivity, distance and difference (Robertson, 2010: 28). The children are thus exposed as the most idealized victims of the Gaza War, whereas elite sources such as involved experts and adults—for example Palestinian parents, medical staff, politicians, NGOs and Palestinian armed groups—are conspicuously absent from the report. Also, the Israeli authorities, identified as the perpetuators in the introduction to the report, are silenced in this story. A strong political subtext is thus constructed for this representation of children's suffering—they are the innocent victims of the Israeli war machine. In her studies of audience compassion, Höijer finds that the visualization of the suffering is imperative and compassion is dependent on visuals, as documentary pictures become evidence of suffering (Höijer 2004: 520–1). Secondly, Höijer documents that the viewer's perception of the victim as helpless and innocent is a condition for being moved (ibid.). The Gaza report presents the children as innocent and helpless, and the visualization of suffering is highly dramatic. The report thus meets all Höijer's most important criteria for generating audience compassion.

EXPOSING AND COUNTERING THE OFFICIAL NARRATIVE

In the previous chapter, it was demonstrated that AJE's editorial management stressed the importance of preparing for political spin and strategic communication from Israeli and Palestinian spokespeople. It was particularly underlined that the Israeli information campaigns and official spokespersons are especially accessible and professional and that the relative strength of the Israeli information campaigns reflected the broader asymmetry of the conflict. As summarized in the previous chapter, the AJE news anchors were markedly critical and tough when interviewing Israeli officials. More importantly for the purpose of the present chapter, however, is how the studio interviews were framed visually, and the interaction between verbal and visual communication. Verbally, the anchor would offer critical investigations, while the interviewee would offer versions of the core frame. Visually, different uses of split screen dominated the interviews, either split between (a) interviewee and anchor (traditional two-way studio interview between two authoritative figures—the news anchor and the interviewee), (b) interviewee and map or (c) interviewee and moving images. Throughout AJE's coverage of the Israeli ground invasion, the channel interviewed 12 Israeli officials, and 8 out of 12 of these interviews were combined with moving (often 'live') images from the ground. What is noteworthy in the AJE split-screen with Israeli officials is the fact that the moving images do not primarily document or correspond with the official statements; it systematically counters and questions the official core message. On one half of the screen we see a professional Israeli spokesperson repeating the official line but, as this authoritative figure is engaging with the news anchor, she or he is also challenged by the chaotic, grim images from the warzone.

One compelling example here is the extensive live two-way between Israeli military spokeswoman Avital Leibovitch and AJE news anchor Sami Zeidan, aired on 11 January 2009 (see Faldalen and Figenschou [forthcoming] for comprehensive analysis and theoretical discussion). In the extensive live interview, Zeidan interrogates Leibovitch over claims that the Israeli army is using white phosphorous on Gaza. It is a veritable duel between two professional communicators that have met often in this situation, before, during and after the war (see previous chapter). Israeli spokeswoman Leibovitch is linked up from Jerusalem, in a classic static medium close shot that marks a controlled, staged situation. She is accorded authority and is seemingly in control and, in uniform, she looks straight into the camera at the viewer. In the interview, interrogated by AJE news anchor Sami Zeidan, Leibovitch repeatedly denies any knowledge of Israel breaking international law. Although Zeidan asks her directly to confirm or deny that Israel employs white phosphorous, she does not address the question directly. Then, her argumentation is countered visually as the right part of the split-screen shows images of what appears to be white phosphorous; the AJE control room keeps airing the grainy, documentary style 'phosphorous' images from the streets of Gaza throughout the entire interview.

The image of the 'phosphorous' in Gaza counters and exposes Leibovitch's official narrative due to the perceived authenticity of (live) images discussed at the beginning of this chapter. Due to its seemingly analogical character, images are efficient pieces of evidence and legitimization strategies employed to criticize or support particular military actions (Dobernig et al. 2010: 89). Live images from inside Gaza expose what seems to be contradictions in the Israeli official core message in real time as Leibovitch professionally articulates the Israeli core frame on the other half of the screen. The visual rhetoric employed in this studio interview thus illustrates how 'the new visibility' in international news challenges the military and political spin. AJE's visualization of official statements and studio two-ways represent a strong and efficient editorial strategy. It is also undoubtedly a controversial editorial strategy. In the above-mentioned interview, Leibovitch seems neither to be aware of the 'phosphour' images nor the fact that it is being broadcast to the viewers as she speaks. In the case of AJE, it reflects the channel's aim to cover the world from the perspective of the voiceless (the people in Gaza) by exposing the atrocities and suffering under Israeli occupation. On the other hand, it questions the channel's sincerity when it comes to covering all sides of a story ("Every Angle, Every Side"): Is it ethical to frame interviewees and guests with images that counter what they are saying? If it systematically undermines the Israeli statements by means of editorial context and visualization, does it then represent the Israeli side of the story?

THE RISKY STRATEGY AND ETHICS OF GIVING A "VOICE TO THE VOICELESS"

In the war on Gaza, Al Jazeera English literally gets closer and zooms in, exposes, personalizes and dramatizes, politicizes and authorizes the perspective of the victims on the ground. These editorial techniques are not necessarily or essentially more charitable or benevolent than those of the Western media. It seems clear, however, that they reflect an editorial agenda and strategy that is qualitatively different from that of the mainstream media in the West. According to Berenger and Taha (2013) the contextual ethics of the Arab world is influenced by the key characteristics of the Arab public sphere and media systems (outlined in chapters 1 and 2 of this volume) and hence the practices of Arab media ethics differ from the Western media ethics as a consequence (also see Hafez 2002 for a comparison). As discussed in chapter 3 of this volume, AJE aims to balance the information flow between the South and the North—a flow that historically has run from North to South, from rich countries to poor. The channel has an explicit editorial emphasis on reporting forgotten stories from the perspective of the voiceless—the global South, the underprivileged, the subaltern, the underdog, and the disenfranchised.

The editorial exposure and individualization of suffering 'up close' brings about a new set of ethical concerns. To avoid charges of sensationalism and indecency, the representation of violence, pain and suffering in the news must be justified as being in the public interest (Wells 2007: 57). For Al Jazeera Network editorial management and staff interviewed for this book, it is vital to document the atrocities of wars and international conflicts. For AJN, this is based on an understanding that the mainstream Western media is not depicting the realities on the ground—an analysis that has been widely confirmed in the extant studies of visual representations of wars and international conflict outlined in this chapter. According to AJN sources, the public needs to know what happens when and where the bombs hit the ground, in someone's kitchen, in a market or in a military facility.

According to the Al Jazeera Network's *Code of Ethics* (2010), it will "[a]dhere to the journalistic values of honesty, courage, fairness, balance, independence, credibility and diversity, giving no priority to commercial or political considerations over professional ones." (AJN 2010c) The network's ethics code does not specifically address images. In their study of images addressed in US media ethics codes, Keith et al. (2006) find that the special problems of violence and truth telling in wars and conflicts, particularly the controversial issue of how to handle graphic images, receive virtually no attention. And this lack of strict guidelines is confirmed in Fahmy's (2005b) survey among photographers and photo editors covering the US-led "war on terror." Moreover, Keith et al. (2006) identify several unaddressed issues concerning images that require comprehensive ethical discussion in the contemporary media landscape (ibid.: 257–8). First, the news media must acknowledge and address the fact that war and politically motivated violence produce images that raise special ethical concerns. Second, ethical codes of visuals should articulate the inbuilt tension in visual journalists' roles as truth tellers, compassionate humans, and employees sensible to audience concerns. Third, it is vital to advocate greater accountability and discourse with audiences about images of violence and tragedy. Fourth, ethical codes should recognize that images are shared across media platforms and from the local to the international media and vice versa, and, related to this, the current media technology facilitates user-generated content, graphic images taken by witnesses and survivors, which should be addressed comprehensively in visual codes (ibid.). These recommendations are particularly pertinent for the Al Jazeera Network, whose visual depictions of suffering and death have been both controversial and vital for its position in the international news landscape.

This editorial agenda carries a heavy responsibility, as the editorial emphasis on the voiceless potentially risks overusing the emotive stories of suffering and, consequently, leading to a habituation to and normalization of mediated atrocity (Sontag 2003, Zelizer 1998). Corresponding with this, Moeller (1999: 313–2) argues that it is not the volume of stories of death, famine, pestilence or war that causes indifference or 'compassion fatigue' but, rather, the formulaic, repetitive nature of the coverage of crisis. She finds that foreign crises are covered briefly, and without the necessary contextual information. As a result, the coverage levels the particularities and anomalies of each crisis into a uniform formula. Moeller (1999) concludes that the answer to compassion fatigue basically comes down to how the story is told and thus also how the media professionals themselves perceive the story—how a news event is narrated and visualized. It is only when the exposure and documentation of civilian suffering is combined with editorial techniques to personalize and authorize the exposed pain that the suffering is brought closer to the viewer.

As demonstrated above, the editorial assessment over when, how and where to publish violent and/or casualty images is not explicit in contemporary visual ethics codes. From the extant literature on graphic images, we know that these editorial decisions are founded on a combination of several considerations: in essence, the journalists' duty to tell the truth versus the journalistic duty to be compassionate, the public's interest in showing the truth versus the interest of protecting the audience, the privacy of those portrayed in the images and the interests of national security. The limits of good taste and decency are shaped by the context of the events and the news media's perceived sensibilities of the (domestic) audience (Wells 2007: 58), implying that the context of the images changes with time and place. In a survey of American photographers and photo editors, Fahmy (2005b: 159–60) finds that situational context was perceived to be more important for the visual gatekeeping process than the written ethical codes. The decisions over which images to select for publication are embedded in political, economic and organizational constraints but, as the instructions and guidelines are not clear cut, photographers and (photo) editors often face practical dilemmas about where to draw the line (ibid.).

In the Western media, the responsibility to protect the audience, which most often prefers to avoid gruesome images (Silcock et al. 2008: 37), has been particularly powerful. The visual conservatism among American viewers and media professionals, aiming to protect its target audience and its advertisers and commercial interests, has been well documented in the literature of mediated human suffering. In their ethical code, the Al Jazeera Network states that it will "[t]reat our audiences with due respect and address every issue or story with due attention to present a clear, factual and accurate picture" (AJN 2010c). For AJE, which does not have a closely defined target audience and aims to reach global viewers worldwide with diverging sensibilities and definitions over what defines a 'graphic image,' this is more complicated. The limited empirical audience studies on graphic visuals indicate that viewers around the world may not share the American understanding of 'good taste.' In the survey of audience perceptions among Al Jazeera Arabic viewers, Fahmy and Johnson (2007a) found overwhelming support for the channel's editorial policy of broadcasting graphic images. Nearly 9 out of 10 supported the channel's use of graphic visuals and, in hindsight, a similar percentage agreed that watching the graphic visuals from the recent conflicts in Iraq war and the Palestinian/Israeli conflict was the right decision for them (ibid.: 258). The study found that the viewers wanted the channel to air graphic images showing the ugliness of war because they perceived the suffering to be part of the full and complete coverage. To them, the problem was not the sensationalism of the graphic images but the act of atrocity and violence in the ongoing conflicts in the Arab world (ibid.: 259). In a related study, Johnson and Fahmy (2010) examined how readers of Al Jazeera English's website, examined in 2004,[6] perceived graphic images published on the website. First, the respondents, who represented an international elite audience with high education and international experience, did not perceive the website as presenting 'graphic images,' albeit 9 out of 10 supported the broadcasting of such visuals and regarded such visuals valuable, and missing from the Western media (ibid.: 54). Overall, the respondents' argumentation for why the Al Jazeera websites should show these images echo the editorial staff's argumentation outlined in the beginning of this chapter. To these viewers, these visuals simply reflect the disturbing realities of war (ibid.: 57–8). Moreover, the respondents concurred with the AJN editorial staff's criticism of the sanitized Western media outlined above (ibid.). These two studies thus demonstrate that the exposure of suffering is politicized, and that the tolerance for close-ups of civilian suffering may be politically motivated and varies between different audience groups, and that it is not solely decided by geography and ethnicity. Furthermore, because the Al Jazeera Network is not dependent on commercial advertisers, and thus not as sensitive to audience or commercial interests, they are freer to challenge the limits of 'good taste.'

For Al Jazeera English, the privacy and protection of those individuals and casualties that are exposed in images of violence appears to be the most relevant responsibility in assessing its visual editorial policy. The concern for the people in the news is also expressed in its ethical code stating the imperative of "giving full consideration to the feelings of victims of crime, war, persecution and disaster, their relatives and our viewers, and to individual privacies and public decorum" (AJN 2010c). The consideration for the victims' privacy was not foregrounded in the interviews with AJN sources, who predominantly related the discussion on 'graphic images' to military and political power. By documenting the atrocities and realities of war and exposing power misuse, AJE undoubtedly follows its editorial agenda, and the channel's teams go further in both exposing the sufferers and in aligning themselves with sufferers than mainstream Western media. Both being exposed and being strategically co-opted carries a risk for those exposed. How do the media of attachment handle these dilemmas? Victims of catastrophes, war and violence are marked by their traumatic experience and should be treated with particular respect and consideration by the media. At the same time, these victims' stories are often the most powerful testimonies challenging the official narratives and truths about conflict and wars. This poses a delicate ethical dilemma for AJE, illustrated by the channel's Gaza coverage: In aiming to expose the realities of war, does AJE risk 'sacrificing' the privacy of those victims foregrounded for this purpose? On one hand, documenting and exposing the pain of others is an important reminder of the realities of life and death. On the other hand, although the exposure of the pain of ordinary people may evoke intimacy, the close-up also positions them as less powerful (Graddol 1994: 146). Elaborating on the dilemma of exposure, Boltanski (1999: 33) writes: "A picture which goes too far in the realistic description of details, one which might be described as repulsive, may actually be denounced on the one hand as *reductive*, inasmuch as the person is entirely defined by their suffering, and on the other hand as taking the suffering away from the person inflicted by it in order to *exhibit* this suffering to those who do not suffer."

8 Beyond the Arab Spring
The Structural Contradictions of the Al Jazeera Project

The Arab uprisings of 2011–12 formed the perfect story for Al Jazeera English and gave the channel its major international breakthrough. This book has aimed to elucidate *how* and *why* AJE became the channel of choice in order to understand the massive protests across the Arab world. It has demonstrated that the editorial agenda and strategies that made the channel stand out during the intense 'Arab Spring' media frenzy had in fact developed over a long period preceding the Arab Spring. As demonstrated in chapters 3 through 5 of this volume, the channel had experimented and striven to professionalize an alternative, southern news agenda, most of the time below the radar of the international media. The AJE staff had been covering the Global South, on the ground, searching for alternative voices and dramatic images, and circumventing censorship for years while waiting for their big break in the competitive environment of international news. Particularly important in preparation for a reputation for mediation of protest was the channel's coverage of the political protests in authoritarian Asian states like Burma (2007) and Malaysia (2007), where their reporters on the ground were 'embedded' with the protesters, empathically telling the story from the view of the demonstrators and documenting the authorities' violent reactions and killing of protestors, relying on social media activists and largely validating the protestors as legitimate and peaceful (see Powers and El-Nawawy's 2008 case study of AJE's coverage of the November 2007 clashes in Malaysia).

Before the Arab uprisings, AJE had first received international recognition (and criticism) for its coverage of the Gaza War, 2009, and their professional approach to the war was strikingly similar to the way the channel covered the protests two years later. The sheer magnitude of the Arab uprisings, the hundreds of thousands of people taking to the streets for democracy and reform and the rapid, dramatic fall of many of the Arab world's most repressive dictators explains why this story dominated headlines across the globe. In contrast to the Gaza War, coverage of which was also a major journalistic achievement by AJE, the 'Arab Spring' story was perceived as highly newsworthy, popular and uncontroversial in major mainstream Western media, in contrast to the deep, hyperpoliticized Israeli–Palestinian conflict. Not only did *the* story take place in AJE's home region, where they had more bureaus, local reporters, extensive source networks and regional expertise—the channel's framing of the events as legitimate, democratic and peaceful was widely shared by the international media. The first phase of the Arab uprisings was characterized by international and regional consensus (Ulrichsen 2012). It was one of the rare news stories in which most people, journalists and political elites around the world shared an understanding of who were the 'bad guys' and who were the 'good guys' (see Cottle 2011 for discussion). In this unprecedented story, AJE capitalized fully on its comparative advantages and became among the most recognized international sources of information.

There are a number of forthcoming studies of the new media's role in the Arab uprisings, and, as underlined in the introduction of this book, there is a strong need for more empirically-substantiated, systematic analysis of the Al Jazeera Network's role in and coverage of the different uprisings and internal struggles that at the time of writing are still ongoing throughout the Arab world. The main contribution of this present chapter will be to illuminate some of the structural limitations and contradictions inherent in the Al Jazeera English project and how these have been accentuated in the aftermath of the 2011–12 upheavals. It first argues that the channel's resource-intensive production strategies make it highly dependent on its Qatari sponsor. It is a remarkable paradox that AJE's editorial boldness is dependent on expensive production strategies and the goodwill of its owners. It is only as long as the Al Jazeera Network serves the regional and international ambitions of Qatar that it will be granted today's generous budgets and political goodwill from its owners. This built-in contradiction in the Al Jazeera project—in which an autocratic, wealthy owner with strategic ambitions and a team of elite media professionals runs an alternative news channel—has vital theoretical implications as it blurs the traditional alternative vs. mainstream, contra vs. dominant dichotomy. The chapter argues that these built-in challenges in the Al Jazeera model have only deepened and become more pressing in the aftermath of the 'Arab Spring.' First, the Al Jazeera–Qatari relations analyzed in chapter 2 of this volume were dramatically altered when the Al Jazeera Network's visionary and powerful Director General Wadah Khanfar unexpectedly announced his retirement on Twitter on 20 September 2011 and was replaced by a member of the extended Qatari ruling family—Sheikh Ahmed bin Jassim Al Thani. How the replacement will influence Al Jazeera English's editorial freedom in the long run remains to be seen, but the appointment's profound effect on the Al Jazeera model will be discussed in this chapter. Moreover, it argues that the Arab Spring has profound implications on both Qatari domestic and foreign policy and that these changes make it even more difficult in the future for the Al Jazeera Network to be independent within the Qatari political context.

PROFESSIONALIZING THE 'SOUTHERN' ALTERNATIVE

Alternative news media have traditionally been in explicit opposition to professional, mainstream media, whereas AJE's editorial agenda and production strategies aim to professionalize the alternative perspective. In contrast to the 'native reporters' in alternative media, who identify with an activist cause and characterize themselves as activists, AJE informants are professional journalists reporting to an international audience. The channel has been characterized by a big margin of editorial freedom, similar to the independence found by Zayani and Sahraoui (2007) in its Arabic sister channel. At the same time, most AJE employees are critical of the development in mainstream international reporting symbolized by the pressure toward domestication, corporate ownership and commercial imperatives. The channel's editorial core values are broad ideals that can have a wide variety of interpretations. In practice, AJE informants interviewed for this book have conflicting interpretations of the editorial core values, employ diverging production strategies, and evaluate the output differently. In its formative years, AJE employees have been concerned that the output has been desultory and inconsistent, underlining the need to narrow down the editorial agenda, articulate the editorial vision and institutionalize newsroom practices (AJN 2009b). In January 2013, AJE finally found a way into the US market by buying the Current TV cable network for 500 million. According to a network press release, "the assets of Current Media, an independent television and online network founded in 2005, include distribution agreements with cable and satellite TV partners" reaching a potential 40 million American viewers (AJN 2013a). Early in 2013, the network was hiring around 100 management and editorial staff to work in bureaus across the US for a new 'Al Jazeera America' news channel. The new channel is aiming to double the network's US-based staff to more than 300 employees (ibid.), including a team of investigative reporters. Moreover, at the Seventh Al Jazeera Forum (Doha, 15–18 March 2013), the new director general publicly announced that the network was planning to launch a number of new news channels among others Al Jazeera UK (competing for the UK market) and Al Jazeera French (targeting French-speaking audiences worldwide). At present, it is not clear to what extent the American Al Jazeera will be domesticated/localized or whether it will continue a 'Southern' perspective (AJE press office information request, May 2013). What the network's ambitious new American, UK and French market plans epitomize is the fact that its heavy investments into new markets will increase the diversity and heterogeneity of its audience substantially. A wider global audience, in turn, exacerbates AJE's need to define its target audience and decide on its editorial line, as discussed in chapter 3 of this volume. This need to professionalize and institutionalize the organization has been a recurrent ambition for the top management throughout AJE's short history. The inherent risk is that these streamlining processes may 'mainstream' the news production.

Much of AJE's editorial distinctiveness has come as a result of the channel's progressive production strategies, and it is imperative that the channel's editorial management protects the 'Southern' perspective. The fundamental dilemma in AJE's editorial strategy and organization is that the channel is a competitive contra-flow, because of its size and resources, at the same time as the size of the organization potentially threatens alternative production strategies. While an alternative media organization is small, it can operate within an egalitarian structure and with a certain level of autonomy. Given its size and resources, AJE is an anomaly within the alternative media ecology, and this pushes the channel toward mainstream production values and strategies. Staffing is one example. Although AJE emphasizes that it reports the world through its local correspondents, in its formative years the top and middle management teams have been dominated by white, British, middle-aged men on the rationalization that to operate AJE's ambitious, complex, decentralized production structure, the channel needed senior staff with extended experience from international media. Operating AJE's extensive global presence and four headquarters is capital-intensive, and it is mainly as a result of these resource-intensive production strategies that AJE challenges the 'dominant' Western news channels. A lack of a participatory internal communications strategy, characterized as hierarchical and top-down in internal evaluation, has been undermining the channel's progressive editorial agenda further (AJN 2009b).

A more fundamental structural contradiction in the Al Jazeera model is the fact that the channel's progressive production strategies, demonstrated in its coverage of the Gaza War 2009 (chapters 6 and 7, this volume) and the Arab uprisings (chapter 1), are dependent on conditional privileges that are fully controlled by the Qatari authorities. Arguing that it is particularly important to examine the strategic motivation behind, and the inherent structural limitations of, the new, non-Western satellite news channels that are sponsored and owned by nondemocratic states like Qatar, the chapter problematizes how the recent regional developments have changed the foreign and domestic policy of Qatar, which, in turn, challenges the Al Jazeera Network's editorial independence. After the initial euphoric first phase of the Arab Spring, the escalation from demonstrations to violent conflicts in Libya, Bahrain and Syria have dramatically exposed Qatar's new power and influence in the Arab world, which may turn critical for the reputation of both Qatar and the Al Jazeera Network (Barakat 2012, Ulrichsen 2012). Together, these drastic changes have put Qatari–Al Jazeera relations under regional and international scrutiny.

AJE AND QATAR'S MEDIATED PUBLIC DIPLOMACY

As argued earlier, in order to understand AJE, it is imperative to study the political ambitions of the Qatari authorities. The Qatari vision has been underpinned by three key strategies: controlled, top-down economic and political liberalization, the pursuit of an independent foreign policy, and a 'state branding' project (Barakat 2012). Analysts have particularly highlighted the state branding strategy, as the promised domestic reforms have served more like showcases than substantial changes (see, among others, Bahry & Marr 2005, Kamrava 2011). One illustrative example is the highly publicized manner in which Qatari authorities have embraced international norms on democracy and gender equality in order to attract international attention and legitimacy. Lambert (2011: 98–9) points to the irony of the Qatari regime being willing to censor national newspaper criticism of its democratization and gender equality strategy in a move to ensure that the latter was viewed as successful by the international community—raising questions about how deeply the Qatari authorities and society have internalized these new normative policies.

Through its distinct, alternative agenda in international affairs, AJE demonstrates its editorial boldness and Qatari 'media freedom' in practice. The channel's editorial distinctiveness has attracted vast international media interest with mostly positive spillover effects on its owner. When the international media cover the Al Jazeera Network, journalists tend to list the ruling family's other 'showcases of reform' and state branding tools as well, and most media do not stay long enough in Qatar to conduct investigative, critical reporting. As discussed in chapter 2 of this volume, Qatari authorities have underlined the Al Jazeera network's independence, publicly distanced themselves from the Al Jazeera Network, and consistently stated that they do not wish to interfere in the network's editorial decisions. For Qatar, AJE is most important as a showcase of Qatari media freedom, and it is through its role as a satellite news contra-flow that AJE serves Qatar's strategic interests. The prominent position of the brave Al Jazeera Network, which pushes editorial limits, diverts attention from the local, loyal, national media and the fact that there is no substantial media freedom within the national Qatari mediasphere. In order to reflect the national strategies underlying AJE's role as a contra-flow and shed light on the structural contradiction between AJE's alternative agenda and its autocratic owner, AJE is best characterized as a *strategic* contra-flow.

In this context, the sudden and unexpected departure of former Director General Wadah Khanfar in early September 2011 raises many questions: Why did the network owner replace a highly respected director general immediately after he had led the network through the its biggest story since it went on air in 1996, and at a time when the network was in the international spotlight?[1] Did the replacement of a correspondent-turned-executive with a member of the extended Qatari ruling family signal a tighter grip on the network? The replacement of Khanfar, who had worked his way up since he joined the Arabic channel in South Africa 1997 and had acquired field experience from Afghanistan and Iraq, with a Qatari national without any journalistic experience undermines the Al Jazeera model. Because the new director general, Sheikh Ahmed bin Jassim Al Thani, is a member of the country's ruling elite, analysts have started to watch the network's coverage of Qatar and Qatari foreign interests more closely. In itself, even before the new Qatari director general has made his mark on the network, the appointment of Al Thani questions the network's independence, weakens the journalistic credibility of the Al Jazeera Network and thus, conversely, its strategic position in Qatar's public diplomacy. Recent events related to the Arab Spring have impacted Qatar's reputation and position in the region in ways that invite critical investigation—by Al Jazeera English as well, if they are to be seen as professional journalists.

FROM IMPARTIALITY TO MILITARY INTERVENTION

In the first phase of the Arab uprisings, the Al Thani family of Qatar managed to capitalize on the Arab Spring despite being one of the region's most autocratic rulers (Davidson 2012: 226). When the uprisings started, Qatar held a unique position in the Arab world—it had regional and international legitimacy, stability at home, a relatively progressive government, the ability to make swift policy decisions, extensive experience in mediation and a reputation for impartiality (Barakat 2012: 25). Qatar's mediation policy has been essential in the country's efforts to carve out an image of an experienced mediator, a regional diplomatic powerhouse, an honest broker, and a wise and mature defender of peace and stability (Kamrava 2011: 542). Qatari mediators have often selected high-profile mediation cases, and mediation has emerged as one of the central tools for enhancing Qatari soft power and its global image (Kamrava 2011: 556, Rabi 2009). Since early 2011, Qatari authorities chose a high-profile role in peacemaking and have been at the forefront of attempts to control and shape the direction of changes coursing through the region, most evidently in its drastic shift from neutral mediation to actual political and military intervention (Barakat 2012, Ulrichsen 2012). The Qatari authorities have taken an aggressive new stance against violent oppression of protestors in Libya and Syria (Barakat 2012: 2). In Libya, the Qatari rulers lobbied for military intervention within the Arab League and the UN, was the first Arab state to recognize the rebel government, and supported the opposition with resources, war jets, weapons and ground troops (ibid.: 26–7). When the uprising spread to Syria, Qatar took a leadership role in the Arab League, called on the Syrian president to step down and advocated the international community's intervention in Syria (ibid.: 27–9). It is primarily Qatar's high-profile support for the Syrian opposition that places in jeopardy its regional and international standing (Ulrichsen 2012: 15). In contrast to the unprecedented international consensus on the uprisings in Tunisia, Egypt and Libya, the lack of consensus within the Syrian opposition and among the international community at large "expose[s] Qatar to significant reputational risk" (ibid.). Analysts have explained the shift in foreign policy differently: some interpret the interventionist line as a reaction to human rights violations, others maintain that Qatar is just adapting to the changing circumstances, while the most cynical interpretations underline Qatar's strategic, long-term goal of becoming a leader in a stronger Arab diplomacy, its ambition to be an emerging world player and its aim to protect national security and resources (see Barakat 2012: 29–35 for an overview).

Perhaps more important for the analysis of Al Jazeera–Qatari relations is the fact that Qatar's shift from diplomatic mediation to a more aggressive, assertive foreign policy has positioned it as an unconventional leader in the Arab world, but it has also put Qatar in the critical spotlight (Barakat 2012, Colombo 2012, Ulrichsen 2012). Since 2011, Qatar has revealed itself as a much more "self-interested foreign policy actor" intent on expanding its clout (Colombo 2012: 118). More fundamentally, these actions have broken with Qatar's traditional position as a neutral and impartial mediator, analyzed in chapter 2 of this volume, and potentially undermine both its carefully built reputation of treating everyone without bias, and its pragmatic, carefully balanced security policy (Barakat 2012). Qatar has challenged and displeased a variety of regional actors in the last couple of years and the loss of impartiality (one of its key foreign policy principles) may prove damaging in the long term. According to Ulrichsen (2012), reports on deteriorating diplomatic relations between Qatar and Algeria and Mauretania are initial evidence suggesting that the regional reservoir of goodwill towards Qatar and Al Jazeera, resulting from its vital role in the first phase of the Arab Spring, may be rapidly shrinking (Ulrichsen 2012: 16). Within the Arab Gulf monarchies, Qatari diplomatic relations with both Bahrain and Saudi Arabia has been complicated due to Qatar's emergence as an increasingly assertive Arab power (Colombo 2012: 117).

DOUBLE STANDARDS: THE COUNTERREVOLUTION IN THE ARAB GULF MONARCHIES

How the autocratic Arab Gulf kingdoms met the regional uprisings has attracted substantial critical attention. In essence, the repressive counterrevolution in the Arab Gulf has made it much harder for the Gulf monarchies to "keep disguising the authoritarian nature of their politics" (Davidson 2012: 112), and its pragmatic, inconsistent approach to both domestic and regional post-Arab Spring development has been exposed as revealing double standards (Colombo 2012). In their immediate, initial reactions to the uprisings, the Gulf kingdoms largely sided with the authorities (Davidson 2012). After recovering from the initial shock, the Gulf Cooperation Council (GCC) played an important, supportive role for the popular mobilizations through a variety of media, economic and diplomatic means. The striking contrast between the response in its own (physical and symbolic) space and that in other Arab states has nurtured claims of a double standard (Barakat 2012, Colombo 2012, Ulrichsen 2012).

Although the regional uprisings were mostly focused on North Africa and the Levant, the conservative autocratic Gulf kingdoms did not escape the political mobilization altogether and faced escalating public and political protest, most violent and visible in Bahrain, Saudi Arabia, Oman and Kuwait (Ulrichsen 2012: 12). Within the GCC states, the reaction to the Arab Spring has been a mix of economic handouts, patronage, limited political and economic reforms, domestic repression and military intervention (Colombo 2012). Aiming to explain the Gulf kingdoms' various responses to the many variations of political and military mobilization across the region, Colombo (2012) distinguishes between uprisings inside vs. outside the GCC, in monarchies vs. republics, and initiated by Sunni movements vs. Shiite movements. She finds that, faced with unprecedented challenges from their own populations, the ruling Gulf monarchies stepped up their conservative counterrevolutionary approach: on the one hand, the authorities have met the challenges with state patronage through financial inducement on key sectors, most heavily employed in the states with highest potential destabilization such as Saudi Arabia, Oman and Bahrain (ibid.: 114), although Qatari authorities also raised the salary for citizens working in the public sector by 60 percent, and 120 percent for the police and military (Gengler 2012: 68). These massive expenditures have raised questions about their long-term sustainability, particularly when coupled with the mounting internal pressures facing the Gulf kingdoms, such as declining hydrocarbon reserves, rising domestic energy consumption, rapid demographic growth, the lack of ambition among the national population and the widening gap between rich and poor (see Davidson 2012: 111–54 for in-depth critical analysis of these challenges).

The counterrevolution in the Gulf kingdoms has made it harder for international partners and institutions to justify their engagement in the Arab Gulf and, recently, there have been several examples of terminated partnerships and conflicts further undermining the international reputation of the Gulf kingdoms (Ulrichsen 2012: 17). According to Davidson (2012: 112) the lack of transparency about national budgets, government spending and investments, and, more than anything, the accumulation of personal wealth by the ruling families and their closest allies, has become critical at a time when questionable sustainability threatens the state-patronage strategy in the longer term.

Massive state patronage is not only unsustainable for economic and fiscal reasons, concludes Colombo (2012: 124), it also expands entitlements and raises public expectations to levels unsustainable for the GCC states. The ruling families have implemented limited political and social reform while increasingly relying on repressive politics of censorship and brutal oppression. Colombo (2012: 118) concludes that, overall, the GCC countries pragmatically aim to manage instability by shoring up friendly regimes

on the inside and expanding its clout from the outside, thus appearing counterrevolutionary inside the Gulf and pro-revolutionary outside the Gulf
area. She further finds that this 'rally-around-the-flag' strategy is extended
to other Arab monarchies such as Morocco and Jordan, which have both
been promised extensive economic aid from the GCC (ibid.: 121) and were
offered GCC memberships in May 2011 (Davidson 2012: 204–5). Moreover, the GCC ruling families are all founded on a puritan form of Wahhabi
Sunni Islam and have strategically framed the popular mobilizations, particularly in Bahrain and Saudi Arabia, as examples of Shiite sectarianism
(Colombo 2012: 122).

More than anything, GCC reactions to the brutal clampdown of the
'Bahraini Spring' have exposed the Gulf kingdoms' pragmatism and double
standards. The Bahraini clampdown on the demonstrations in the capital
city Manama, escalating from February 2011, was remarkably violent, with
continuous reports of killings and arrests of activists (see Davidson 2012:
204–9 for details). As pointed out by Ulrichsen (2012: 14) Qatar's mobilization of Arab intervention to support the Libyan opposition in mid-March
2011 happened at the exact same time as GCC forces (1,000 troops from
the Saudi Arabian armed forces and about 500 police officers from the UAE)
crossed into Bahrain to suppress the demonstrations at the Pearl Round-
about. Unlike its neighbors, Qatar did not send forces to Bahrain, but its
GCC membership has rendered it very vulnerable to accusations of double
standards (ibid.). Facing criticism that the Al Jazeera Network emphasized
the uprisings where Qatar played a key role while muting the internal conflict
in Bahrain, AJE published a documentary depicting human rights violations
and police brutality, which led to a diplomatic dispute between the two
neighbors (Davidson 2012: 208). On the other hand, Qatar did not publicly
condemn the brutal repression of Bahraini protestors and Al Jazeera Arabic has been strongly criticized for muting the dramatic events in Manama
(ibid.: 227). These pragmatic, inconsistent moves illustrate the Qatari aim to
balance its loyalty to its close GCC allies with publicly distancing themselves
from their neighbors' anti-Arab Spring positions (Davidson 2012).

A QATARI SPRING?

As explained in chapter 2 of this volume, Qatar has a tiny homogenous,
national population, one of the world's highest GDP per capita and vast
reserves of natural gas, and has largely avoided significant calls for political
reform (Davidson 2012). Qatar's natural gas is among the cheapest in the
world to extract, and this makes the country better prepared for falling gas
prices (Fromherz 2012: 149). In Qatar, in contrast to its Gulf neighbors,
the ruling family can continue a policy of state patronage as it can actually
sustain high spending and wealth distribution among its citizens (Davidson
2012: 237). This does not mean, however, that the ruling family does not

face domestic challenges ahead. Most pertinent is the authorities' need to balance its top-down rapid modernization with national traditions, cultural identity and heritage (Fromherz 2012, Gengler 2012, Wright 2011). Despite the relative popularity of Emir Sheikh Hamad bin Khalifa Al Thani and his closest family, their ambitions have tended to conflict with social interest groups who feel left out of the dreams and aspirations of the elite (Fromherz 2012: 122). There is a considerable problem with 'voluntary unemployment' (young men who do not go to university or work in the booming private sector), and these disaffected young men often disapprove of the country's development. One contested issue related to the modernization program is the politicization of the immigration debate and growing xenophobia among the national population (Gengler 2012). Qatar's astounding population growth is largely attributable to large-scale, state-initiated immigration, and men substantially outnumber women among inhabitants over 15 (Berrebi et al. 2009: 430–1).

Qatar's newfound prosperity has not come without potential problems, as expatriate workers dominate the labor market and Qatari workers are almost exclusively engaged in public sector jobs (Berrebi et al. 2009, Davidson 2012, Fromherz 2012, Wright 2011). Berrebi et al. (2009: 440) summarize the core of the Qatari dilemma:

> On the one hand Qataris will want fewer foreign workers because of the associated negative externalities on infrastructure (housing, sewage, security), society (discrimination, potential assimilation, loss of culture), stability (source of discontent, political pressure), and national pride (dependence on foreigners for key functions and associated vulnerability). On the other hand foreign workers, as a source of both high-skilled and cheap unskilled labor, contribute to Qatar's international competitiveness, its ability to attract investments and, more generally, its economic growth. In addition, expatriates fill demand in the household service industry (e.g. nannies, domestic cleaners, drivers and cooks), a segregated sector in which native Qataris do not participate (ibid.).

In recent years, the large scale immigration to the GCC countries has been associated with rising alcohol consumption, gambling and prostitution, and criticism of these issues has become increasingly loud (Davidson 2012: 161). In his analysis of recent political polls, Gengler (2012: 69–70) finds that Qatari mobilization against the ruling family—albeit very small, fragmented and subdued—has been playing on group identity and conflict between Qatari citizens and the foreign expatriate population. Historically, the privileged national Qatari minority and the expatriate majority have been largely separated and mutually suspicious of one another, but in the last couple of years, the tense relationship has deteriorated into a more open conflict (ibid.). After five years of massive, unprecedented immigration, the issue of immigration has become increasingly politicized as conservative, family-oriented national citizens react to what they view as strongly Western cultural and political-military influence (ibid.). Immigration is expected to increase further in the coming decade due to massive construction and infrastructure projects in preparation for the 2022 FIFA World Cup (ibid.: 74). One site of contest has been the prestigious Education City complex, which has been renamed as Hamad bin Khalil University, honoring the Emir and downplaying the international 'partners' previously highlighted in the national branding campaigns (ibid.: 72). Similarly, alcohol was banned from the prestigious tourist and real-estate project—the Pearl—in early 2012 (Davidson 2012: 162).

This growing ambivalence towards the socioeconomic politics and massive immigration (emerging antigovernment and anti-Western attitudes) does not suggest the impending rise of organized political opposition in Qatar (Gengler 2012). The major risk for the Emir is that power becomes too concentrated in a small part of the Al Thani family (Fromherz 2012: 160). For the Qatari Emir, the biggest threats remain within his own extended family, particularly those family members who sympathize with his deceased father, whom he replaced in a palace coup, and those with Saudi Arabian interests (ibid.: 144). The effects of the swift and sudden transfer of power from Emir Hamad bin Khalifa Al Thani to his young son, the current Emir Sheikh Tamim, in late June 2013, remain to be seen. As this book goes into print, the new Emir has given a message of continuity, stating that he aims to follow his father's policy. Sheikh Hamad was unconventional, strategic and smart, but Sheikh Tamim has also inherited his father's problems in the aftermath of the Arab uprisings. In recent years, there have been several reports in regional media about attempted coups in 2009, 2011 and 2012, and, although it is difficult to assess whether these reports are rumors or uncomfortable truths silenced in the local media, they undermine Qatar's regional reputation (Davidson 2012: 183–4). According to Davidson (2012) the Gulf monarchies remain highly vulnerable to foreign aggressors (especially Iran) and to internal GCC disputes (supporting military coups in neighboring states). As such, they will remain dependent on external security guarantees and will have to meet the internal criticism of its dependency on the Western powers.

CONCLUDING REMARKS

The last couple of years have been dramatic for both Qatar and the Al Jazeera Network. The aftermath of the Arab Spring has demonstrated that Qatar is not just punching above its weight as analysts repeatedly claim—it has become a heavyweight (Allaf 2011 in Barakat 2012: 43). In interviews with Al Jazeera Network staff from 2003 to the present, questions about their sensitivities towards domestic Qatari affairs have consistently been countered with reference to its relatively minor size, its stability and dullness.

Interviewees have recurrently explained that Al Jazeera will start to cover Qatar critically if there is news of international or regional importance involving the country. The events of the Arab Spring have positioned Qatar as a controversial, unconventional regional power, and both the country's involvement and military intervention and its position among the repressive GCC states should be investigated thoroughly by international media, including AJE. In the coming years, as more Qatari prestige projects are finalized, the conflicts between expatriates and nationals and liberal and traditional values will be exacerbated.

The 2022 FIFA World Cup epitomizes these challenges: The impressive Qatari stadiums and the new cities built to host the teams and supporters will be built by Asian migrant workers. Today, the low-skilled expatriate labor force represents 85 percent of the population in Qatar, but their difficult working and living conditions are not covered comprehensively on AJE (see Figenschou 2010b for discussion about the migrant worker issue). The expatriate workers are regularly exploited by their Qatari sponsors and there will be intense international media attention in the years leading up to the world cup. These breaches of international labor rights are systematically neglected by the Qatari authorities and, arguably, affect the disenfranchised majority to whom alternative, counter-hegemonic media strive to give a voice. Moreover, since most Al Jazeera employees see the migrant workers every day and are themselves noncitizens under the Qatari sponsor system, this silencing of the issue is particularly striking. Given that AJE promotes itself as "the voice of the voiceless," the limited coverage of the issue illustrates the ways in which the channel's self-censorship practices prevent it from fully exposing the negative aspects of Qatar's economic boom and rapid development. Because Al Jazeera rarely raises controversial issues that directly affect the status quo in Qatar, it protects Qatari political concerns and interests over time (Rugh 2007: 12). Today, Qatar has become a regional player, and the Al Jazeera Network will have to start covering its host more thoroughly and substantially. As the royal family has taken the top position within the network and Qatar has increasingly come under international media scrutiny—it cannot afford not to.

Appendix
List of Interviews

Personal interviews by the author. The informants are identified by the title and affiliation they had at the time of the interview.

Hashem Ahelbarra, Correspondent, Doha, 2007
Lamis Andoni, Middle East Consultant, Doha, 2007
Al Anstey, Deputy Director of News, Doha, 2007
Omar Bec, Managing Editor, Doha, 2007
Bhanu Bhatnagar, Interview Producer News, London, 2008
Tony Burman, Managing Director, Doha, 2009
Steve Clark, Director of News, Doha, 2007
Nazar Daw, Producer *Inside Story*, Doha, 2007
Mike Dillon, Senior Editor of Programmes, Doha, 2007
Alan Fisher, Correspondent, London, 2008
Imran Garda, Presenter & Producer, Doha, 2007
Rob Gilles, Programme Editor, London, 2008
Richard Gizbert, Program Host *The Listening Post*, London, 2008
Maria Hadjiconstanti, Planning Desk, London, 2008
Mike Hanna, Correspondent, Doha, 2007
Dawoud Hassan, Producer AJA, Doha, 2007
Ibrahim Helal, Deputy Managing Director, Doha, 2009
Arif Hijawi, Head of Programming, AJA, Doha, 2007
Saira Jaffer, Deputy News Editor, London, 2008
Corinna Katsarka, Planning Editor London, 2008
Majed Khader, Head of Assignment Desk, AJA, Doha, 2007
Samir Khader, Program Editor, AJA, Doha, 2007
Waddah Khanfar, Director General, Doha, 2007
Claudio Lavanga, Deputy News Editor, London, 2008
Laurence Lee, Correspondent, London, 2008
Sylvia Lennan, Producer News, London, 2008
Rebecca Lipkin, Executive Producer Programming, London, 2008
Hamish MacDonald, Presenter & Correspondent, London, 2008
Richard Martin, Assistant Programme Editor, News, London, 2008
Gaven Morris, Head of Planning, Doha, 2007
Sue Phillips, Bureau Chief London, London, 2008

John Pullman, Head of Output, Doha, 2007
Ben Rayner, Head of News London, London, 2008
Mark Seddon, Diplomatic Correspondent, London, 2008
Amani Soliman, Middle East Editor, 2007
Lauren Taylor, Presenter, Doha, 2007
Mohamed Vall, Correspondent, 2007
Nick Walshe, Head of Input, Doha, 2007
May Yin Welsh, Producer, Middle East Desk, Doha, 2007
Sami Zeidan, Presenter & Correspondent, Doha, 2007

BACKGROUND INTERVIEWS:

Maher Abdallah, Talk Show Host/Correspondent, Al Jazeera Channel, Doha, 2003
Ahmed Abdullah, Senior Producer/Journalist, Al Arabiya Channel, Dubai, 2005
Sirin Abu Aqleh, Correspondent, Al Jazeera Channel's Ramallah bureau, Ramallah, 2005
Jihad Ali Ballout, Section Head Communications & Media Relations, Al Jazeera Channel, Doha, 2003 and 2005
Hesham Badawy, Correspondent Abu Dhabi TV's Baghdad bureau, Abu Dhabi, 2003
Najib Bencherif, Head of Assignment, Al Arabiya Channel, Dubai, 2005
Nart Bouran, Director of News Centre, Abu Dhabi TV, Abu Dhabi, 2003 and 2005
Nakle El Haje, Director of News and Current Affairs, Al Arabiya Channel, Dubai, 2005
Hassan Ibrahim, Senior Program Producer, Al Jazeera Channel, Doha, 2005
Amr El-Kahky, Senior Correspondent, Al Jazeera Channel, Doha, 2003
Samir Khader, Senior Producer, Al Jazeera Channel, Doha, 2005
Nabil Khatib, Executive Editor, Al Arabiya Channel, Dubai, 2005
Raed Khattar, Cameraman, Abu Dhabi TV's Baghdad bureau, Abu Dhabi, 2003
Hafez Al Mirazi, Bureau Chief, Al Jazeera Channel's Washington bureau, Washington D.C., 2004
Salah Nejm, News Director, Al Arabiya Channel, Dubai, 2003
Diyar Al Omari, Senior Correspondent, Al Jazeera Channel, Dubai, 2003
Walid Omary, Bureau Chief, Al Jazeera Channel's Ramallah bureau, Ramallah, 2005
Hassan Rachidi, Senior Journalist, Al Jazeera Channel, Doha, 2003
Hasan Sari, Producer/Editor, Abu Dhabi TV, Abu Dhabi, 2003
Saeed Shouli, Deputy Editor-in-Chief, Al Jazeera Channel, Doha, 2003
Mawafak F. Tawfik, Head of Translation Department, Al Jazeera Channel, Doha, 2003 and 2005
Wajd Waqfi, Correspondent, Al Jazeera's Washington bureau, Washington D.C., 2004
May-Ying Welsh, Producer, Al Jazeera's Baghdad bureau, (phone interview), 2003

Notes

NOTES TO CHAPTER 1

1. Although this book focuses on transnational satellite news channels, it is necessary to note that the majority of transnational cross-border channels specialize in entertainment genres such as music, children's programs, movies and sports (Chalaby 2003).
2. The abbreviation CNN in this book refers to *CNN International* and the abbreviation BBC to *BBC World News*.
3. It should be added that the innovative *World Report* program format, where broadcasters globally contribute with locally produced reports, collected and presented by CNN anchors, is not representative of the channel's general program profile.
4. According to channel websites, CNN is available to over 270 million households, while the BBC is available in more than 300 million households, both spanning 200 territories and countries globally in May 2013 according to channel websites (BBC 2011, CNN 2013). It is vital to emphasize that distribution is not equivalent to audience size, for it measures the number of homes that can receive the channel, not the number of households that actually watch the channel (Sparks 2005: 41).
5. For analysis of the different localization models, from basic translation to global multilingual networks, see Chalaby (2003, 2005a, 2005b) and Straubhaar (2007). For an in-depth study of domestication processes in foreign news production, see Clausen (2003).
6. The link between localization, hybridity and global power imbalances is investigated further by Kraidy's (2005) innovative "critical transculturalism" approach. In particular, his notion of "corporate transculturalism," a demonstration of how the hybridity literature has been used to promote a neoliberal agenda in the US, is valuable to the debate on localization (ibid: 72–96).
7. All vision statements are cited from the official channel websites. See Jirik (2010), Kuhn (2010), and Robertson (2013) for further analysis of the Chinese, French and Russian English-language new channels.
8. In the first five years post launch, the news on AJE were anchored in turn from Kuala Lumpur, Doha, London and Washington, before management decided to transmit full time out of Doha from the beginning of 2011 (AJE press office information request, May 2013).

9. In a survey-based study among Egypt's Tahrir Square protests, Tufekci and Wilson (2012) find that half of the respondents first heard about the demonstrations from someone face-to–face, and a quarter first heard it from Facebook. More importantly, they found that social media use greatly increased the odds of participating in the protests and that almost half of the respondents were actively documenting and sharing the developments on the ground via social media (ibid.: 376). Comparing the use of Internet-based communication to organize the protests in Iran (2009) and Egypt (2011), Tusa (2013) finds that social media were more important in framing the events than for organizing the protests. He concludes that the Egyptian protest movement was the more successful of the two because it relied on traditional organization and mobilization methods (ibid.: 17). Media-use studies further nuance the role of social media, documenting that the links posted on social media outlets (operationalized as bit.ly traffic), were primarily consumed outside the countries where the protests took place and outside the Arab region and most probably did not matter in the direct mobilization and organization (Aday et al. 2012: 13).

10. The study focused exclusively on AJA and the central network management. AJE had only just been launched when the book went into print and was not studied empirically.

NOTES TO CHAPTER 2

1. Looking chiefly at European and US media, Hallin and Mancini (2004) categorized media systems as belonging to either the polarized pluralist model, the democratic corporatist model or the liberal model.

2. Rugh's classification has mainly been criticized for being Western-centric and simplistic and for disregarding the socialization and professionalization of Arab journalists, the journalistic culture and news production (see Mellor 2005: 49–74 and Iskandar 2007 for a detailed discussion).

3. Although a complete list is impossible, since there are other Qatari initiatives taking place behind the scene, away from the media spotlight, both Fromherz (2012: 89–91) and Barakat (2012: 16–22) provide insightful overviews of Qatar's mediation activities.

4. Reporters Without Borders explained their withdrawal in the following statement: "We are disappointed by the attitude of the Qatari authorities, who did not really want to play along and did everything possible to prevent the Centre from being independent. Robert Ménard and his staff were targeted as soon as they criticized press freedom violations in Qatar although it was a prerequisite for the Centre to be credible. Several of the Emir's aides did not understand this" (Reporters Without Borders 2009b). In leaked US embassy cables, Sheikh Hamad bin Thamer Al Thani, who is the chairman of the center's board as well as the chairman of the Board of the Al Jazeera Network and the Qatar Radio and Television Corporation, was identified as the official laying restrictions on the center's operations (Booth 2010).

5. Saudi Arabia is by far the most important television advertising market in the Arab world, combining a large population (20 million viewers watch television at least six times a week) and high incomes (Kraidy & Khalil 2009: 12).

As a result, catering to the tastes of the Saudi market remains the top priority for Arab advertisers and the regional television industry (ibid.).

NOTES TO CHAPTER 3

1. It is vital to emphasize that not all alternative media are democratic, progressive and radical. Defining the radicalism of different media must be done case by case. Alternative media may also be repressive and change their political orientation with time, but these ultra-rightist, fascist media are not discussed in-depth in this book (see Downing 2001: 88–96 for an overview of repressive alternative media).
2. The striking resemblance to AJE's mission, outlined in the introduction, is worth noting, although a more comprehensive, comparative study of the two will not be pursued further.
3. The IPS has been noted as an early example of a news contra-flow and as a facilitator of South-South news flows (Boyd-Barrett & Thussu 1992: 31, 137–43). The editorial agenda of the IPS includes promoting information flows among developing nations, distributing southern news to northern clients, and promoting equal gender representation and a balanced representation of ethnic diversity and geographical distribution (Rauch 2003: 89). About two-thirds of IPS reports pertain to the developing world (Giffard & van Horn 1992), and IPS has gained credibility for its coverage of Third World issues, particularly in Latin America. In contrast to the major mainstream news agencies, IPS emphasizes southern nations' cooperation, achievement and goals (Rauch 2003: 98).
4. Atton (2002a: 51) argued that, given their limited financial resources, most alternative media stress an emphatically anticommercial 'black or green' economic agenda rather than direct competition with the mainstream media, whether in terms of markets or of production economics.
5. Former Managing Director, Tony Burman, who initiated the renewal project in October 2008, gave a copy of the report to the author in 2009 for research purposes. The report (completed in March 2009) is written by seven working groups of channel employees and includes internal briefings from the management (AJN 2009b).
6. "Clarifying the Editorial Vision of Al Jazeera English," written by Ian Alexander, for Managing Director Tony Burman, March 2009 (AJN 2009b). Mr. Burman reconfirmed the main points in the document in an interview with the author in Doha (15 March 2009). The document targets AJE staff and is thus an internal, institutional document (Syvertsen 2004) intended to legitimize the internal institutionalization processes chaired and initiated by the managing director himself.
7. The Al Jazeera Network is in the process of integrating its bureaus closer. How this will affect the number of bureaus and bureau structure within the different channels remains to be seen, but the total network number of bureaus is expected to grow significantly in the coming years with the planned launch of 'Al Jazeera America' (AJN 2013a).
8. Allen and Hamilton (2010) find that foreign news have always been limited (10 percent of total news coverage) and argue that the decline of foreign news is overstated, as foreign news is relatively more important vs. the total coverage.

9. Discussing the changing role of foreign correspondents in humanitarian crisis, Cooper (2011) finds that the mainstream media are challenged by increasingly mediatized, camera-ready NGOs and people on the ground (through user-generated content [UCG] on social media and traditional news media).

10. They distinguish between: traditional foreign correspondent, parachute journalist, foreign-foreign correspondent (hired foreign staff), local foreign correspondent (covering foreign news from home), foreign local correspondent (non-Americans working for foreign news organizations), in-house foreign correspondent, premium service foreign correspondent (information to subscribers) and amateur correspondents (unaffiliated and often untrained de facto journalists reporting on international news) (ibid.).

11. The study focused exclusively on AJA and the central network management. AJE had only just been launched when the book went into print and was not studied empirically.

12. It should be noted, however, that AJE has not always followed this strategy of local correspondents in practice. One example is the recruitment of two high-profile British correspondents, Jacky Rowland (from the BBC) and David Chater (ITN/Sky News) to fill key positions in the channel's strategically important Jerusalem bureau (AJN 2009a).

13. It should be noted that Ndege herself had worked extensively for the BBC before joining AJE in 2007.

14. It should be noted that both reporters had established journalistic careers before joining AJE: Odeh from the Palestine Broadcasting Corporation and Ramattan News Agency, and Mutasa from the South African Broadcasting Corporation (SABC), CNN, Television New Zealand (TVNZ), Associated Press Television News (APTN) and the Star Sports Network. Mutasa was nominated for the Royal Television Society Journalism Awards' (2008) *RTS Young Journalist of the Year* for her reporting for AJE, but lost to her colleague Hamish MacDonald.

15. Issues concerning logistical, technical and organizational challenges to integration are not analyzed here, although they are key obstacles for improved coordination and network efficiency (AJN 2009b).

NOTES TO CHAPTER 4

1. Due to the vast number of academic publications on media flows in the last 90 years (Gerber et al. 1993, Tsang et al. 1988, Wilke 1987), this review will have to highlight the main contributions and does not claim to be exhaustive.

2. Key works in this tradition are Daniel Lerner's *The Passing of Traditional Society: Modernizing the Middle East* (1958), Everett M. Rogers *Diffusion of Innovations* (1962) and Wilbur Schramm's *Mass Media and National Development* (1964) (see Mody & Lee 2002 for a comprehensive discussion).

3. Mustapha Masmoudi was Information Minister of Tunisia and a member of the MacBride Commission. He defined the global information imbalances as: 1) a flagrant quantitative imbalance between North and South; 2) an inequality in information resources; 3) a de facto hegemony and a will to dominate; 4) a lack of information on developing countries; 5) survival of the colonial era; 6) an alienating influence in the economic, social and

cultural spheres and 7) messages ill-suited to the areas in which they are disseminated (Masmoudi 1979: 172–175).

4. In their evaluation of these efforts, Boyd-Barrett & Thussu (1992) concluded that the news exchange mechanisms do not appear to have had any significant impact on the structures over the past two decades (ibid.: 141).

5. Like Galtung and Ruge, many of the early contributions to news flow determinants research present hypotheses about factors that facilitate or obstruct news flows between nations without testing these empirically (e.g., Hester 1973, Östgaard 1965).

6. In cultural studies, the term 'flow' was proposed to describe the distinctive nature of television in Williams's (1974: 78–118) classic study of the television medium. Emphasizing the continuity in broadcasting, he found that the *planned flow* of sequences is "the defining characteristic of broadcasting, both as a technology and as a cultural form" (ibid. 86). For a comprehensive overview and critique of the cultural studies tradition, which attempts to capture and explain the unique quality of television textuality, see White (2003).

7. Interestingly, the project problematizes the operationalization of the categories and illustrates how "many domestic programmes contain foreign inserts" (ibid. 11). In national newscasts, to take one example, the pictures may often be of foreign origin. Sports programming, coproductions, entertainment shows and adaptations of imported program concepts posed further problems to the categorization.

8. According to Tunstall's (2008: 250) "pecking order" in global television, big media nations such as India, China and Japan export to smaller neighboring countries, and the larger Arab players such as Egypt and Saudi Arabia import some from the US and Europe—but do more exporting to smaller and poorer Arab nations. Africa has its own pecking order, depending on imports from the US and Europe, while the two largest African media nations, Nigeria and South Africa, export to other sub-Saharan countries.

9. One illustrative example is the British news 'contra-flow' in the US after 9/11, where British elite media such as the BBC and *The Guardian* have gained popularity among American audiences as 'alternative' news sources (Wall & Bicket 2008, Bicket & Wall 2009).

10. After Al Jazeera launched its English-language website in 2003, Samual-Azran (2010) found that Al Jazeera news on civilian suffering was picked up by alternative news outlets, fighting the 'bias' of mainstream media and adopting Al Jazeera as an ally and contributor to an emerging counter-public (ibid: 99–100).

11. In her innovative and comprehensive study, Clausen (2003, 2004) documented how 'domestication processes' in international news production occur at different levels in the production process: at the global level, media institutions serve as mediators between the international and the national through the dissemination of international information into their economic political environment. At the national level, competing news institutions provide and process information according to statutory rules and political systems in their country. At the organizational level, information is negotiated in accordance with house norms and particular production strategies in each media institution; and at the professional level, individual producers, anchors and correspondents negotiate and 'bring information home' before it is communicated to the public at large (ibid. 2003: 83).

12. Taken together, these three studies have mapped Al Jazeera English newscasts aired around the clock from 09.00 to 00.00 GMT, from November 2006 to May 2008.

13. The Global South was not covered evenly, and quantitative mappings find that Africa (including North Africa) was among the least covered regions on AJE (10 percent of the stories broadcast in Figenschou 2010a, 6 percent in Painter 2008: 30 and 8.5 percent in Uysal 2011: 11. See also Arsenault 2012: 83). More comprehensive analysis of the channel's coverage of South-Saharan Africa find that AJE aimed to have a broader representation on the ground, more diverse coverage and African, everyday experiences and voices incorporated in the reporting; but although AJE is "more expansive than its competitors, [it] does not measure up to its rhetoric" (Arsenault 2012: 85).

14. The political news from the South (37 percent of the total coverage) highlights internal political crisis (13 percent of total coverage), politics between nations/diplomacy (11 percent), election coverage (8 percent) and other political processes, such as legislation (5 percent). The political news relating to North America and Europe (37 percent of total coverage) was on diplomacy (14 percent), elections (12 percent), other political processes (6 percent) and internal political crisis (5 percent).

15. The third largest news topic in the sample, legal affairs (13 percent of all news items), is also unevenly distributed geographically. From the global North, legal affairs were the main topic in 21 percent of the news items, compared to 9 percent of the coverage out of the South. Further, there are more economic news items originating in the North than in the South, and more news items about aid (development aid and disaster relief) from the South than in the North, although all these topics receive limited coverage.

16. It should be mentioned here that AJE offered a number of current affairs programs on these topics in its first years on air, such as *Everywoman* (gender and social issues), *The Pulse* (health issues), *People & Power* (political, economic and social issues from a grass-roots perspective), *24* (travel and culture), *The Fabulous Picture Show* (movies and visual culture) and *The Listening Post* (media).

17. Concurring with these analyses of the AJE broadcasts, Loomis' (2009: 156) study of the AJE website finds that the Middle East was the most covered region and further that the region was covered with the most emotionally charged language.

NOTES TO CHAPTER 5

1. See, among others, Alterman (1998), El-Nawawy & Iskandar (2002), Ghareeb (2000) for discussion.

2. The 'neo-Gramscian' perspective on international relations initiated by Cox (1993) has reinterpreted Gramsci and transposed his concept of hegemony from the national to the international level.

3. See Manning (2001: 174–201) for an in-depth analysis of these strategies, and Benford and Snow (2000) for a comprehensive overview of the framing processes of social movements.

4. Revising his insider-outsider-distinction Grant (2004) found that the formal political establishment remains strong, but that the traditional political structures are increasingly challenged and bypassed by loosely coordinated pressure groups and social movements.

5. Defined as commanding "the field in all subsequent treatment and set[ting] the terms of reference within which much [of] all further coverage or debate takes place. Arguments *against* a primary interpretation are forced to insert themselves to *its* definition of 'what is at issue'—they must begin from this framework of interpretation as their starting-point" (Hall et al. 1978: 59).

6. In his analysis of conservative American politics in the 1980s, Kellner (1990: 139) found that the lack of substantial television criticism of the Republican Reagan government was partly due to the lack of a significant and vocal political opposition.

7. The indexing hypothesis has been substantiated by broad empirical data: empirically testing the hypothesis on the media coverage of eight US military interventions in the post-Vietnam era, Mermin (1999) documented the ways in which the spectrum of debate in Washington determined the debate in the news and the ways in which critical viewpoints were marginalized. Moreover, Entman and Page's (1994) analysis of the indexing of the 1990 US Iraq war debate, found that even in a time of unusually vocal and lengthy elite dissent, support for military intervention was systematically prioritized over more critical elite voices. Extending the indexing thesis to event-driven satellite news, Livingston and Bennett (2003) demonstrated the ways in which officials work to 'reinstitutionalize' rolling news stories (see Thune 2009: 46 for an extensive overview of international indexing studies).

8. Wojcieszak (2007) questioned the extent to which traditional framing research is generalizable to Al Jazeera and other transnational channels. She argued that framing analysis has presupposed the influence of domestic elites on the framing process, conceived the media as hegemonic, been idiosyncratic to the American media and power arrangements, and not taken new media into account. Although her problematization of the applicability of national theories was appropriate, she underestimated the key role of Arab elites in Arab satellite broadcasting, as demonstrated in chapters 1 and 2, this volume.

9. The program selected for analysis, the *NewsHour* at 18.00 GMT, is the flagship news program for the channel, linking up the Doha headquarters with the London and the Washington broadcasting centers. Sixty newscasts are included in the study and were recorded over two periods of two months (October–December 2007 and May–July 2008) (see Figenschou 2010a for further details).

NOTES TO CHAPTER 6

1. Hundreds of those killed were unarmed civilians, including some 300 children (Amnesty International 2009). Palestinian casualty numbers and how to categorize victims as combatants, noncombatants and minors was highly disputed, ranging from almost 1,200 from Israeli authorities to around 1,440 by the Palestinians (see, among others, Fahmy & Neumann 2012:16 for an overview of various casualty data).

2. The staff briefing from Managing Director Tony Burman was e-mailed to the editorial staff on 2 January 2009, one day before Israel started the ground offensive. Briefings and e-mails were collected in the AJE renewal report (AJN 2009b; see also Chapter 3, this volume).

3. See Reporters Without Borders' report *Gaza/Israel. Operation 'Cast Lead': News Control as Military Objective* (2009) for discussion.

4. See: *http://www.mfa.gov.il/GazaFacts/*.

5. Media statements by Hamas officials and interviews with Hamas representatives referred to in the *Ending the War in Gaza* (2009) report by the International Crisis Group were primary sources to construct the Gaza frame (International Crisis Group 2009). Secondly, key Hamas documents, such as the Hamas Charter (1988) and the Change and Reform List (the Hamas election manifesto for the legislative elections 2006), op-ed articles by the Hamas leadership in international newspapers and recent academic analyses of the movement (found in Schanzer 2008, Tamimi 2007) have been used as background material.

6. *Haaretz* had permanent correspondents living in the West Bank and systematically reported Palestinian views (Korn 2004, 2007, Rinnawi 2007, Wolfsfeld 2003), from time to time giving the personal details of the Palestinian victims and reporting the cumulative number of Palestinian casualties (Korn 2007: 252–3). Korn (2007: 258) finds that although *Haaretz* emphasizes Palestinian suffering more than the other Israeli newspapers, it still underplays the dimensions of Palestinian victimization as these articles are framed as 'the Palestinian perspective,' placed in the back and never appeared as 'competitive information' that challenged or undermined the official version of events, but rather as 'additional' information' (Korn 2004: 220).

7. See Deprez and Raeymaeckers (2011) for an informative overview and systematization of the extant literature on 'international' studies of the conflict, but note that they include studies of Israeli media while leaving out studies of the Arab and Palestinian media.

8. The editorial management and senior editorial staff from the most important Arab news and current channels, Al Jazeera Channel, Al Arabiya Channel and Abu Dhabi TV, were interviewed in Qatar, Dubai and Abu Dhabi in February 2005 and in Ramallah (the occupied West Bank) in May 2005.

9. The weekdays selected for analyses were 7, 8, 9, 13, 14, 15 and 16 January 2009. Weekends were excluded to have as directly comparable newscasts as possible, as CNN and BBC World diverged from their regular schedule during weekends. The newscasts were recorded from Europe by the author, and it is therefore the localized European version of the global newscasters that is analyzed (see the localization debates in the Introduction to this volume).

10. There are ongoing methodological debates over which intercoder reliability measurements are the most precise and comprehensive in content analysis studies, although *Krippendorffs alpha* (Hayes & Krippendorff 2007) has largely been established as the most suitable model in recent years. The variables included in this analysis have a Krippendorffs alpha coefficients ranging from 0.907 to 0.708, and are all within the acceptable level of agreement (in general higher than 0.8, although higher than 0.667 is acceptable in more tentative arguments). Variables that did not reach this level were omitted from the analysis. Contact the author for a complete overview of the reliability scores.

11. Ayish (2010) does not discuss how and by which criteria these news items were selected, and it is therefore impossible to know to what extent the sample analyzed is representative of AJA's coverage of the war. His findings are still included here as they illustrate how the channel covered the story.

12. Defined as media attention relative to casualty data (see Bahador 2011 and Hawkins 2011 for details).

13. Critics argue that live coverage has become an empty routine in 24/7 rolling news. The news crews themselves, the audience and analysts are critical towards "going live for the sake of going live" (see, among others, Cushion 2010, Lewis 2010, Paterson 2010, and Tuggle et al. 2010). It must be noted, however, that this criticism is primarily directed at commercial national or local Anglo-American networks that prioritize liveness and visual drama over relevance, importance and analysis, and not on the international news channel's coverage of international conflicts and wars.

14. Ayish (2010) employed three broad issue categories (political, humanitarian, military) compared to the eight topic categories used in this book, and this may explain why the three main topics seems to be employed more frequently on AJA than its English-language competitors. For instance, Ayish includes demonstrations against the war in his politics category while these news items are coded as peace protests in this analysis. The relative importance accorded to the three topics within each channel remains important, notwithstanding.

15. AJE sent interviews with or statements by 10 officials (three Hamas officials, three Fatah officials and four Israeli officials), the BBC aired eight officials (four Israeli, one Hamas and three Fatah), and CNN interviewed/broadcasted statements from five officials—all of them Israeli. AJE interviewed Ahmed Youssef, political advisor to Ismail Haniya (Hamas) (1 July 2009); Daniel Taub, senior legal advisor to the Israeli Government (7 January 2009); Riyad Mansour, Palestinian envoy to the UN (13 January 2009) and aired statements from Rafic Al Husseini, Chief of Staff, President Mahmoud Abbas (Fatah) (8 January 2009); Mark Regev, Israeli government spokesman (9 January 2009); Yigal Palmer, spokesman Israeli Foreign Ministry (9 January 2009); Mahmoud Abbas, Palestinian President in a live press conference (14 January 2009); Tzipi Livni, the Israeli Foreign Minister (15 January 2009) and Khaled Meshal, a Hamas political leader (15 January 2009). The BBC interviewed Isaac Herzog, the Israeli welfare minister (7 January 2009); Sabri Saidam, advisor to the Palestinian President (7 January 2009/9 January 2009); David Siegel, the Israel Foreign Ministry spokesman (9 January 2009); Mark Regev, the Israeli Government Spokesman (14 January 2009); Yigal Palmor, the spokesman for the Israeli Foreign Ministry (15 January 2009); Manuel Hassassian, a Palestinian representative, UK (15 January 2009) and aired statements from Taha Nounou, a Hamas spokesman (8 January 2009) and Mark Regev, the Israeli government spokesman (9 January 2009). CNN interviewed Shimon Peres, the Israeli President (7 January 2009); Mark Regev, the Israeli government spokesman (9 January 2009/15 January 2009) and aired statements by Maj. Avital Leibovitch, IDF (8 January 2009) and Shimon Peres, the Israeli President, in a live press conference with the UN Secretary General (15 January 2009).

NOTES TO CHAPTER 7

1. It is imperative to note that the influence of visual images is rarely systematically tested empirically. One notable exception is Domke et al.'s (2002) experimental study, which concludes that images most often interact with the viewers' existing understandings of the world.
2. For a more fine-grained analysis of images of death in still photographs, Hanusch (2012) has developed a scale of graphicness in which all categories depict increasing levels of visibility of death in news images, from implied death to contorted death (see Hanusch 2012: 662 for details). His model is not directly adaptable for television images.
3. Most of the iconic images from the war that are perceived to be the 'defining images of the Vietnam war' exposing civilian suffering and death, did in fact not reach the US public because the images were omitted by the major media at the time (Griffin 2010: 13–20), only to be made available years later when the context was changed (Griffin 2010, Wells 2007).
4. Researchers find that the major US news media did not challenge the US Administration's claim that Abu Ghraib was an isolated case of dreadful abuse perpetrated by a few low-level soldiers, and thus largely muted claims that the photos documented deliberate torture of suspected terrorists (Bennett et al. 2006, Griffin 2010, Rowling et al. 2011). Bennett et al. (2006: 482) conclude: "The photos may have driven the story, but the White House communication staff ultimately wrote the captions."
5. This story has previously been analyzed in an article published in *The International Journal of Communication* (see Figenschou 2011 where it was compared with a story from 2008 the Sichuan [China] earthquake.
6. This study was conducted before the 2006 launch of AJE and is not representative of the current English-language Aljazeera.com news site.

NOTE TO CHAPTER 8

1. Khanfar's resignation has led to extensive speculation and conspiracy theories, particularly since Khanfar was directly linked to accusations that the Al Jazeera Network had served as a foreign policy tool for Qatar under his leadership in numerous leaked US diplomatic cables (see Chatriwala 2011 for an analysis of what the 30 WikiLeaks cables on Al Jazeera reveals about the network).

References

LITERATURE

Aday, S., H. Farrell, M. Lynch, J. Sides & D. Freelon (2012) New media and conflict after the Arab spring, Peaceworks 80, July 2012, Washington: United States Institute of Peace.

Allen, C.J. & J.M. Hamilton (2010) "Normalcy and foreign news," *Journalism Studies* 11(5): 634–649.

Al-Najjar, A. (2009) "How Arab is Al-Jazeera English? Comparative study of Al-Jazeera Arabic and Al-Jazeera English news channels," Global Media Journal.

Alterman, J.B. (1998) "*New media, new politics? From satellite television to the internet in the Arab world,*" Policy Paper No. 48, The Washington Institute for Near East Policy.

——— (2002) "The effects of satellite television on Arab domestic politics," *Transnational Broadcasting Studies,* No. 9, Fall/Winter 2002.

——— (2011) "The revolution will not be tweeted," *The Washington Quarterly* 34(4): 103–116.

Altheide, D.L. (1984) "Media hegemony: a failure of perspective," *Public Opinion Quarterly* 48: 476–490.

Amara, M. (2006) "A 'modernization' project from above? Asian Games—Qatar 2006," *Sport in Society* 8(3): 495–514.

Amin, H. (1996) "Egypt and the Arab world in the satellite age," pp: 101–125, in Sinclair, J., E. Jacka & S. Cunningham (eds) *New patterns in global television: peripheral vision,* Oxford University Press.

Amin, H. Y. (2002) "Transnational broadcast services and their impact on the peace process in the Middle East," *Transnational Broadcasting Studies,* No. 9, Fall/Winter 2002.

Amin, H. (2012) "The nature of the channel's global audience," pp: 29–40, in Seib, P. (ed) *Al Jazeera English: global news in a changing world,* New York: Palgrave Macmillan.

Amnesty International (2009) *Operation 'Cast Lead': 22 days of death and destruction,* London: Amnesty International Publishing.

Arafa, M.M. (1994) "Qatar," in Kamalipour, Y.R. & H. Mowlana (eds) *Mass media in the Middle East. A comprehensive handbook,* Westport, Connecticut & London: Greenwood Publishing Group.

Archetti, C. (2012) "Which future for foreign correspondence?" *Journalism Studies* 13(5–6): 847–856.

Arsenault, A. (2012) "Covering and reaching Africa," pp.79–96, in Seib, P. (ed) *Al Jazeera English: Global news in a changing world,* New York: Palgrave Macmillan

Artz, L. (2003) "Globalization, media hegemony, and social class," pp: 3–32, in Artz, L. & Y.R. Kamalipour (eds) (2003) *The globalization of corporate media hegemony,* State University of New York Press.

Artz, L. & Y. R. Kamalipour (eds) (2003) *The globalization of corporate media hegemony*, State University of New York Press.

Atton, C. (2002a) *Alternative media*, Los Angeles, London, New Delhi & Singapore: SAGE Publications.

—— (2002b) "News cultures and new social movements: radical journalism and the mainstream media," *Journalism Studies* 3(4): 491–505.

—— (2009) "Alternative and citizen media," pp: 265–278, in Wahl-Jorgensen, K. & T. Hanitzsch (eds) *The handbook of journalism studies*, New York and London: Routledge.

Atton, C. & E. Wickenden (2005) "Sourcing routines and representation in alternative journalism: a case study approach," *Journalism Studies* 6(3): 347–359.

Ayish, M. I. (2002) "Political communication on Arab world television: evolving patterns," *Political Communication* 19: 137–154.

—— (2005) "Media brinkmanship in the Arab world: Al Jazeera's *The opposite direction* as a fighting arena," pp: 106–126, in Zayani, M. (ed) *The Al Jazeera phenomenon: critical perspectives on new Arab media*, Boulder: Paradigm Publishers.

—— (2010) "Morality vs. politics in the public sphere: how the Al Jazeera satellite channel humanized a bloody political conflict in Gaza," pp: 221–242, in Cushion, S. & J. Lewis (eds) *The rise of 24-hour news television: global perspectives*, New York: Peter Lang.

Baabood, A. (2008) "Sport and identity in the Gulf," pp: 97–120, in Alsharekh, A. & R. Springborg (eds) *Popular culture and political identity in the Arab Gulf states*, London: SAQI/London Middle East Institute, SOAS.

Bahador, B. (2007) *The CNN effect in action: how the news media pushed the west toward war in Kosovo*, New York: Palgrave MacMillan.

—— (2011) "Did the global war on terror end the CNN effect?" *Media, War & Conflict* 4(1): 37–54.

Bahry, L. Y. (2001) "The new Arab media phenomenon: Qatar's Al-Jazeera," *Middle East Policy* VIII (2): 88–99.

Bahry, L. Y. & P. Marr (2005) "Qatari women: a new generation of leaders?" *Middle East Policy* 12(2): 104–119.

Bailey, O. G., B. Cammaerts & N. Carpentier (2008) *Understanding alternative media*, Maidenhead: Open University Press.

Barakat, S. (2012) "*The Qatari spring: Qatar's emerging role in peacemaking*," Research paper, Kuwait Programme on Development, Governance and Globalisation in the Gulf States, LSE.

Barkho, L. (2008a) *Strategies of power in multilingual global broadcasters: how the BBC, CNN and Al Jazeera shape their Middle East news discourse*, Dissertation, Jönköping International Business School.

—— (2008b) "The BBC's discursive strategy and practices vis-à-vis the Palestinian-Israeli conflict," *Journalism Studies* 9(2): 278–294.

Bell, M. (1998): "The truth is our currency," *Harvard International Journal Press/Politics* 3(1): 102–109.

Benford, R. D. & D. A. Snow (2000) "Framing processes and social movements," *Annual Review of Sociology* 26: 611–639.

Bennett, W. L. (1990) "Toward a theory of press-state relations in the United States," *Journal of Communication* 40(2): 103–125.

Bennett, L. W., R. G. Lawrence & S. Livingston (2006) "None dare call it torture: indexing and the limits of press independence in the Abu Ghraib scandal," *Journal of Communication* 56: 467–485.

Berkowitz, D. & J. V. TerKeurst (1999) "Community as interpretive community: rethinking the journalist-source relationship," *Journal of Communication* 49(3): 125–136.

Berrebi, C., F. Martorell & J. C. Tanner (2009) "Qatar's labor markets at a crucial crossroad," *The Middle East Journal* 63(3): 421–442.

Bicket, D. & M. Wall (2009) "BBC News in the United States: a 'super-alternative' news medium emerges," *Media, Culture & Society* 31(3): 365–384.

Bielby, D. D. & C. L. Harrington (2008) *Global TV: exporting television and culture in the world market,* New York and London: New York University Press.

Biltereyst, D. & P. Meers (2000) "The telenovela debate and the contra-flow argument: a reappraisal," *Media, Culture & Society* 22(4): 393–413.

Bishara, A. (2006) "Local hands, international news: Palestinian journalists and the international media," *Ethnography* 7(1): 19–46.

Blanchard, C. M (2008) "*Qatar: background and U.S. relations,*"CRS Report for Congress, Congressional Research Service.

Blondheim, M. & L. Shifman (2009) "What officials say, what media show, and what publics get: Gaza, January 2009," *The Communication Review* 12(3): 205–214.

Boltanski, L. (1999) *Distant suffering: morality, media and politics,* Cambridge University Press.

Boudana, S. (2010) "On the values guiding the French practice of journalism: interviews with thirteen war correspondents," *Journalism* 11(3): 293–311.

Boyd-Barrett, J. O. (1977) "Media imperialism: towards an international framework for an analysis of media systems," pp: 116–35, in Curran, J., M. Gurevitch & J. Woollacott (eds) *Mass communication and society,* London: Edward Arnold.

Boyd-Barrett, O. (1998) "Media imperialism reformulated," pp: 157–176, in Thussu, D. K. (ed) *Electronic empires: global media and local resistance,* London: Arnold.

––––––– (2002) "Global communication orders," pp: 325–342, in W. B. Gudykunst & B. Mody (eds) *Handbook of international and intercultural communication,* Thousand Oaks, London & New Delhi: SAGE Publications.

Boyd-Barrett, C. & Boyd-Barrett O. (2010) "24/7 news as counter-hegemonic soft power in Latin America," pp: 199–220, in Cushion, S. & J. Lewis (eds) *The rise of 24-hour news television: global perspectives,* New York: Peter Lang.

Boyd-Barrett, O. & D. K. Thussu (1992) *Contra-flow in global news. International and regional news exchange mechanisms,* Academia research monograph 8, UNESCO, London, Paris, & Rome: John Libbey.

Booth, R. (2010) "WikiLeaks cables claim al-Jazeera changed coverage to suit Qatari foreign policy." *The Guardian,* December 5. (Consulted May 2013: hhttp://www.guardian.co.uk/world/2010/dec/05/wikileaks-cables-al-jazeera-qatari-foreign-policy).

Braman, S. (2002) "A pandemonic age: the future of international communication and research," pp: 399–413, in Gudykunst, W. B. & B. Mody (eds) *Handbook of international and intercultural communication,* Thousand Oaks, London & New Delhi: SAGE Publications.

Brandchannel.com (2004) "Brand Ranking by Impact 2004," Reader's Choice 2004, (Consulted May 2013: http://www.brandchannel.com/start1.asp?fa_id=248).

Brantner, C., K. Lobinger & I. Wetzstein (2011) "Effects of visual framing on emotional responses and evaluations of news stories about the Gaza conflict 2009," *Journalism & Mass Communication Quarterly* 88(3): 523–540.

Bunce, M. (2011) *The new foreign correspondent at work: local-national "stringers" and the global news coverage of conflict in Darfur,* Report, Reuters Institute for the Study of Journalism, University of Oxford.

Burch, S. (2007) "Telesur and the new agenda for Latin American integration," *Global Media and Communication* 3(2): 227–232.

Carlsson, U. (2005) "From NWICO to global governance of the information society," pp: 193–214, in Hemer, O. & T. Tufte (eds) *Media & global change: rethinking communication for development,* NORDICOM.

Carragee, K. M. & W. Roefs (2006) "The neglect of power in recent framing research," *Journal of Communication* 54(2): 214–233.

Chalaby, J. K. (2003) "Television for a new global order: transnational television networks and the formation of global systems," *Gazette: the International Journal for Communication Studies* 65(6): 457–72.

——— (2005a) "Towards an understanding of media transnationalism," pp: 1–13, in Chalaby, J. K. (ed) *Transnational television worldwide: towards a new media order*, London and New York: I. B. Taurus.

——— (2005b) "The quiet invention of a new medium: twenty years of transnational television in Europe," pp: 43–65, in Chalaby, J. K. (ed) *Transnational television worldwide: towards a new media order*, London and New York: I. B. Taurus.

——— (2006) "American cultural primacy in a new media order: a European perspective," *International Communication Gazette* 68(1): 33–51.

Chang, W. H., P. J. Shoemaker & N. Brendinger (1987) "Determinants in international news coverage in the US media," *Communication research* 14(84): 396–414.

Chatriwala, O. (2011) "What WikiLeaks tells us about Al Jazeera," *Foreign Policy,* September 19, 2011.

Chouliaraki, L. (2006) *The spectatorship of suffering,* London, Thousand Oaks & New Delhi: SAGE Publications.

Christensen, C. (2008) "Uploading dissonance: *YouTube* and the US occupation of Iraq," *Media, War & Conflict* 1(2): 155–175.

Clausen, L. (2003) *Global news production,* Copenhagen Business School Press: Copenhagen.

——— (2004) "Localizing the global: 'domestication' processes in international news production," *Media Culture Society* 26(1): 25–44.

Cohen, S. (2001) *States of denial: knowing about atrocities and suffering,* Cambridge: Polity.

Colombo, S. (2012) "The GCC and the Arab spring: a tale of double standards," *The International Spectator: Italian Journal of International Affairs* 47(4): 110–126.

Cook, T. E. (1998). *Governing with the news: the news media as a political institution,* Chicago, IL: University of Chicago Press.

Cooper, G. (2011) *"From their own correspondent? New media and the changes in disaster coverage: lessons to be learnt,"* Report, Reuters Institute for the Study of Journalism, University of Oxford.

Cottle, S. (2008) "Reporting demonstrations: the changing media politics of dissent," *Media, Culture & Society* 30(6): 853–872.

——— (2009) *Global crisis reporting,* Maidenhead: Open University Press.

——— (2011) "Cell phones, camels and global call for democracy," pp: 196–210, in J. Mair & R. L. Keeble (eds) *Mirage in the desert? Reporting the 'Arab Spring,'* Suffolk: Abramis Academic Publishing.

Cottle, S. & Rai, M. (2008) "Global 24/7 news providers: emissaries of global dominance or global public sphere?" *Global Media and Communication* 4(2): 157–181.

Cox, R. W (1993) "Gramsci, hegemony and international relations: an essay in method," pp: 49–66, in Gill, S. (ed) *Gramsci, historical materialism and international relations,* Cambridge: Cambridge University Press.

Coyer, K. (2005) "If it leads it bleeds: the participatory newsmaking of the independent media centre," pp: 165–178, in Jong, M., M. Shaw & N. Stammers (eds) *Global activism: global media,* London: Pluto Press.

Curran, J. (2002) *Media and power,* London & New York: Routledge.

Curran, J. & Park, M. (eds) (2000) *De-westernizing media studies,* London and New York: Routledge.

Curtin, M. (2003) "Media capital: towards the study of spatial flows," *International Journal of Cultural Studies* 6(2): 202–228.

Cushion, S. (2010) "Three phases of 24-hour news television," pp: 15–30, in S. Cushion & J. Lewis (eds) *The rise of 24-hour news television: global perspectives,* New York: Peter Lang.

Dajani, M. (2003) "Press reporting during the second intifada: Palestinian coverage of Jenin," *Palestine-Israel Journal of Politics, Economics and Culture* 10(2).

Da Lage, O. (2005) "The politics of Al Jazeera or the politics of Doha," pp: 49–65, in Zayani, M. (ed) *The Al Jazeera phenomenon: critical perspectives on new Arab media*, Boulder: Paradigm Publishers.

Daraghmeh, M. (2003) "Effects of the conflict on the Palestinian media," *Palestine-Israel Journal of Politics, Economics and Culture* 10(2).

Dargin, J. (2007) "Qatar's natural gas: the foreign-policy driver," *Middle East policy* 14(3): 136–142.

Davidson, C.M. (2008) *Dubai: the vulnerability of success*, New York: Columbia University Press.

—— (2009) *Abu Dhabi: oil and beyond*, London: Hurst & Company.

—— (2012) *After the sheikhs*, London: Hurst & Company.

Deprez, A. & K. Raeymaeckers (2010) "Bias in the news? Representation of Palestinians and Israelis in the coverage of the first and second intifada," *International Communication Gazette* 72(1): 91–109.

—— (2011) "Bottlenecks in the coverage of the Israeli-Palestinian conflict: the coverage of the first and second intifada in the Flemish press," *Media, War & Conflict* 4(2): 185–202.

Doberning, K., K. Lobinger & I. Wetzstein (2010) "Covering conflict: differences in visual and verbal news coverage of the Gaza crisis 2009 in four weekly news media," *Journal of Visual Literacy* 29(1): 88–105.

Domke, D., D. Perlmutter & M. Spratt (2002) "The primes of our times?: An examination of the 'power' of visual images", *Journalism* 3(2): 131–159.

Dor, D. (2003) "All the news that fits: the Israeli media and the second intifada," *Palestine-Israel Journal of Politics, Economics and Culture* 10(2).

Downing, J.D.H. (2001) *Radical media: rebellious communication and social movements*, Thousand Oaks, London & New Delhi: Sage Publications.

Dresch, P. (2005) "Introduction: societies, identities and global issues," pp: 1–33, in Dresch, P. & J. Piscatori (eds) *Monarchies and nations: globalisation and identity in the Arab states of the Gulf*, London and New York: I.B. Taurus.

Dunsky, M. (2008) *Pens and swords: how the American mainstream media report the Israeli-Palestinian conflict*, New York: Columbia University Press.

Eakin, H. (2011) "The strange power of Qatar." *The New York Review of Books*, October 27. (Consulted May 2013: http://www.nybooks.com/articles/archives/2011/oct/27/strange-power-qatar/?pagination=false).

Ehteshami, A. & S. Wright (2007) "Political change in the Arab oil monarchies: from liberalization to enfranchisement," *International Affairs* 83(5): 913–932.

El-Nawawy, M. & Iskandar, A. (2002) *Al-Jazeera: the story of the network that is rattling governments and redefining governments and redefining modern journalism*, Cambridge: Westview.

El-Nawawy, M. & L.A. Gher (2003) "Al Jazeera: bridging the east-west gap through public discourse and media diplomacy," *Transnational Broadcasting Studies* 10, Spring/Summer.

El-Nawawy, M. & S. Powers (2008) *Mediating conflict. Al-Jazeera English and the possibility of a conciliatory media*, Los Angeles: Figueroa Press.

—— (2010) "Al-Jazeera English: a conciliatory medium in a conflict-driven environment?" *Global Media and Communication* 6(1): 61–84.

El-Obeidi, I. (2003) "A Palestinian perspective on satellite television coverage of the Iraq war," *Transnational Broadcasting Studies*, 10, Spring/Summer.

El Tounsy, A. (2002) "Reflections on the Arab satellites, the Palestinian intifada, and the Israeli war," *Transnational Broadcasting Studies*, 8, Spring/Summer.

Enderlin, C. (2003) "Enemies of Israel: the foreign press and the second intifada," *Palestine-Israel Journal of Politics, Economics and Culture* 10(2).

Entman, R.M. (1993) "Framing: toward clarification of a fractured paradigm," *Journal of Communication* 43: 51–58.

—— (2004) *Projections of power: framing news, public opinion and U.S. foreign policy,* Chicago & London: University of Chicago Press.

—— (2008) "Theorizing mediated public diplomacy: the U.S. Case," *The International Journal of Press/Politics* 13(2): 87–102.

Entman, R.M. & B.I. Page (1994) "The news before the storm: the Iraq war debate and the limits of media independence," pp: 82–101, in Bennett, W.L. & D. L Paletz (eds) *Taken by storm: the media, public opinion, and U.S. foreign policy in the Gulf War,* Chicago & London: The University of Chicago Press.

Entman, R.M., J. Matthes & L. Pellicano (2009) "Nature, sources and effects of news framing," pp: 175–190, in Wahl-Jorgensen, K. & T. Hanitzsch (eds) *The handbook of journalism studies,* New York and London: Routledge.

Esser, F. (2008) "History of media effects," in Wolfgang Donsbach (ed) *The international encyclopedia of communication,* Blackwell Publishing (Consulted May 2013: http://www.communicationencyclopedia.com/subscriber/tocnode.html?id=g9781405131995_yr2013_chunk_g978140513199518_ss32–1).

Evans, M.R. (2002) "Hegemony and discourse: negotiating cultural relationships through media," *Journalism* 3(3): 309–329.

Fahmy, S. (2005a) "Emerging alternatives or traditional news gates: which news sources were used to picture the 9/11 attack and the Afghan war?" *Gazette* 67(5): 383–400.

—— (2005b) "Photojournalists' and photo editors' attitudes and perceptions: the visual coverage of 9/11 and the Afghan war," *Visual Communication Quarterly* 12(3–4): 146–163.

Fahmy, S. & R. Neumann (2012) "Shooting war or peace photographs? An examination of newswires' coverage of the conflict in Gaza (2008–2009)," *American Behavioral Scientist* 56(2): 1–26.

Fahmy, S. & T. J. Johnson (2007a) "Show the truth and let the audience decide: a web-based survey showing support among viewers of Al-Jazeera for use of graphic imagery", *Journal of Broadcasting & Electronic Media* 51(2): 245–264.

—— (2009) "How embedded journalists in Iraq viewed the arrest of Al-Jazeera reporter Taysir Alouni," *Media, War & Conflict* 2(1): 47–65.

Faldalen, J.I. & T.U. Figenschou (forthcoming) "Visual war: conflict and collision in the split screen on Al Jazeera English." (working title)

Fandy, M. (2000) "Information technology, trust, and social change in the Arab world," *Middle East Journal,* 54(3): 378–394.

—— (2007) *(Un)civil war of words: media and politics in the Arab world,* Westport, Connecticut & London: Praeger Security International.

Fialka, J.J. (1991): *Hotel warriors: covering the Gulf War,* Washington D.C.: The Woodrow Wilson Center Press.

Figenschou, T.U. (2005) *Courting, criticism, censorship and bombs: a study of the relationship between the Al Jazeera Channel and the US administration during the war in Iraq 2003,* Report, Oslo University College.

—— (2007) "*In the shadow of Iraq and Palestine: challenges and self-criticism in the Arab news room,*" Paper presented at the 18th Nordic Conference for Media and Communication Research (Helsinki, August 2007) and at Arab Satellite TV and Cultural Identity (international conference, American University of Sharjah), Sharjah, December 2007.

—— (2010a) "A voice for the voiceless? A quantitative content analysis of Al-Jazeera English's flagship news," *Global Media and Communication* 6(1): 85–107.

—— (2010b) "The South is talking back: Al Jazeera English as a strategic contra-flow,"PhD Thesis, Department of Media and Communication, Faculty of Humanities, University of Oslo. April 2010.

———— (2010c) "Young, female, Western researcher vs. senior, male, Al Jazeera officials: critical reflections on accessing and interviewing media elites in authoritarian societies," *Media, Culture & Society* 32(6): 961–978.

———— (2012) "Content: the messages of AJE's news" pp: 41–56, in Seib, P. (ed) *Al Jazeera English: global news in a changing world*, New York: Palgrave Macmillan.

Fisher, A. (2011) "The 'Arab spring,' social media and Al Jazeera," pp: 149–159, in Mair, J. & R.L. Keeble (eds) *Mirage in the desert? Reporting the 'Arab spring,'* Suffolk: Abramis Academic Publishing.

Flournoy, D.M. & R.K. Stewart (1997) *CNN: making news in the global market*, University of Luton Press.

Ford, T.V. & G. Gil (2001) "Radical internet use," pp: 201–234, in J.D.H. Downing (2001) *Radical media: rebellious communication and social movements*, Thousand Oaks, London & New Delhi: Sage Publications.

Fromhertz, A.J. (2012) *Quatar: a modern history*, Washington DC: Georgetown University Press.

Frosh, P. & A. Pinchevski (2009) "Introduction: why media witnessing? Why now?" pp. 1–22, in Frosh, P. & A. Pinchevski (eds) *Media witnessing*, Houndmills: Palgrave Macmillan.

Gaber, I., E. Seymour & L. Thomas (2009) "Review commentary: is the BBC biased? The corporation and the coverage of the 2006 Israeli–Hezbollah war," *Journalism* 10(2): 239–259.

Galtung, J. & M.H. Ruge (1965) "The structure of foreign news: the presentation of the Congo, Cuba and Cyprus crises in four Norwegian newspapers, *Journal of Peace Research* 2(1): 64–90.

Gamson, W. (1985) "Goffman's legacy to political sociology," *Theory and Society* 14: 605–621.

Gamson, W.A. & A. Modigliani (1987) "The changing culture of affirmative action," *Research in Political Sociology* 3: 137–177.

Gamson, W.A., D. Croteau, W. Hoyes & T. Sassen (1992) "Media images and the social construction of reality," *Annual Review of Sociology* 18: 373–393.

Gasher, M. & S. Gabriele (2004) "Increasing circulation? A comparative news-flow study of the Montreal Gazette's hard-copy and on-line editions," *Journalism Studies* 5(3): 311–323.

Gengler, J. (2012) "The political costs of Quatar's western orientation," *Middle East Policy* 13(4): 68–76.

Gerbner, G., H. Mowlana & K. Nordenstreng (1993) "Preface," pp: i-xii, in Gerbner et al. (eds) *The global media debate: its rise, fall and renewal*, Norwood, New Jersey: Ablex Publishing Corporation.

Ghareeb, E. (2000) "New media and the information revolution in the Arab world: an assessment," *Middle East Journal* 54(3): 395–418.

Giffard, C.A. (1998) "Alternative news agencies," pp: 191–201, in Boyd-Barrett, O. & T. Rantanen (eds) *The globalization of news*, London: SAGE.

Giffard, C.A. & van Horn, C. (1992) "Inter press service and the MacBride report: heading the call?" *Gazette* 50: 147–168.

Gilboa, E. (2005a) "The CNN effect: the search for a communication theory of international relations," *Political Communication* 22(1): 27–44.

———— (2005b) "Global television news and foreign policy: debating the CNN effect," *International Studies Perspectives* 6(3): 325–341.

———— (2008) "Searching for a theory of public diplomacy," *The ANNALS of the American Academy of Political and Social Science* 616: 55–77.

———— (2012) "Covering Gaza, 2008–2009: an Israeli view," pp: 143–162, in Seib, P. (ed) *Al Jazeera English: Global news in a changing world*, New York: Palgrave Macmillan.

Ginsberg, T. (2002) "Rediscovering the world," *American Journalism Review*, January/February. (Consulted May 2013: http://www.ajr.org/article.asp?id=2443).

Gitlin, T. (1980) *The whole world is watching: mass media in the making & unmaking of the new left,* Berkeley, California: University of California Press.

Golding, P. & P. Harris (1997) *Beyond cultural imperialism: globalization communication and the new international order,* London: Sage.

Graddol, D. (1994) "The visual accomplishment of factuality," pp: 136–157, in Graddol, D. & O. Boyd-Barrett (eds) *Media texts: authors and readers,* Clevedon: Multilingual Matters Limited.

Gramsci, A. (1971) *Selections from the prison notebooks of Antonio Gramsci,* edited and translated by Hoare, Q & G.N. Smith, London: Lawrence and Wishart.

Grant, W. (1989) *Pressure groups, politics and democracy in Britain,* New York, London, Toronto, Sydney & Tokyo: Philip Allan.

—— (2004) "Pressure politics: the changing world of pressure groups." *Parliamentary Affairs* 57(2): 408–19.

Griffin, M. (2004) "Picturing America's 'war on terrorism' in Afghanistan and Iraq: photographic motifs as news frames," *Journalism: Theory, Practice & Criticism* 5(4): 381–402.

—— (2010) "Media images of war," *Media, War & Conflict* 3(1): 7–41.

Habermas, J. (1989) *The structural transformation of the public sphere,* Cambridge: Polity Press.

Hafez, K. (2002) "Journalism ethics revisited: a comparison of ethics codes in Europe, North Africa, the Middle East, and Muslim Africa," *Political Communication* 19: 225–50.

—— (2006) "Arab satellite broadcasting: democracy without political parties?" *Transnational Broadcasting Studies* 15, Jan–June.

—— (2007) *The myth of media globalization,* Cambridge & Malden: Polity Press.

—— (2008) "Arab media: power and weakness," pp: 1–14, in Hafez, K. (ed) *Arab media: power and weakness,* New York & London: Continuum.

Hahn, O. & J. Lönnendonker (2009) "Transatlantic foreign reporting and foreign correspondents after 9/11," *The International Journal of Press/Politics* 14: 497–515.

Hall, S. (1977) "Culture, the media and the 'ideological effect,' " pp: 315–348, in Curran, J., M. Gurevitch & J. Woollacott (eds) *Mass communication and society,* London: Edward Arnold.

Hall, S., C. Critcher, T. Jefferson, J. Clarke & B. Roberts (1978) *Policing the crisis: mugging, the state and law and order,* London: Macmillan.

Hallin, D.C. (1989) *'Uncensored war': the media and Vietnam,* Berkley, Los Angeles & London: University of California Press.

Hallin, D C. & P. Mancini (2004) *Comparing media systems: three models of media and politics,* Cambridge University Press.

Ham, P. V. (2008) "Place branding: the state of the art," *The ANNALS of the American Academy of Political and Social Science* 616: 126–149.

Hamdy, N. & E.H. Gomaa (2012) "Framing the Egyptian uprising in Arabic language newspapers and social media," *Journal of Communication* 62(2012): 195–211.

Hamilton, J.M. & E. Jenner (2004) "Redefining foreign correspondence," *Journalism* 5(3): 301–21.

Hamilton, J.M., R.G. Lawrence & R. Cozma (2010) "The paradox of respectability: the limits of indexing and Harrison Salisbury's coverage of the Vietnam war," *The International Journal of Press/Politics* 15(1): 77–103.

Hamilton, J.T. (2010) "The (many) markets for international news: how news from abroad sells at home," *Journalism Studies* 11(5): 650–666.

Hammond, A. (2007) "Saudi Arabia's media empire: keeping the masses at home," *Arab Media & Society,* October 2007.

Hannerz, U. (2004) *Foreign news: exploring the world of foreign correspondents,* Chicago & London: University of Chicago Press.

—— (2007) "Foreign correspondents and the varieties of cosmopolitanism," *Journal of Ethnic and Migration Studies* 33(2): 299–311.

Hansen, A., S. Cottle, R. Negrine & C. Newbold (1998) *Mass communication research methods,* Hampshire & New York: Palgrave.

Hanusch, F. (2008) "Valuing those close to us: a comparison of German and Australian quality newspapers' reporting of death in foreign news," *Journalism Studies* 9(3): 341–356.

—— (2010) *Representing death in the news: journalism, media & mortality,* New York: Palgrave.

—— (2012) "The visibility of disaster deaths in news images: a comparison of newspapers from 15 countries," *The International Communication Gazette* 74(7): 655–672.

Hanusch, F. and Obijiofor, L. (2008) "Toward a more holistic analysis of international news flows," *Journal of Global Mass Communication* 1(1/2): 9–21.

Harcup, T. (2003) "The unspoken—said: the journalism of alternative media," *Journalism* 4(3): 356–376.

Harcup, T. & D. O'Neill (2001) "What is news? Galtung and Ruge revisited," *Journalism Studies* 2(2): 261–280.

Hawkins, V. (2011) "Media selectivity and the other side of the CNN effect: the consequences of not paying attention to conflict," *Media, War & Conflict* 4(1): 55–68.

Hayes, A. F. & K. Krippendorff (2007) "Answering the call for a standard reliability measure for coding data," *Communication Methods and Measures* 1: 77–89.

Herman, E. S. & N. Chomsky (1988) *Manufacturing consent: the political economy of the mass media,* London: Vintage Books.

Hester, A. (1973) "Theoretical considerations in predicting volume and direction of international information flow," *International Communication Gazette* 19(4): 239–247.

Hickey, N. (2002): "Access denied. The Pentagon's war reporting rules are the toughest ever," *Columbia Journalism Review,* January/February 2002.

Hjarvard, S. (1995) "TV news flow studies revisited," *The Electronic Journal of Communication* 5(2/3).

—— (2001) "News media and the globalization of the public sphere," pp: 17–40, in Hjarvard, S. (ed) *News in a globalized society,* Göteborg: NORDICOM.

—— (2002) "The study of international news," pp: 91–97, in Jensen, K. B (ed) *A handbook of media and communication research: qualitative and quantitative methodologies,* London & New York: Routledge.

Höijer, B. (2004) "The discourse of global compassion: the audience and media reporting of global suffering," *Media, Culture & Society* 26(4): 513–531.

Hvidt, M. (2009) "The Dubai model: an outline of key development-process elements in Dubai," *International Journal of Middle East Studies* 41(3): 397–418.

—— (2011) "Economic and institutional reforms in the Arab Gulf countries," *The Middle East Journal* 65(1): 85–102.

Ibrahim, D. (2003) "Individual perceptions of international correspondents in the Middle East: an obstacle to fair news?" *International Communication Gazette* 65(1): 87–101.

International Crisis Group (2009) *Ending the war in Gaza,* Middle East Briefing No. 26, 5 January. (Consulted May 2013: http://www.crisisgroup.org/~/media/Files/Middle%20East%20North%20Africa/Israel%20Palestine/b26_ending_the_war_in_gaza.pdf).

Iskandar, A. (2006) "Is Al Jazeera alternative? Mainstreaming alterity and assimilating discourses of dissent," *Transnational Broadcasting Journal,* Number 15, January–June 2006.

—— (2007) "Lines in the sand: problematizing Arab media in the post-taxonomic era," *Arab Media & Society* 2, May 2007.

Ismail, A. (2009) "In the shadow of a leader," *Journalism Studies* 10(2): 253–267.

Jamal, A. (2009) "Media culture as counter-hegemonic strategy: the communicative action of the Arab minority in Israel," *Media Culture & Society* 31(4): 559–577.

Jirik, J. (2010) "24-hour television news in the People's Republic of China," pp: 281–298, in Cushion, S. & J. Lewis (eds) *The rise of 24-hour news television: global perspectives,* New York: Peter Lang.

Johnson, T. J. & S. Fahmy (2010) "When blood becomes cheaper than a bottle of water: how viewers of Al-Jazeera's English-language website judge graphic images of conflict," *Media, War and Conflict* 3(1) 43–66.

Jong, M., M. Shaw & N. Stammers (eds) (2005) *Global activism: global media,* London: Pluto Press.

Kallender, A. A. (2013) "From TUNeZINE to Nhar 3la 3mmar: a reconstruction of the role of bloggers in Tunisia's revolution," *Arab Media and Society* 17.

Kamrava, M. (2009) "Royal factionalism and political liberalization in Qatar," *The Middle East Journal,* 63(3): 401–420.

——— (2011) "Mediation and Qatari foreign policy," *The Middle East Journal,* 65(4): 539–556.

Karim, K. H. (2003) *Islamic peril: media and global violence,* Montreal, New York & London: Black Rose Books.

Kayser, J. (1953) *One week's news: comparative study of 17 major dailies for a seven-days period,* Paris: UNESCO.

Keith, S., C. B. Schwalbe & B. W. Silcock (2006) "Images in ethics codes in an era of violence and tragedy," *Journal of Mass Media Ethics: Exploring Questions of Media Morality* 21(4): 245–264.

Kellner, D. (1990) *Television and the crisis of democracy,* Colorado: Westview.

Kellner, D. & M. G. Durham (2001) "Adventures in media and cultural studies: introducing the key works," pp: 1–47, in Durham, M. G. & D. M. Kellner (eds) *Media and cultural studies: key works,* Malden, MA: Blackwell Publishing.

Kennedy, L. (2008) "Securing vision: photography and US foreign policy," *Media, Culture & Society* 30(3): 279–294.

——— (2009) "Soldier photography: visualising the war in Iraq," *Review of International Studies,* 35(4): 817–833.

Kester, B. (2010) "The art of balancing: foreign correspondence in non-democratic countries: the Russian case," *International Communication Gazette* 72(1): 51–69.

Khamis, S. (2007) "The role of new Arab satellite in fostering intercultural dialogue: can Al Jazeera English bridge the gap," pp: 39–51, in Seib, P. (ed) *New media and the new Middle East,* New York: Palgrave Macmillan.

Khamis, S. & K. Vaughn (2011) "Cyberactivism in the Egyptian revolution: how civic engagement and citizen journalism tilted the balance," *Arabic Media & Society* 14.

Khanfar, Wadah (2011) *A historic moment in the Arab world,* TED Talk, March 2. (Consulted May 2013: http://www.ted.com/talks/wadah_khanfar_a_historic_moment_in_the_arab_world.html).

Khatib, L. (2007) "Television and public action in the Beirut spring," pp: 28–43, in Sakr, N. (ed) *Arab media and political renewal: community, legitimacy and public life,* London: I. B. Tauris.

Kim. K. & G. A. Barnett (1996) "The determinants in the international news flow: a network analysis," *Communication Research* 23(3): 323–352.

King, J. M. & M. Zayani (2008) "Media, branding and controversy: perceptions of Al Jazeera in newspapers around the world," *Journal of Middle East Media* 1(4): 27–43.

Kitch, C. & J. Hume (2008) *Journalism in a culture of grief,* New York: Routledge.

Kleinwatcher, W. (1993) "Three waves of the debate," pp: 21–34, in Gerbner et al. (eds) *The global media debate: its rise, fall and renewal,* Norwood, New Jersey: Ablex Publishing Corporation.

Knightley, P. (2002): *The first casualty: the war correspondent as hero and myth-maker from the Crimea to Kosovo,* Baltimore & London: John Hopkins University Press.

Konstantinidou, C. (2008) "The spectacle of suffering and death: the photographic representation of war in Greek newspapers," *Visual Communication* 7(2): 143–169.

Korn, A. (2004) "Israeli press and the war against terrorism: the construction of the 'liquidation policy,' " *Crime, Law & Social Change* 41: 209–233.

——— (2007) "Reporting Palestinian casualties in the Israeli press: the case of Haaretz and the intifada," *Journalism Studies* 5(2): 247–262.

Kraidy, M.K. (2005) *Hybridity, or the cultural logic of globalization,* Philadelphia: Temple University Press.

——— (2007) "Saudi Arabia, Lebanon, and the changing Arab information order," *International Journal of Communication* 1(1): 139–156.

——— (2008) "From activity to interactivity: the Arab audience," pp: 91–102, in Hafez, K. (ed) *Arab media: power and weakness,* New York & London: Continuum.

——— (2010) *Reality television and Arab politics: contention in public life,* Cambridge University Press.

——— and J.F. Khalil (2009) *Arab television industries,* London: Palgrave Macmillan.

Kugelman, M. (2012) "Covering and reaching South Asia," pp: 97–119, in Seib, P. (ed) *Al Jazeera English: global news in a changing world,* New York: Palgrave Macmillan

Kunh, R. (2010) "France 24: too little, too late, too French?" pp: 265–279, in Cushion, S. & J. Lewis (eds) *The rise of 24-hour news television: global perspectives,* New York: Peter Lang.

Küng-Shankleman, L. (2000) *Inside the BBC and CNN: managing media organisations,* London: Routledge.

Lambert, J. (2011) "Political reform in Qatar: participation, legitimacy and security," *Middle East Policy* 18(1): 89–101.

Larson, J.F. (1984) *Television's window on the world: international affairs coverage on the U.S. networks,* Norwood, New Jersey: Ablex Publishing Corporation.

Laustsen, C.B. (2008) "The camera as a weapon: on Abu Ghraib and related matter," *Journal of Cultural Research* 12(2): 123–142.

Lawson, R. (2011) "*The death of Osama Bin Laden: global TV news and journalistic detachment,*" Reuters Institute Fellowship Paper, University of Oxford.

Leonard, M. (2002) "Diplomacy by other means," *Foreign Policy* September/October: 48–56.

Leonard, M. & C. Smewing (2003) *Public diplomacy and the Middle East,* London: The Foreign Policy Centre.

Lewis, J. (2010) "Democratic or disposable? 24-hour news, consumer culture, and built-in obsolescence, pp: 81–98, in Cushion, S. and J. Lewis (eds) *The rise of 24-hour news television: global perspectives,* New York: Peter Lang.

Liebes, T (1997) *Reporting the Arab-Israeli conflict: how hegemony works,* London & New York: Routledge.

Liebes, T. & Z. Kampf (2009) "Black and white shades of gray: Palestinians in the Israeli media during the 2nd intifada," *The International Journal of Press/Politics* 14(4): 434–453.

Lim, M. (2012) "Clicks, cabs, and coffee houses: social media and oppositional movements in Egypt 2004–2011," *Journal of Communication* 62(2012): 231–248.

Livingston, S. & G. Asmolov (2010) "Networks and the future of foreign affairs reporting," *Journalism Studies* 11(5): 745–760.

Livingston, S & W.C. Bennett (2003) "Gatekeeping, indexing and live-event news: is technology altering the construction of news?" *Political Communication* 20: 363–380.

Lombard, M., Snyder-Duch, J. & Bracken, C.C. (2002) "Content analysis in mass communication: assessment and reporting of intercoder reliability," *Human Communication Research* 28: 587–604.

Loughborough University Communications Research Centre (2006) *The BBC's reporting of the Israeli-Palestinian conflict August 1 2005 – January 31 2006*. Report.

Loughborough University Communications Research Centre (2012) *A BBC Trust report on the impartiality and accuracy of the BBC's coverage of the events known as the "Arab Spring": Content Analysis*. Report.

Lowstedt, A. & H. Madhoun (2003) "The intifada, *Hasbara* and the media," *Palestine-Israel Journal of Politics, Economics and Culture* 10(2).

Lynch, M. (2003) "Taking Arabs seriously," *Foreign Affairs*, 82(5): 81–94.

—— (2005a) "Assessing the democratizing power of satellite TV," *Transnational Broadcasting Studies* 14, Spring/Summer 2005.

—— (2005b) "Reality is not enough: the politics of Arab reality TV," *Transnational Broadcasting Studies* 15, Fall.

—— (2006) *Voices of the new Arab public: Iraq, Al-Jazeera and Middle East politics today*, New York: Colombia University Press.

—— (2007) "Talk shows and the Arab public sphere," pp: 101–118, in Seib, P. (ed) *New media and the new Middle East*, New York: Palgrave Macmillan.

—— (2008) "Political opportunity structures: effects on Arab media," pp: 17–32, in Hafez, K. (ed) *Arab media: power and weakness*, New York and London: Continuum.

Lynch, Mark (2011a) "After Egypt: the limits and promise of online challenges to the authoritarian Arab state," *Perspectives on Politics* 9(2): 301–310.

—— (2011b) "The big think behind the Arab spring," *Foreign Policy* December.

MacBride, S. (1980): *Many voices one world. Towards a new more just and more efficient world information and communication order*, Paris: Unesco.

MacBride, S. & C. Roach (1993) "The new international information order," pp: 3–20, in Gerbner et al. (eds): *The global media debate: its rise, fall and renewal*, Norwood, New Jersey: Ablex Publishing Corporation.

Maiola, G. & D. Ward (2007) "Democracy and the media in Palestine: a comparison of election coverage by local and pan-Arab media," pp: 96–117, in Sakr, N. (ed.) *Arab media and political renewal: community, legitimacy and public life*, London/New York: I.B. Tauris Publishers.

Mair, J. (2011) "Reporter or provocateur? The 'Arab Spring' and Al Jazeera's 'CNN moment," pp: 172–183, in Mair, J. and R.L. Keeble (eds) *Mirage in the desert? Reporting the 'Arab spring*,' Suffolk: Abramis Academic Publishing.

Maltby, S. (2013) "The mediatization of the military," *Media, War & Conflict* 5(3): 255–268.

Manning, P. (2001) *News and news sources: a critical introduction*, London, Thousand Oaks & News Delhi: SAGE Publications.

Mansour, A.M.E. (2007) "Public policy and privatization: the case of the Qatari experience," *Public administration and development*, 27: 283–292.

Manzo, K. (2008) "Imagining humanitarianism: NGO identity and the iconography of childhood," *Antipode* 40(4): 632–657.

Markham, T. (2011) "The political phenomenology of war reporting," *Journalism* 12(5): 567–585.

Marmura, S.M.E. (2008) *Hegemony in the digital age: the Arab/Israeli conflict online*, Lanham, Boulder, New York, Toronto & Plymouth: Lexington Books.

Masmoudi, M (1979) "The new world information order," *Journal of Communication*, 29(2): 172–185.

Mattern, S. (2008) "Font of a nation: creating a national graphic identity for Qatar," *Public Culture* 20(3): 479–496.

McDowell, S.D. (2002) "Theory and research in international communication," pp: 295–308, in Gudykunst, W.B. and B. Mody (eds) *Handbook of international and intercultural communication*, Thousand Oaks, London & New Delhi: SAGE Publications.

McGreal, C. (2009) "Why Israel went to war in Gaza." *The Guardian,* January 5. (Consulted May 2013: http://www.guardian.co.uk/world/2009/jan/04/israel-gaza-hamas-hidden-agenda).

McLaughlin, G. (2002): *The war correspondent,* London & Sterling Virginia: Pluto Press.

McManus, J. (2003) "The newsworthiness of death." *Grade the News,* December 18. (Consulted May 2013: http://www.gradethenews.org/pages/middleeastpv.htm).

Mellor, N. (2005) *The making of Arab news,* Lanham, Boulder, New York, Toronto & Oxford: Rowman & Littlefield Publishers.

—— (2008) "Arab journalists as cultural intermediaries," *The International Journal of Press/Politics* 13(4): 465–483.

—— (2011) "Arab media: an overview of recent trends," pp: 12–28, in Mellor, N., M. Ayish, N. Dajani & K. Rinnawi (eds) *Arab media: globalization and emerging media industries,* Cambridge: Polity Press.

—— (2012) "The culture of witnessing: war correspondents rewriting the history of the Iraq War," *Language and Intercultural Communication* 12(2): 103–117.

MENA Report (2009) *Media freedom in the Middle East and North Africa,* Doha Centre for Media Freedom, Doha, Qatar.

Mermin, J. (1999) *Debating war and peace: media coverage of U.S. intervention in the Post-Vietnam era,* Princeton, New Jersey: Princeton University Press.

Meyer, W.H. (1989) "Global news flows: dependency and neoimperialism," *Comparative International Studies* 22: 243–264.

Miles, H. (2005) *Al-Jazeera: the inside story of the Arab news channel that is challenging the West,* New York: Grove Press.

—— (2011) "The Al Jazeera effect," *Foreign Policy* February 8. (Consulted May 2013: http://www.npr.org/2011/02/09/133615792/foreign-policy-the-al-jazeera-effect).

Mir, M. (2011) "Was Al Jazeera English's coverage of the 2011 Egyptian revolution 'campaign journalism'?" pp: 160–171, in Mair, J. & R.L. Keeble (eds) *Mirage in the desert? Reporting the 'Arab spring',* Suffolk: Abramis Academic Publishing.

Mody, B. (2012) "The marketization of foreign news," *Global Media and Communication,* 8(2): 99–115.

Mody, B. and A. Lee (2002) "Differing traditions of research on international media influence," pp: 381–398, in Gudykunst, W.B. & B. Mody (eds) *Handbook of international and intercultural communication,* Thousand Oaks, London & New Delhi: SAGE Publications.

Moeller, S.D. (1999) *Compassion fatigue: how the media sell disease, famine, war and death,* New York & London: Routledge.

—— (2002) "A Hierarchy of innocence: the media's use of children in the telling of international news," *The Harvard Journal of Press/Politics* 7(1): 36–56.

Moran, A. (2009) *New flows in global TV,* Bristol, UK & Chicago, USA: Intellect.

Morley, D. (2001) "Belongings: place, space and identity in a mediated world," *European Journal of Cultural Studies* 4(4): 425–448.

Müller, J. & R. Schröder (2010) "*Economics of foreign correspondence,*" Paper presented at the 3rd European Communication Conference (ECREA), Hamburg, 15 October 2010.

Murrell, C. (2010) "Baghdad bureau: an exploration on the interconnected world of fixers and correspondents at the BBC and CNN," *Media, War & Conflict* 3(2): 125–137.

Nagy, S. (2006) "Making room for migrants, making sense of difference: spatial and ideological expressions of social diversity in urban Qatar," *Urban studies* 43(1): 119–137.

Neumann, R. & S. Fahmy (2012) "Analyzing the spell of war: a war/peace framing analysis of the 2009 visual coverage of the Sri Lankan civil war in western newswires," *Mass Communication & Society* 15(2): 169–200.

Nordenstreng, K. (1984) "The 'World of news' study: bitter lessons," *Journal of Communication*, pp. 138–142.

Nordenstreng. K. & T. Varis (1974) *Television traffic—a one-way street*, Reports and Papers in Mass Communication, Paris: Unesco.

Nye, J. S. (1990) "Soft power," *Foreign Policy* 80: 153–171.

—— (2004a) "The decline of America's soft power: why Washington should worry," *Foreign Affairs*, 83(3): 16–20.

—— (2004b) *Soft power: the means to success in world politics*, New York: Public Affairs.

—— (2008) "Public diplomacy and soft power," *The ANNALS of the American Academy of Political and Social Science* 616: 94–109.

O'Neill, D. & T. Harcup (2009) "News values and selectivity," pp: 161–174, in Wahl-Jorgensen, K. & T. Hanitzsch (eds) *The handbook of journalism studies*, New York and London: Routledge.

Orgad, S. (2009) "Watching how others watch us: the Israeli media's treatment of international coverage of the Gaza war," *The Communication Review* 13(3): 250–261.

Otto, F. & C. O. Meyer (2012) "Missing the story? Changes in foreign news reporting and their implications for conflict prevention," *Media, War & Conflict* 5(3): 205–221.

Östgaard, E. (1965) "Factors influencing the flow of news," *Journal of Peace research*, 2(1): 39–63.

Painter, J. (2008) *Counter-hegemonic news: a case study of Al-Jazeera English and Telesûr*, Reuters Institute of the study of Journalism, University of Oxford.

Palmer, J. & V. Fontan (2007) "Our ears and our eyes: journalists and fixers in Iraq," *Journalism* 8(1): 5–24.

Parry, K. (2010) "A visual framing analysis of British press photography during the 2006 Israel- Lebanon conflict," *Media, War & Conflict* 3(1): 67–85.

Paterson, Chris (2010) "The hidden role of television news agencies: "going live" on 24-hour news channels," pp: 99–112, in Cushion, S. & J. Lewis (eds) *The rise of 24-hour news television: global perspectives*, New York: Peter Lang.

—— (2011) *The international television news agencies*. New York: Peter Lang

Philo, G. & M. Berry (2004) *Bad news from Israel*, London/Sterling, Virginia: Pluto Press.

Pintak, L. (2008) "Satellite TV news and Arab democracy," *Journalism Practice* 2(1): 15–26.

—— (2009) "Gaza: of media wars and borderless journalism," *Arab Media & Society* January.

—— (2010) "Arab media and the Al-Jazeera effect," pp: 290–304, in McPhail, T.L. (ed) *Global communication: theories, stakeholders, and trends*, Wiley-Blackwell.

—— (2011) *The new Arab journalist: mission and identity in a time of turmoil*, London & New York: I. B. Tauris.

Pintak, L. & J. Ginges (2008) "The mission of Arab journalism: creating change in a time of turmoil," *The International Journal of Press/Politics* 13(3): 193–227.

—— (2009) "Inside the Arab newsroom," *Journalism Studies* 10(2): 157–177.

Potter, J. & S. Smith (2000) "The context of graphic portrayals of television violence," *Journal of Broadcasting & Electronic Media* 44(2): 301–323.

Powers, S. (2012) "The origins of Al Jazeera English," pp: 5–28, in Seib, P. (ed.) *Al Jazeera English: global news in a changing world*, New York: Palgrave Macmillan

Powers, S. & E. Gilboa (2007) "The public diplomacy of Al Jazeera," pp: 53–80, in Seib, P. (ed) *New media and the new Middle East*, New York: Palgrave Macmillan

Powers, S. & M. El-Nawawy (2008) "New media and the politics of protest: a case study of Al Jazeera English in Malaysia," in M. Kugelman (ed.) *Kuala Lumpur calling. Al Jazeera English in Asia*, Woodrow Wilson International Center for Scholars, Asia Program.

Rabi, U. (2009) "Qatar's relations with Israel: challenging Arab and Gulf norms," *The Middle East Journal* 63(3): 443–459.

Rai, M. & S. Cottle (2007) "Global mediations: on the changing ecology of satellite television news," *Global Media and Communication,* 3(1): 51–78.

—— (2010) "Global media revisited: mapping the contemporary landscape of satellite television news," pp: 51–80, in Cushion, S. & J. Lewis (eds) *The rise of 24-hour news television: global perspectives,* New York: Peter Lang.

Rantanen, T. (2005) *The media and globalization,* London, Thousand Oaks & New Delhi: SAGE Publications.

Rauch, J. (2003) "Rooted in nations, blossoming in globalization? A cultural perspective on the content of a 'northern' mainstream and a 'southern' alternative news agency," *Journal of Communication Inquiry* 27(1): 87–103.

—— (2007) "Activists as interpretive communities: rituals of consumption and interaction in an alternative media audience," *Media, Culture & Society* 29(6): 994–1013.

Reese, S.D. & S.C. Lewis (2009) "Framing the war on terror: the internalization of policy in the US press," *Journalism* 10(6): 777–797.

Reporters Without Borders (2009a) *Press Freedom Index 2009.* (Consulted May 2013: http://en.rsf.org/press-freedom-index-2009,1001.html).

—— (2009b) *Robert Ménard and staff leave Doha Centre for media freedom,* June 23. (Consulted May 2013: http://en.rsf.org/qatar-robert-menard-and-staff-leave-doha-23–06–2009,33548.html).

—— (2009c) *Israel/Gaza: operation "Cast Lead": news control as military objective,* Middle East and Northern Africa Desk, February. (Consulted May 2013: http://en.rsf.org/palestinian-territories-operation-cast-lead-news-control-15–02–2009,30310.html

—— (2013) *Press Freedom Index 13.* (Consulted May 2013: http://fr.rsf.org/IMG/pdf/classement_2013_gb-bd.pdf).

Ricchiardi, S. (2006) "The limits of the parachute," *American Journalism Review,* October/November. (Consulted May 2013: http://www.ajr.org/article.asp?id=4211).

—— (2008a) "Covering the world," *American Journalism Review,* December/January. (Consulted May 2013: http://www.ajr.org/article.asp?id=4429).

—— (2008b) "Whatever happened to Iraq?" *American Journalism Review,* June/July. (Consulted May 2013: http://www.ajr.org/article.asp?id=4515).

—— (2011) "The Al Jazeera effect," *American Journalism Review,* March & April 2011. (Consulted May 2013: http://ajr.org/Article.asp?id=5077).

Richardson, J.E. & L. Barkho (2009) "Reporting Israel/Palestine," *Journalism Studies* 10(5): 594–622.

Rinnawi, K. (2006) *Instant nationalism: McArabism, Al-Jazeera and transnational media in the Arab world,* Lanham, Boulder, New York, Toronto & Oxford: University Press of America.

—— (2007) "De-legitimization of media mechanisms: Israeli press coverage of the Al Aqsa intifada," *International Communication Gazette* 69(2): 149–178.

—— (2012) "Cyber uprising: Al-Jazeera TV channel and the Egyptian uprising," *Language and Intercultural Communication* 12(2): 118–132.

Robertson, A. (2010) *Mediated cosmopolitanism: the world of television news,* Cambridge & Malden, MA: Polity Press.

—— (2012) "Narratives of resistance: comparing global news coverage of the Arab spring," *New Global Studies* 6(2): 1–20.

—— (2013) "Connecting in crisis: 'old' and 'new' media and the Arab spring," *The International Journal of Press/Politics,* April 22.

Robertson, L. (2004) "Images of war," *American Journalism Review,* October/November. (Consulted May 2013: http://www.ajr.org/article.asp?id=3759).

Robinson, P. (2002) *The CNN effect: the myth of news, foreign policy and intervention,* London and New York: Routledge.

—— (2005) "The CNN effect revisited," *Critical Studies in Media Communication* 22(4): 344–349.

Roger, Nathan (2013) *Image warfare in the war on terror,* New York: Palgrave MacMillan.

Rønning, H. (2009) "Strengths and weaknesses: political change and the media in Africa since the 1990s," pp: 25–65, in Rønning, H. & K. Orgeret (eds) *The power of communication: changes and challenges in African media,* Oslo: Unipub.

Rosengren, K.E. (1974) "International news: methods, data and theory," *Journal of Peace Research* 11(2): 145–156.

Rowling, C.M., T.M. Jones & P. Sheets (2011) "Some dared call it torture: cultural resonance, Abu Ghraib, and a selectively echoing press," *Journal of Communication* 61: 1043–1061.

Rugh, W.A. (2004) *Arab mass media: newspapers, radio, and television in Arab politics,* Westport, Connecticut and London: Praeger.

—— (2007) "Do national systems still influence Arab media?" *Arab Media & Society* 2, May.

—— (2009) "Repairing American public diplomacy," *Arab Media & Society* 7, February.

Sakr, N. (2001) *Satellite realms: transnational television, globalization & the Middle East,* London/New York: I.B. Tauris Publishers.

—— (2002) "Arab satellite channels between state and private ownership: current and future implications," *Transnational Broadcasting Studies* 9, Fall/Winter.

—— (2004) "Al-Jazeera satellite channel: global newscasting in Arabic," in Paterson, C. & A. Sreberny (eds) *International news in the twenty-first century,* Luton: University of Luton Press.

—— (2005) "Arab satellite broadcasting and the state: who curbs whom, why and how?" *Transnational Broadcasting Studies* 14, Spring.

—— (2007a) "Approaches to exploring media-politics connections in the Arab world," pp: 1–13, in N. Sakr (ed) *Arab media and political renewal: community, legitimacy and public life,* London and New York: I.B. Taurus Publishers.

—— (2007b) "Challenger or lackey? The politics of news on Al-Jazeera," pp: 116–132, in Thussu, D.K. (ed) *Media on the move: global flow and contra-flow,* London and New York: Routledge.

—— (2008) "Gaps in the market: insights from scholarly work on Arab media economics," pp: 185–198, in Hafez, K. (ed) *Arab media: power and weakness,* New York and London: Continuum.

Samuel-Azran, T. (2008) "The advent of counter-hegemonic contra-flow," *Journal of Global Mass Communication* 1(3/4): 235–250.

—— (2010) *Al Jazeera and US war coverage,* New York: Peter Lang.

Schanzer, J. (2008) *Hamas vs. Fatah: the struggle for Palestine,* New York: Palgrave Macmillan.

Schiller, H.I. (1976) *Communication and cultural domination,* New York: International Arts and Sciences Press.

Seib, P. (2005) "Hegemonic no more: western media, the rise of Al-Jazeera, and the influence of diverse voices," *International Studies Review* 7: 601–615.

—— (2008) *The Al Jazeera effect: how the new global media are reshaping world politics.* Dulles, VA: Potomac Books.

—— (2012) "Conclusion: AJE in the world," pp: 187–197, in Seib, P. (ed) *Al Jazeera English: global news in a changing world,* New York: Palgrave Macmillan.

Shaw, M. (2005) "Peace activism and western wars: social movements in mass-mediated global politics," pp: 133–146, in Jong, M, M. Shaw & N. Stammers (eds) *Global activism: global media,* London: Pluto Press.

Sheafer, T. & I. Gabay (2009) "Mediated public diplomacy: a strategic contest over international agenda building and frame building," *Political Communication* 26(4): 447–467.

Sheafer, T. & S.R. Shenhav (2009) "Mediated public diplomacy in a new era of warfare," *The Communication Review* 12(3): 272–283.

Sick, G.G. (1998) "Policy imperatives in Washington," pp: 69–81, in Hollis, R. (ed) *Oil and regional developments in the Gulf*, London: The Royal Institute of International Affairs.

Siebert, F.S. et al. (1956) *Four theories of the press: the authoritarian, libertarian, social responsibility and Soviet communist concepts of what the press should be and do*, Urbana, Ill.: University of Illinois Press.

Silcock, B.W., C.B. Schwalbe & S. Keith (2008) "Secret casualties: images of injury & death in the Iraq war across media platforms," *Journal of Mass Media Ethics: Exploring Questions of media Morality* 23(1): 36–60.

Sinclair, J., E. Jacka & S. Cunningsham (1996) "Peripheral vision," pp: 1–32, in Sinclair, J., E. Jacka & S. Cunningsham (eds) *New patterns in global television: peripheral vision*, Oxford University Press.

Sontag, S. (2003) *Regarding the pain of others*, London: Penguin Books.

Sparks, C. (2005) "Media and the global public sphere," pp: 34–49, in Jong, M., M. Shaw & N. Stammers (eds) *Global activism: global media*, London: Pluto Press.

Spivak, G.C. (1988) "Can the subaltern speak?" pp: 271–313, in Grossberg, L. & C. Nelson (eds) *Marxism and the interpretation of culture*, Houndmills: MacMillan.

Sreberny, A. & C. Paterson (2004) "Introduction. Shouting from the rooftops: reflections on international news in the 21st century," pp: 3–27, in Paterson, C. & A. Sreberny (eds.) *International news in the 21st century*, London: John Libbey.

Sreberny, A. & G. Khiabany (2010) *Blogistan: the internet and politics in Iran*, London: I.B. Taurus.

Sreberny-Mohammadi, A. (1984) "The 'World of news' study: results of international cooperation," *Journal of Communication*, 34(1): 121–134.

—— (1991) "The global and the local in international communication," pp: 118–138, in Curran, J. & M. Gurrevitch *Mass media and society*, London: Edward Arnold.

Sreberny-Mohammadi, A. & A. Mohammadi (1994) *Small media, big revolution: communication, culture, and the Iranian revolution*, Minneapolis: University of Arizona Press.

Sreberny-Mohammadi, A. et al. (eds) (1985) *Foreign news in the media: international reporting in 29 Countries*, Reports and Papers on Mass Communication, No. 93. Paris: UNESCO.

Stein, L. (2001) "Access television and grassroots political communication in the United States," pp: 299–324, in Downing, J.D.H. (2001) *Radical media: rebellious communication and social movements*, Thousand Oaks, London & New Delhi: Sage Publications.

Stevenson, R.L. (1984) "The 'World of news' study: pseudo debate," *Journal of Communication*, 34(1): 134–138.

Stevenson, R.L. & R.R. Cole (1984) "Patterns of foreign news," pp: 37–62, in Stevenson, R.L. & D.L. Shaw (eds) *Foreign news and the new world information order*, Iowa: Iowa State University Press.

Straubhaar, J.D. (2007) *World television: from global to local*, Los Angeles, London, New Delhi and Singapore: SAGE.

Syvertsen, T. (2004) *Mediemangfold: styring av mediene i et globalisert marked*, Kristiansand: IJ Forlaget.

Tamimi, A. (2007) *Hamas: a history from within*, Northampton: Olive Branch Press.

Telhami, S. (2004) *The stakes. America in the Middle East*, Westview Press.

Thomas, A. O. (2010) "Adapting global television to regional realities: traversing the Middle East experience," pp: 151–161, in Moran, A. (ed) *TV formats worldwide: localizing global programs*, Bristol & Chicago: Intellect.

Thompson, J. B. (2005) "The new visibility," *Theory, Culture & Society* 22(6): 31–51.

Thompson, M. (2002): "The brief, ineffective life of the Pentagon's media pool," *Columbia Journalism Review* March/April.

Thune, H. (2009) *Beyond the CNN effect: towards a constitutive understanding of media power in international politics*. PhD Dissertation, Department of Political Science, Faculty of Social Science, University of Oslo.

Thussu, D. K (2007a) "Introduction," pp: 1–8, in Thussu, D.K. (ed) *Media on the move. global flow and contra-flow*, London & New York: Routledge.

——— (2007b) "Mapping global media flow and contra-flow," pp: 11–32, in Thussu, D.K. (ed) *Media on the move. Global flow and contra-flow*, London & New York: Routledge.

——— (2007c) *News as entertainment: the rise of global infotainment*, Los Angeles, London, New Delhi & Singapore: SAGE Publications.

——— (2008) *News as entertainment: the rise of global infotainment*, Los Angeles, London, New Delhi & Singapore: SAGE Publications.

Tomlinson, J. (1991) *Cultural imperialism: a critical introduction*, Continuum International Publishing Group.

Tsang, K., Y. Tsai & S. Liu (1988) "Geographic emphases of international news studies," *Journalism Quarterly* 65(1): 191–4.

Tufecki, Z. & C. Wilson (2012) "Social media and the decision to participate in political protest: observations from Tahrir Square," *Journal of Communication* 62: 363–379.

Tuggle, C. A., P. Casella & S. Huffman (2010) "Live, late-breaking, and broken: TV news and the challenge of live reporting in America," pp: 133–150, in Cushion, S. & J. Lewis (eds) *The rise of 24-hour news television: global perspectives*, New York: Peter Lang.

Tumber, H. & J. Palmer (2003): *Media at war. The Iraqi crisis*, London, Thousand Oaks& New Delhi: SAGE Publications

Tunstall, J. (1977) *The media are American: Anglo-American media in the world*, London: Constable.

——— (2008) *The media were American: U.S. mass media in decline*, New York & London: Oxford University Press.

Tusa, F. (2013) "How social media can shape a protest movement: the cases of Egypt in 2011 and Iran in 2009," *Arab Media and Society* 17.

Ulrichsen, K.C. (2012) *"Small states with a big role: Quatar and the United Arab Emirates in the wake of the Arab spring,."* Discussion Paper, Durham University, H. H. Sheikh Nasser Al-Sabah Programme, Durham.

US Bureau of Democracy, Human Rights, and Labor (2009) *2008 Human rights report: Qatar*, Department of State, February 25. (Consulted May 2013: http://www.state.gov/g/drl/rls/hrrpt/2008/nea/119125.htm

Utley, G. (1997) "The shrinking of foreign news: from broadcast to narrowcast," *Foreign Affairs* 76(2): 2–10.

Uysal, A. (2011) "The new frontier in international politics: the nature of Al-Jazeera's prime-time broadcasting in Arabic and English," pp: 1–18, in Zweiri, M. & E.C. Murphy (eds) *The new Arab media; technology, image and perception*, UK: Ithaca Press.

van Veeren, E. (2011) "Captured by the camera's eye: Guantanamo and the shifting frame of the global war on terror," *Review of International Studies* 37(4): 1721–1749.

Varis, T. (1984) "The international flow of television programs," *Journal of Communication* 34(1): 143–152.

—— (1986) "Trends in international television flow," *International Political Science Review* 7: 235–249.

Varis, T. & K. Nordenstreng (1974) "Television traffic—a one-way street? A survey and analysis of the international flow of television programme material," *Reports and Papers on Mass Communication* 70, Unesco.

Viser, M. (2003) "Attempted objectivity: an analysis of the *New York Times* and *Ha'aretz* and their portrayals of the Palestinian-Israeli conflict," *Press/Politics* 8(4): 114–20.

Volkmer, I. (1999) *News in the global sphere: a study of CNN and its impact on global communication,* Luton: University of Luton Press.

—— (2000) "International communication theory in transition. Parameters of the new global public sphere," pp: 65–76, in Hjarvard, S. (ed) *News in a globalized Society,* Göteborg: NORDICOM.

—— (2002) "Journalism and political crisis in the global network society," pp: 235–247, in Zelizer, B. & Allan, S. (eds) *Journalism after September 11,* London and New York: Routledge.

Wall, M. & D. Bicket (2008) "A window on your world: rise of British news in the US," *Journalism Practice* 2(2): 163–178.

Wallis, R. & S. J. Baran (1990) *The known world of broadcast news,* Routledge.

Ward, S. (2010) "Emotion in reporting: use and abuse," Report Center for Journalism Ethics,ttp://ethics.journalism.wisc.edu/2010/10/14/ethics-center-co-authors-report-on-nonprofit-journalism-10/

Ward, W. (2009) "Social media in the Gaza conflict," *Arab Media & Society* January.

Wells, K. (2007) "Narratives of liberation and narratives of innocent suffering: the rhetorical uses of images of Iraqi children in the British press," *Visual Communication* 6(1): 55–71.

Wessler, H. & Adolphsen, M. (2008) "Contra-flow from the Arab world? How Arab television coverage of the 2003 Iraq war was used and framed on western international news channels," *Media, Culture & Society* 30(4): 439–461.

White, M. (1995) "Reconsidering television program flows, or whose flow is it anyway?" *The Electronic Journal of Communication* 5(2/3).

—— (2003) "Flows and other close encounters with television," pp: 94–110, in Parks, L. & S. Kumar (eds) *Planet TV,* New York & London: New York University Press.

Wilke, J. (1987) "Foreign news coverage and international news flow over three centuries," *International Communication Gazette* 39: 147–180.

Williams, R. (1973) "Base and superstructure in Marxist cultural theory," *New Left Review* 85.

—— (1974) *Television: technology and cultural form,* Collins: Fontana Original.

Willnat, L. & D. Weaver (2003) "Through their eyes: the work of foreign correspondents in the United States," *Journalism* 4(4) 403–422.

Wilson, C. & A. Dunn (2011) "Digital media in the Egyptian revolution: Descriptive Analysis from the Tahrir Square," *International Journal of Communication* 5.

Wojcieszak, M. E. (2007) "Al Jazeera: a challenge to traditional framing research," *The International Communication Gazette* 69(2): 115–128.

Wolfsfeld, G. (2003) "The news media and the second intifada," *Palestine-Israel Journal of Politics, Economics and Culture* 10(2).

Wolfsfeld, G., P. Frosh & M. T. Awabdy (2008) "Covering death in conflicts: coverage of the second intifada on Israeli and Palestinian television," *Journal of Peace Research* 45(3): 401–417.

Wright, S. (2009) *Foreign policies with international reach: the case of Qatar* (unpublished article).

—— (2011) "Qatar," pp: 113–134, in C. M. Davidson (ed.) *Power and politics in the Persian Gulf monarchies,* New York: Columbia University Press.

Wu, H.D. (1998) "Investigating the determinants of international news flow: a meta-analysis," *International Communication Gazette* 60(6): 493–512.

———— (2003) "Homogeneity around the world: comparing the systematic determinants of international news flow between developed and developing countries," *International Communication Gazette* 65(1): 9–24.

———— (2007) "A brave new world for international news? Exploring the determinants of the coverage of foreign nations on US websites," *International Communication Gazette*, 69(6): 539–551.

Youmans, W. (2012) "AJE after the Arab spring: the politics of distribution in the United States," pp: 57–78, in Seib, P. (ed) *Al Jazeera English: global news in a changing world*, New York: Palgrave Macmillan

Zahlan, R. S. (1998) *The making of the modern Gulf States: Kuwait, Bahrain, Qatar, the United Arab Emirates and Oman*, Reading: Ithaca Press.

Zayani, M. (2004) "Arab satellite television and politics in the Middle East," *The Emirates Occasional Papers no. 54*, The Emirates Center for Strategic Studies and Research.

———— (2011) "Toward a cultural anthropology of Arab media: reflections on the codification of everyday life," *History and Anthropology* 22(1): 37–56.

Zayani, M. & S. Sahraoui (2007) *The culture of Al Jazeera: inside an Arab media giant*, Jefferson, North Carolina & London: McFarland & Company.

Zelizer, B. (1993) "Journalists as interpretive communities," *Critical Studies in Mass Communication* 10(3): 219–237.

———— (1998) *Remembering to forget: Holocaust memory through the camera's eye*, Chicago & London: The University of Chicago Press.

———— (2004) *Taking journalism seriously: news and the academy*, Thousand Oaks, London & New Delhi: SAGE Publications.

———— (2005) "Death in wartime: photographs and the 'other war' in Afghanistan, *The Harvard Journal of Press/Politics* 10(3): 26–55.

POLICY DOCUMENTS/PRESENTATIONS

Al Jazeera English (2011a) *FAQ: the Palestine papers*. (Consulted May 2013: http://www.aljazeera.com/palestinepapers/2011/01/2011123114726552723.html).

Al Jazeera Network (2009a) *Al Jazeera Network—media pack 2009*.

———— (2009b) *AJE renewal project: Al Jazeera English 2008–2011*, Phase One Report, March 2009.

———— (2010a) *Corporate profile, about us*. (Consulted May 2010: http://english.aljazeera.net/aboutus/).

———— (2010b) *I want Al Jazeera*. (Consulted May 2013: http://iwantaje.com/).

———— (2010c) *Code of ethics*, modified 7 November 2010. (Consulted May 2013: http://www.aljazeera.com/aboutus/2006/11/2008525185733692771.html).

———— (2013a) *Al Jazeera America*, Media pack.

———— (2013b) *Work for us, corporate profile*. (Consulted May 2013: http://www.aljazeera.com/aboutus/2009/10/2009103081456514230.html).

BBC (2010) *About BBC World News*. (Consulted April 2010: http://www.bbcworldnews.com/Pages/About.aspx).

———— (2011) *About BBC World News*. (Consulted May 2013: http://www.bbcworldnews.com/Pages/About.aspx).

CNN (2013) *CNN International—Europe, Middle East & Africa*, Turner Press Room. (Consulted May 2013: http://news.turner.com/press_kits.cfm?presskit_id=72).

IPS (2013) *Our mission*. (Consulted May 2013: http://www.ips.org/institutional/get-to-know-us-2/our-mission/).

MOFA (2010) *Qatar: social development: media*, Ministry of Foreign Affairs, State of Qatar. (Consulted May 2013: http://english.mofa.gov.qa/Sarticle.cfm?CatId=114&article_ID=1).

Index